BATH MUNICIPAL
REFERENCE LIBRARY

This book must not be removed
from the library

International Heraldry

The Stuarts of Traquair
The House of Wavell
The Middle Sea
The Story of Heraldry
Trace Your Ancestors
The Golden Book of the Coronation
They Came with the Conqueror
The Story of the Peerage
Tales of the British Aristocracy
The House of Constantine
Teach Yourself Heraldry
The Twilight of Monarchy
A Guide to Titles
Princes of Wales
American Origins
Your Family Tree
Ramshackledom
Heirs of the Conqueror
Heraldry, Ancestry and Titles : Questions and Answers
The Story of Surnames
After Their Blood
Tradition and Custom in Modern Britain
The Genealogist's Encyclopedia
The Story of Titles

International Heraldry

by

L. G. PINE

DAVID & CHARLES
NEWTON ABBOT

7153 4790 X

Set in eleven on thirteen point Baskerville
and printed in Great Britain
by Clarke Doble & Brendon Limited
for David & Charles (Publishers) Limited
South Devon House Newton Abbot Devon

Contents

Illustrations

7

CHAPTER 1

A Medieval Survival

IN Madrid, at the entrance to a park and in front of an office building over thirty storeys high, stands a gigantic sculptured group of the most famous figures in Spanish literature. There they are, the gaunt Knight of La Mancha in armour which appears almost as attenuated as his figure; his poor half-broken-down steed Rosinante; and the squat Sancho Panza on his mule. There they are, immortal figures riding into the hearts of humanity. When we first meet them in our childhood we think how amusing they are; probably Cervantes thought of Don Quixote in the same way, yet with a touch of satire, laughing at the follies which accompanied the end of chivalry. Cervantes was, after all, a professional writer of poems, plays and novels, 'exemplary' novels as he called them; but, as sometimes happens with really great writers, his characters gradually assumed a mastery independently of his own intentions. Long before the end of his greatest work, Don Quixote had taken control of his creator, and he, as we in our mature years, sees only the sadness of a noble soul, full of honour and ideals, who is out of accord with his age.

Cervantes published *Don Quixote* in 1605,[1] the year before his death, but the conception of knight errantry—of knights in

---

[1] The success of the book was immediate, though it did not bring the author much money and, like many other successful writers, Cervantes wrote a sequel.

armour riding out to redress wrongs, slay giants and enchanters, and rescue damsels in distress—had lost connection with reality more than a century before. The Chevalier Bayard (1473–1524) was perhaps the last exponent of the older kind of chivalric warfare. He disdained the infantry, at whose side he refused to fight; he detested guns and cannon and by a bitter irony it was an arquebus ball that caused his death (See note at end of chapter). The mad career of Charles the Bold (1433–77) may have impressed realistic soldiers with the folly of carrying medieval methods of warfare into an age when artillery, hand firearms and a highly disciplined infantry were turning the knight into a dangerous anachronism. The infantry in question were the Swiss spearmen who had defeated the Austrians on several occasions, and the Burgundians under Charles the Bold three times. Strange episode in the development of warfare was the triumph of the Welsh longbow as used by English archers with success against French knights, Scottish schiltrons (squares of pikemen), and Spanish cavalry and slingers. No one in Europe seems to have copied the tactics of Edward I, of the Black Prince or of Henry V; they were useful to the English alone.

By 1500, the conception of the knight as the most important figure on the battlefield was a century out of date; by 1600, the ideas of medieval knighthood, often betrayed and shamefully traduced, but nonetheless real had passed out of practical reckoning in human conduct, except in so far as the concept of chivalry towards women and the weak had left an impress on good manners.

The accoutrements of the knight—his suit of complete steel, his helmet, shield, the defensive armour of his horse, the lance, the long and heavy sword, the mace—all had gone out of practical use. A history of armour, in England, usually ends with the reign of James I (died 1625). Even then the complete suit of armour appeared far less on the battlefield than in tournaments, which were more or less mock warfare or preparations for mortal encounters. Anyone who has studied the splendid collection of armour in the Tower of London must have wondered how men ever managed to move with any agility, to swing the huge swords, or even to see through the small apertures of their visors. In the Tower is a model showing Henry VIII, in full armour and mounted. Pity for the beast which had to carry him must surely be our first thought. By comparison, the mounted knights in the Royal Armoury of Madrid appear almost graceful, but then, in the sixteenth century, as armour declined for practical use, it became ever the object of the armour-maker to embellish his work. The splendid suits of late fifteenth- and sixteenth-century armour which survive in the various European collections were for the most part not used in warfare at all. Many suits were worn for ceremonial occasions only, and often when the wearer was to have his portrait painted. As early as 1530, a Sir James Smith complained that 'these new fantasied men of warre doo despise and scorne our ancient arming of ourselves, both on horseback and on foot, saying that we armed ourselves in times past with too much armour or pieces of yron (as they terme it)', (quoted by J. Starkie Gardner, *Foreign Armour in England*, 1898, p. 56). So, in the 1500s and 1600s, armour declined for actual use in war until it was represented only by the helmet and cuirass now worn by the Life Guards and Horse Guards of the British Army in peacetime dress.

Tournament armour was not so embellished and was subjected to fairly heavy punishment. As it had only to be worn for a fixed time, and as a jouster could be riding against his best friend, it was made to be all protecting. Tilting armour had a rest for the lance, to assist the tilter to bear its weight, and a special plate to protect the heart.

In England, the tournament probably lingered after it had ceased on the Continent. One of the favourite amusements of Henry VIII was the joust; there was the famous occasion when Sir Henry Norris, lover of Queen Anne Boleyn, gained a point in tilting against the King, whereupon Anne with incredible stupidity dropped her handkerchief to Norris, and he with a parallel folly picked it up. (The King meanwhile rode from the tilting-ground in fury.) Sir Philip Sidney, the Flower of English Chivalry and hero of Zutphen, was an expert tilter. Prince Henry, the elder son of James I, revived the sport of the tilt-yard, no doubt to the approval of those who wanted to use armour in

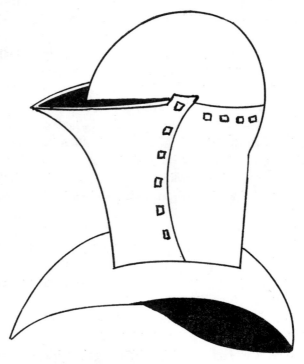

Helmet of an esquire

battle. One of these diehards, a Cavalier, insisted on wearing a full suit of armour to the Civil War. He died of suffocation, and is said, with good reason, to have been the last to use full armour in warfare.

Edmund Spenser, 'the poets' poet', an English contemporary of Cervantes but who died sixteen years before him, also wrote the epitaph of chivalry, but with a very different motive from the

Spaniard's The *Faërie Queene* is an allegory meant, under the guise of knightly adventure, to show forth the twelve moral virtues. Six books were finished and unkind critics have said that, had the author completed his design, no heart less stout than a commentator's could have endured to read it through. Yet the poetry of Spenser is some of the most beautiful in English literature and shows a mastery of the language second to none. Probably the tale of knightly adventures with a moral lesson has proved unacceptable reading for the majority. For my present purpose the opening stanzas of canto I are highly relevant:

> A gentle knight was pricking on the plain
> Yclad in mighty arms and silver shield,
> Wherein old dints of deep wounds did remain,
> The cruel marks of many a bloody field
> Yet arms till that time did he never wield
> His angry steed did chide his foaming bit
> As much disdaining to the curb to yield
> Full jolly knight he seemed and fair did sit
> As one for knightly jousts and fierce encounters fit.
>
> And on his breast a bloody cross he bore
> The dear remembrance of his dying Lord
> For whose sweet sake that glorious badge he wore.
> And dead, as living, ever Him adored;
> Upon his shield the like was also scored ...

Later, Spenser writes of Saracen knights, with devices on their shields and of the lady knight, Britomart, who 'bore a lion passant on a golden shield'.

The armour and the weapons went out of use 400 years ago. Why, then, have the devices survived? Why is it that at this very moment in England, in Scotland, in the United States of America, in South Africa, in Ireland, in Australia, to mention only six countries, men are having coats of arms blazoned for them, with helmets befitting their degree, and with crests bound to the helmets by wreaths of the colours? Why are sane, sensible, highly successful business and professional men paying good money for

their shields of arms, and in many cases for their standards and
their badges? How is it that a large literature has appeared, in
the leading languages of the world, to explain the meaning of
heraldry, its terms and rules? Why do republics which have joy-

Wreath

Wreath and crest

fully repudiated any imperial connections, institute heralds of
their own and why is it possible in country after country to hold
an international congress of heraldry and genealogy, attended by
learned men and women from more than a score of nations?

The answer to all these questions is that, long before armour
went out of practical use, the devices which had been shown
upon it had been put to altogether different uses, and that the

devices so employed were recognised as signs of gentility and noblesse, of what is called 'nobiliary status'.

The language of these devices could not be disassociated from armour, since armour was the original cause of the appearance of armorial devices or bearings. They are found first in the middle of the twelfth century in western Europe—see the next chapter for a detailed account—when armour had developed from a simpler to a much more complex form. The student of armour will know that to distinguish one fully armoured knight from another would be very difficult if not impossible without some guiding signs. These must appear on the armour itself. Hence the term 'shield', for what more natural than that the primitive devices should be shown on the shield borne by the warrior? Owing to the heat of the steel covering, some protection from the sun's rays was necessary, hence a surcoat of linen or some other material. On this surcoat a simple device like that of a lion in red on a golden ground would show up well. This is the origin of the term 'coat of arms'; the surcoat resembled a waistcoat and so was appropriately named a coat of arms. The crest borne on the helmet would be either something similar to, or identical with part of the device on the shield or surcoat, eg, a lion. At first it would be of leather, later of wood. The knight, as his name implies in most European languages, was a horseman. His horse wore trappings bearing the owner's devices, and the man himself carried a lance with an embroidered pennon showing the arms. A body of such knights formed the feudal army.

When William the Conqueror consolidated his conquest of England in 1086 (the date of the Domesday Book) he had parcelled out the land between about 5,000 knights. Each would be likely to have at least ten followers, so that a force of fair size could be summoned, bringing with it provisions for forty days' service, the period of obligation under the feudal system in England. To distinguish these men from one another, badges were useful but as the greater tenants of the Crown, such as the earls in charge of counties, were wont to collect their under-tenants to march in a compact body with them, the greater lord had a banner which served as a rallying centre at all times and especially in battle. Of a great lord of the late twelfth century,

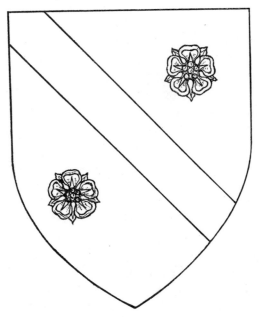

Shield with charges

Strongbow, Earl of Pembroke, it was said that, however hard the battle, his soldiers could always find succour and a rallying point under his banner. Among his soldiers were many simple knights, as much of gentle blood as the earl, but not such wealthy land-owners. They bore arms, which they used, especially in wars, as a means of distinguishing themselves and their following from the other contingents ranged under Pembroke's banner. The greatest lord of all, the King of the whole country, had his standard, as does the present Queen of England, Elizabeth, whose royal standard flies above Buckingham Palace when she is in residence there. Occasionally too, even now, a house flag flies over the principal seat of a noble family, as with the three popinjays of the Curzons, seen over Kedleston when the family is at home.

For some 400 years, from 1150 to 1550, armorial bearings were used in war, and Flodden, in 1513, may have been the last great English battle in which the feudal array was marshalled under the banners of the great lords. The misbehaviour of the barons in the earlier of England's civil wars, the Wars of the Roses, had led the succeeding Tudor sovereigns to enforce and strengthen the laws against the keeping of retainers. The practice ceased in most of England in the reign of Henry VII, the first Tudor, but may have been countenanced to some extent in the north, where trouble with the Scots was perennial. Under Henry VIII the county array was held by the Lord Lieutenant, a royal appointee whose office dates from that reign. When the next great Scottish defeat occurred at Pinkie in 1547, feudal contingents were almost certainly superseded by more modern arrangements, for the English general, the Duke of Somerset, had provided himself with well-drilled mercenaries, Italians, Spaniards and Germans, and the English part of his army must have been similarly arrayed in regiments.

In the four centuries when armour and armorial bearings were contemporary, the latter soon spread from employment in connection with war. The correct term for armorial bearings is 'armory', as in the title of *Burke's General Armory* which is an alphabetical list, under family and institutional names, of blazons or descriptions of coats of arms. The word 'armory', however, is not used now, except in an instance such as the above, or in conversation among specialists. The term now used to denote the science and art of armory or armorial bearings is 'heraldry'. Its original meaning was 'the duties and functions of a herald' and 'the science of blazoning arms', but it has since acquired a tertiary meaning so that it can be used to denote coats of arms and their study.

Heraldry spread from the shield and coat of arms to the castle

B

walls. Over the great gateway in the wall of Bodiam Castle in
Sussex, built about 1386, are the arms of three families connected
with the property—Bodiam, Wardedieux and Dalygrygge. There
are many other instances of arms displayed over castellated gate-
ways, or on walls, as with the royal arms on the southern gate of
York, commemorating the struggles of Yorkist and Lancastrian.
In those days, a fit and proper place to sum up, for the benefit of
the often illiterate noble, the alliances of his ancestors was over the
fireplaces in the baronial hall, and here, in the great mansions of
England, the arms of the family and of their marital connections
are still frequently to be seen. From the hall, the arms spread to
the bedrooms and other living rooms, sometimes being carved in
wood, or coloured on the stonework. Once in a country club I
realised that the house had belonged to the Frere family because
their arms were carved above the dining-room fireplace.

As silver became more commonly used in England, what more
obvious place for arms to be displayed? Tudor silver is somewhat
rare, but from later periods few silver pieces of any age are without a coat of arms. Although anything later than 1600 is demon-
strably after the age of armour, the use of arms on silver was not
a new phenomenon, but points back to an earlier time and its
practices. Armorial porcelain is, of course, much later than
armorial silver but there is no reason to suppose that the rougher
vessels of late medieval times were not ornamented or stamped
(for utilitarian reasons) with their owner's badge. This badge was
also worn by his retainers, and in the latter part of the fifteenth
century many ex-servicemen discharged from the army which
had fought in France were proud to ruffle it with the best as long
as they could wear the badge of a great lord. The bear and ragged
staff of the mighty Richard Neville, Earl of Warwick and twice
an earl in right of his wife, was a badge boasted by thousands.
When the maintenance of such private armies ended, the
numerous servants of the rich still wore their badges and their
liveries. The late A. C. Fox-Davies produced in this century
seven editions of his great work, *Armorial Families,* the last issue

in 1929–30 (2 vols), in which he gave the liveries proper to each family for their servants to wear. I do not think that this fashion prevails anywhere today but it was once widely observed.

Heraldry on jewellery, especially on signet rings, was very common, and still is. Many jewellers and engravers keep *Burke's General Armory*, or *Fairbairn's Book of Crests*, in their shops in readiness to furnish descriptions of arms to clients wishing to have rings or other items marked with their crests. The crest is only a part of a coat of arms, but in modern times it has been used in conjunction with a motto (which is no part of the coat of arms) on rings, spoons, forks and on motor-cars. In the case of rings and small silver, the use of the crest apart from the rest of the arms may have been derived from the difficulty of illustrating armorial bearings in a small space. With the depiction of crest and motto on a car, the argument is more obscure. Carriages preceded cars as the mode of travelling for the rich, and on carriage doors the full heraldic achievement could be given. (I have in my home a coat of arms copied from one such carriage door of 200 years ago.) The true story is told of a British ambassador to Washington in the nineteenth century whose carriage bore his arms. During repairs at a carriage maker's, a visiting American noticed the arms on the panel and inquired as to their origin. 'Mighty fine,' he opined on hearing what they were, and proceeded rapidly to bestow on the ambassador the flattery of imitation. Nor was he alone, and soon the Federal capital was enlivened with a brilliant heraldic display moving on some half-a-dozen carriages.

As the motor-car presented a smaller area much nearer to the ground and hence less suitable to the display of arms than the panels of a horse-drawn carriage, the crest and motto fashion on cars did not last long. Even peers are now content with a simple coronet. But if private individuals have exhibited heraldic humility, corporations and businesses have seen no reason to eschew the use of arms on their vehicles.

It should be explained that from very early days in the history of heraldry corporations and bodies of various kinds have used arms, like individuals and families. Regarded as a legal entity, a city, a bishopric, a university or a school, used arms as a sign of its corporate existence and to prevent forgeries or misuse of its name. This heraldic practice has proliferated on an enormous scale in the last 200 years and, as a later chapter will describe, the type of corporation now bearing arms is a great extension from the sort of body just mentioned.

Consequently, the vehicles of our time often bear heraldic devices. This is true of many governmental bodies like municipalities; and in a class by themselves are the royal warrant holders, about 1,000 firms, who are permitted to display the royal arms. This practice, permission for which has to be renewed in each reign, displays itself very amusingly in the streets of one of the most republican-minded cities in the world, Dublin, which not only possesses royal warrant holders but also numerous institutions which by their constitutions are permitted to style themselves 'Royal' and are in evidence everywhere.

In olden times many houses in England bore distinguishing signs, familiar enough to anyone who has read much of our past literature, and which were necessary owing to the absence of street numbers or other directions. Among these signs were those which showed armorial bearings, indicating that the house was inhabited by a nobleman or enjoyed his patronage in some way, and relics of this usage are to be seen all over England today in the numerous inn signs which bear the arms of some notable family. A revival and reversion to older habits of house signs is to be seen in the display of arms on swinging boards by banks, insurance companies and other commercial undertakings which display their coats of arms in this way.

Consideration of corporate arms also recalls the use of arms on seals. Most corporate bodies employ seals with which to authenticate their documents. The use of seals goes back to very early times, and heraldic seals from the twelfth century are the earliest evidences (apart from an enamel of 1127) that we possess of heraldic designs. Even from the beginnings of heraldry, seals have been used and they have therefore had a continuous life of over 800 years.

Some heraldic usages of the middle ages have not survived. In the fourteenth century, as can be seen from many illuminated manuscripts, it was the fashion for great ladies of the period to wear armorially adorned gowns. In heraldry, the rule is that the arms of husband and wife are shown by dividing the husband's shield into two equal portions by a line drawn from top to bottom of the shield; the husband's arms were shown on the right, those of his wife on the left. This practice was carried over to the gowns of the period, and as the female costume of that age—the long, pointed hat, and the long dress made of rich material and in brilliant colours—was one of the most beautiful and attractive of feminine fashions, the wearing of the heraldic devices of husband or father was a further adornment. Occasionally a beautiful red-head may have experienced some trouble with a predominantly gules (red) coat of arms, or a light brunette may have had complexion difficulties through the darkness of a sable or purpure. Incidentally, it may be noted that although feminism did not flourish in the middle ages, great ladies of ability and character were never debarred from exercising power and authority.

The fashion of armorial clothing for women died out with the medieval way of life, but a much longer lasting practice was that of displaying arms at a funeral and also over the door of a dead person's house. This practice was general right up to the seventeenth century, and some of the cases brought before the Court of Chivalry in that age relate to disputes regarding displays of arms at funerals. The quarrel related sometimes to the precedence of the mourners, at others to the right of the deceased to have borne arms at all. John Bunyan, in his *Life and Death of Mr Badman*, describes the carrying of the dead man's escutcheon at his funeral. Three hundred years earlier we have an account of the funeral of the Black Prince at Canterbury, with references to the bearing of his shields of war and of peace. So long did the custom last. A memorial of it is found in many of the older English churches, where the heraldic monuments of the dead, known as hatchments, are very often seen. These hatchments were placed over the door of the house where the death had occurred, and this practice was followed only a few years ago when Lady Catherine Ashburnham, the last of the ancient Ashburnham family of Sussex, died. The only other relic of the custom is to be found at Oxford where, on the death of masters of colleges, hatchments are, I believe, still set up.

Coincident with these numerous uses of arms in peaceful contexts was the display of heraldry in stained-glass windows, in plaques and on tombs and monuments in churches and elsewhere. As far as places of worship were concerned, heraldry was often more powerful than theology in resisting change. At the Reformation, the Protestants turned against prayers for the dead, and the numerous chantries which had been endowed so that priests should say Masses for the souls of the benefactors were abolished. Yet in a place like Boxgrove in Sussex, while the priory lies in ruins, the chantries still stand in the church, and although they have been unused for 400 years the monuments on them have been restored and their heraldic glories still bear witness to those who endowed the chantries. In many of the Catholic edifices taken over by Protestants the old heraldic windows remain, though usually the windows showing religious scenes have been removed. The Dom in Berne, Switzerland, once Catholic and now Protestant, is rich with magnificent windows devoted to the glories of Swiss nobility, and also possesses many carvings of arms. Even the grimmest forms of Protestant worship, while resolutely refusing to allow representation of the saints, have not forbidden entry to the hero and the noble. St Giles's Cathedral in Edinburgh provides a rich store for the genealogical herald in its memorials of family arms.

Heraldry is a medieval survival but on a vast scale. Apart from its ability to lend itself to artistic display, so that it is both a science and an art, its future was assured when men recognised it to be the hall mark of gentility. No one was more aware of the social value of arms than that up-and-coming actor-manager, William Shakespeare. He sued out a petition to the Earl Marshal to be made an armiger and, his prayer having been heard, he was granted arms in 1599 and thus became entitled to write himself 'Gent', which was duly placed on his monument at Stratford. His view of the matter is well expressed by Katherine in *The Taming of the Shrew*, (Act II, Scene I). Petruchio offers to cuff her, whereupon the lady replies :

> So may you lose your arms
> If you strike me, you are no gentleman
> And if no gentleman why then no arms.

The fortune of heraldry was made. It was associated with gentility. To be armigerous was to be a gentleman, or, of course, a lady. Feminine influence in matters of social advancement must never be under-rated.

The detachment of heraldry from body armour and its continuance in separate and complete independence came at a time when the influence of western Europe was becoming increasingly powerful. From the fifteenth century, as body armour gradually disappeared, heraldry flourished and gave impetus to a practice that was to become world wide. The European voyages of discovery brought the whole of the New World from Canada to Patagonia under European control, and as peoples of European stock took over these vast regions, so their habits of life, including heraldry, went with them.

In the Old World, the peoples of the Celtic fringe—in Wales, the Scottish Highlands and Ireland—had long accepted the armorial system, though it was alien to them in origin. So, too, had one of the Slav peoples, of Poland. In the seventeenth and early eighteenth century, Russia also came within the heraldic orbit. Peter the Great brought heraldry back with him from the west; henceforward arms plus noblesse were to be the reward of an official position, military or civil. With the reduction of the

Ottoman Empire in Europe, some heraldic designs were adopted by the Balkan countries.

During the eighteenth century the English, from being mere traders in India, became the dominant power and until the end of British rule the relationship between the Indian native princes and the English Government remained close and on the whole cordial. The ruling princes were encouraged to adopt western habits of education and their assumption of arms was taken for granted; how could the ruler of a state larger than England be without the gentilicial insignia possessed by a second-lieutenant sahib? Many of the princely coats of arms were registered in the English College of Arms after the Delhi Durbar of 1911, though by that time all the greater princes must have possessed armorial bearings.[1]

In the nineteenth century, the rest of the world was opened up by Europeans. Australia and New Zealand became British possessions and in both of them heraldry now flourishes. In southern Africa, there was a considerable influx of Europeans from Holland and later from the United Kingdom, leading eventually to the formation of the Republic of South Africa. In 1962, the republic set up a bureau of heraldry, a heraldry council and a state herald. In the history of heraldry in the Republic, Dutch, English, Portuguese and German heraldic influences must all be taken into account as all have had a bearing upon the subject.

In other parts of Africa which were formerly British colonies many official state coats of arms existed, and independence has not prevented the continuing use, albeit in modified form, of these arms. In addition, many African states and municipalities, especially those in former French Africa, now possess coats of arms, as was conclusively demonstrated at the IXth Congress of Genealogy and Heraldry in Berne in 1968 by M. André Privé in his paper *Armoiries d'Afrique et d'Orient*. Some of these coats of arms

---

[1] The arms of Indian princes are more fully discussed in Chapter 10.

bear only a distant affinity to true heraldic forms, but they would never have appeared at all but for the spread of European heraldic influences.

Lest anyone should imagine that only a tiny minority of intransigent diehards are studying the rules of heraldry, it should be known that nowhere in the world is there a keener following of heraldic knowledge than in the United States of America. In a later chapter American heraldry will be described at length; suffice it here to state that it is extensive, well informed and is now beginning to be most efficiently organised.

I have not mentioned Japan as having come under European heraldic sway because the Japanese possess an heraldic system of their own which is as old as that of Europe. Though differing in many respects from the European form, as one would expect of a system separately evolved, Japanese heraldry is truly heraldic and will be described later.

The earliest writers on European heraldry, having no proper criterion of historical change or even conception of such a matter, were wont to ascribe arms to all manner of men who could never have possessed them. Yet because the heraldic sphere of influence has widened to an extent which these men of the fourteenth to sixteenth centuries could never have anticipated, it has come about that arms are now in use in many countries where the old writers only imagined them to exist.

NOTE: The Chevalier Bayard. Pierre Terrail, Seigneur de Bayard, the famous French knight, can be considered in many respects the perfect example of the true knight of chivalry. He came of a noble family, the heads of which for two hundred years had usually died in battle. His exploits recall the stories of knights of romance. Once he held the passage of a bridge single-handed against a large body of Spaniards. He was the leader in a famous combat of thirteen French knights against an equal number of Germans. His ardour in pursuit once led him into Milan alone, where he was captured but released by the Duke without ransom. Similar good fortune befriended him at the hands of Henry VIII, to whom he gave his word not to serve against him for six weeks. This was at the famous battle of the Spurs (real name Guinegate) in 1513, so-called because of the precipitate flight of the French cavalry. Finding himself cut off, Bayard summoned an unarmed English knight to surrender and then himself surrendered to his prisoner. He was termed, and rightly, *le chevalier sans peur et sans reproche,* but he was no mere knight errant. His military operations showed great skill and he employed the best methods of gathering intelligence of the enemy's movements by reconnaissance and the employment of spies.

SOURCES AND WORKS USED IN REFERENCE

Miguel de Cervantes Saavedra, *Don Quixote de la Mancha.*
Edmund Spenser, *The Faërie Queene.*
J. S. Gardiner, *Foreign Armour in England.*
Die Innsbrucker Plattnerkunst, an illustrated catalogue (1954), showing many beautiful suits of Continental armour.

The journal of the Arms and Armour Society contains a considerable amount of information on armour, and the society has published a catalogue, entitled *The Art of the Armourer,* of an exhibition of armour, swords and firearms which was held at the Victoria and Albert Museum in 1963.

Also very useful are two guide books : *European Armour* by J. F. Hayward of the Victoria and Albert Museum (1951), and *Arms and Armour in England* by Sir James Mann, Master of the Armouries (1961); both booklets are published by Her Majesty's Stationery Office (HMSO).

CHAPTER 2

The Origins of Heraldry

HERALDRY is, then, a survival from the days of the armoured chivalry of the later middle ages. It is a system of symbolism which became hereditary with individuals, in families, and for institutions. Symbols have been used wherever organised communities have existed, and animals have often been the subjects. In the many volumes of Sir James Frazer there are innumerable examples of the identification which mankind has achieved with different animals, the bear, the lion, the wild cat, and so on. This is much less the case where Buddhist influence has prevailed because of this religion's teaching of the unity of all sentient life. This exception apart, the adoption of animals as symbols has been universal, and in early times when the existence of many impossible creatures was believed in, not only actual, but also imaginary creatures like the phoenix and the sphinx were taken as symbols by different races.

Such symbols are not heraldic. Even when they have passed down through long periods in a nation's history, like the human-headed bulls of Assyria, they are still not heraldic designs. Possibly the nearest approach to the latter in ancient times was in the usage of the twelve tribes of Israel, in the Old Testament. Most of the symbols used to describe the twelve sons of Jacob are of animal origin, and this is the meaning of the passage in the book of Numbers (ch 2, v 2) where the children of Israel are

27

bidden to muster each under the ensign of his father's house. There is here a specious resemblance to the devices of heraldry but the reference can only mean that the symbol of the tribe was used as a rallying or mustering point.

Heraldry can be described with certainty as having originated independently in western Europe and in Japan, in each case in the twelfth century. I shall describe the Japanese heraldic system in a later chapter and it will suffice here to emphasise that the use on armour of the Japanese mon, or crest/badge as we should call it, was not for purposes of identification as in Europe. Japanese armour was very different from the complete defensive covering of the western knights. On banners used in war, however, the Japanese were actuated by the same purpose of identification in hostilities as motivated the Europeans.

How did heraldry originate? Was it the production of a single mind or of a particular race or locality? To the first question the answer must be that the development of armour in the twelfth century made the recognition of friend from foe most difficult, and far more so than it had been in the latter part of the eleventh century.

In determining the time when heraldry began, and to answer the second and third questions, it is essential to study the Bayeux Tapestry. Fortunately, the whole of the Tapestry is reproduced in three English books, one of which is published in the Penguin library. It is also possible to see a diorama of the Tapestry in the Victoria and Albert Museum, London, which is based on photographs of the actual Tapestry taken in 1871 for the British government. In Copenhagen, incidentally, can be seen a Danish version of the conquest of England by the Danes, modelled on the lines of the Bayeux Tapestry and shown opposite a reproduction of it.

The Bayeux Tapestry has been preserved from at least 1476 in the cathedral at Bayeux. The considered view of modern scholarship adheres to the opinion of William Freeman and J. H. Round that the Tapestry was made within living memory of the Norman

Conquest. Odo, Bishop of Bayeux and the Conqueror's half-brother, may have been responsible for the production of the Tapestry, though we shall probably never know the names of the artist and executants of the work.

The Tapestry is an account in pictorial form, with captions, of the relations between Harold and William, rather than of the Norman Conquest. There are seventy-nine scenes beginning with what appears to be an interview between King Edward the Confessor and Harold, and ending with the flight of the English after the battle of Hastings. Few documents in history can possess more fascination than the Tapestry, or more inducements to scholarly ingenuity. What, for instance, is the story behind the seemingly disconnected incident (in Scene XVIII) between a lady named Aelfgifu and a certain cleric? Like so many features of the Norman Conquest, we have in the Tapestry the certainty of events but not their interpretation. Harold, we know, went to Normandy, about 1064. Why? If we knew the answer, the whole story of the Conquest would be much clearer.

Putting these interesting but unanswerable questions on one side, the Tapestry is an invaluable guide to the style of dress, armour, weapons, buildings, ships etc of the period 1066–1100. Now the armour in the Tapestry is that of chain mail covering most of the body, but not the legs below the knee. The armour is shown not only on the soldiers but also as being carried on hangers on to William's ships. The helmets are conical, with the face open but protected by a nose-piece. The shields are kite-shaped.

The soldiers on both sides, Norman and English, are armed alike, but none of the English has a design of any kind on his shield. In a few scenes in the Tapestry shields borne by Normans or Frenchmen show what appear at first sight to be heraldic designs, or at least a resemblance to them. In Scene VIII, four of the followers of Guy, Count of Ponthieu, carry shields: (1) with some kind of creature holding a fish (?) in its mouth; (2) a rough design emerging from the left side of the shield; (3) a cross;

and (4) an animal rather like a sheep. In Scene XII, a messenger from William has a winged creature depicted on his shield, and this reappears in Scene XIII, and again in Scene XV. In Scene XVI, a Norman bears a plain shield, while the cross, or a variant, appears in Scene XVIII, though this is most probably only a boss meant to strengthen the shield as it also appears clearly on the shields of the men of Dinan (Scene XXIV). In Scene XXV there is a shield with a cross in the middle, the cross having rather bulbous ends to the arms. This again may be only a strengthening device, as it is hard to see why a Norman knight, a generation before the First Crusade, would have worn so sacred an emblem as the Cross simply as a symbol. In Scene XLII, where William's fleet is navigating the Channel, the shields which hang from the vessels have the boss arrangement (not the cross) mentioned above in Scene XVIII.

In the other scenes where it is possible to see the front of a shield, as in LVIII, that of the Norman knight has strengthening bosses similar to those of the English knights. In Scene LXXV, an English warrior with the unmistakable boss on his shield is seen in close combat with a mounted Norman whose shield carries the rough design of some bird-like creature. There are, therefore, less than half-a-dozen representations on the foreigners' shields. Could these be the original of the heraldic devices borne by knights some three generations later?

There are many prints which show William the Conqueror wearing on his surcoat the three lions of England, which were assumed by his great-great-grandson, Richard I, towards the end of his reign (1189–99) and are the main part of Queen Elizabeth II's arms today. All such illustrations can be discounted. They are simply a feature of the ascription by medieval and later writers of coats of arms to earlier times. This is a constant phenomenon and one which was excusable in times when there was no understanding of historical studies or of the development of weapons, clothing, etc.

The answer to the question is that at the time of the Norman

Conquest heraldry did not exist, but that possibly some of the rudiments out of which it was to arise were already present. Some rough devices were in use. William did not, presumably, employ a national standard as he fought under the gonfanon of the Pope, and Harold's standard was the famous Fighting Man, the flag of the English hosts, along with the Dragon of Wessex. Earlier, the Viking invaders had used a raven standard, but designs of this kind were only continuations of the type used by the ancient Romans, the famous eagle of the legions derived from the legendary bird of Rome. Constantine the Great, the first Christian emperor, used the Labarum with the Chi Rho symbol for the name of Christ.

One of the battle scenes of the Tapestry depicts William throwing back his conical helmet so that it lay flat across the top of his head, to show that, despite rumours, he is alive. As depicted on the Tapestry, his appearance on this highly important occasion, with the end of the nose-piece in the fingers of his right hand, is almost ludicrous, though the scene does prove that the warrior of 1066 could very easily lift his helmet and reveal his full features. The knight of a hundred years later would have found this operation far from convenient; even if he could have accomplished it unaided, he could not have removed his helmet speedily in the tumult of conflict and amidst all the uncertainties of a wavering army. It is thus clear that the form of armour in use at the Norman Conquest permitted both greater ease of movement and of recognition than the chain-mail-cum-plate mixture of a century later. Here lies the explanation of the beginnings of heraldry. When body armour prevented recognition of leaders, the need arose for signs by which to distinguish them. Added to this was the necessity of distinguishing large bodies of men who had come together from different nations.

The Crusades began in the generation after the Norman Conquest, when the uncertainties of life in the earlier middle ages were giving way in Western Europe to a much more orderly system. The pressure on Europe from the Moslems from the south

and east, the Vikings from the north and the pagans from the
north-east against central Europe, was relaxed. The Vikings were
converted to Christianity, and in the Iberian peninsula the
Spanish kingdoms began to make headway against the Moors.
In eastern Europe and the Levant, where for centuries the
Byzantine Empire had barred the way, the Turks, a new power in
Islam, succeeded in gaining control of Asia Minor. Byzantium
was weakened at the very time when the rising energies of western
Europe and its vigorous religious faith were making pilgrimage
to the Holy Land of Palestine very popular. So when the eastern
emperor, Alexius, appealed to the Pope for assistance against the
Moslems, the time was ripe for the extension into the Near East
of the crusading spirit which had already successfully defended
Christendom against so many foes. Pope Urban II preached the
Crusade as a holy war at the Council of Clermont in 1095, and
such was the enthusiasm which swept Europe that, without wait-
ing for proper organisation, a great multitude set out in the spring
of 1096 under the leadership of the wild preacher, Peter the
Hermit, and of Walter the Penniless. As might have been expected, this crowd of simple folk was destroyed, the greater part on
their way through Hungary and the rest when they eventually
reached Asia Minor. In the autumn of 1096 the army of those
princes who had taken the Cross arrived near Constantinople.
The leaders included Hugh of Vermandois, Godfrey de Bouillon,
the Duke of Lower Lorraine, and his brother Baldwin, sons of
that Count Eustace of Boulogne who is mentioned in the
Tapestry; others were Bohemund and Tancred, Normans from
Sicily, Count Raymund of Toulouse, Robert of Flanders, Robert,
Duke of Normandy, the son of William the Conqueror, Stephen
Count of Blois, and the papal legate, Adhemar, Bishop of Ruy.
All these leaders were French or French-speaking, and although
from the start of the crusading movement men from all Christian
nations participated, the character of the First Crusade was
markedly French. The Pope who initiated the effort was French

and preached his famous sermon in France. Consequently, it was natural for the Moslems to refer to the Crusaders as Franks, a name which remained with them.

With the history of the Crusades, except insofar as they influenced heraldry, we are not concerned, but clearly the collection into one large force of many contingents from different parts of Europe must have raised the problem of identification and thus hastened the development of armorial bearings. No similar gathering of many nations under one banner, that of the Cross, had ever taken place before in Europe; the Romans had mustered recruits from all the races in their empire and their auxiliary forces were drawn from many sources, often from barbarian tribes, but these various contingents were gathered under the legionary standards. To take a much later example, during the 1939–45 war, when the allied forces comprised many nationalities and it was essential to distinguish the different formations, there were over 500 army signs of the British and allied HQ commands and formations. The parallel with the practice which must prevail in any large composite force is obvious.

We have a great deal of exact information on the appearance of the Crusaders when they arrived at Constantinople. This knowledge comes from the pen of the Princess Anna Comnena, daughter of Alexius I, the Byzantine emperor who reigned from 1081 to 1118. In her history, *The Alexiad,* the Princess describes the Franks, as she calls the Crusaders, in language at once exaggerated and at the same time calculated to reduce the self-esteem of western Europeans. After mentioning the approach of innumerable Frankish armies, she goes on: 'And indeed the actual facts were far greater and more terrible than rumour made them. For the whole of the West and all the barbarian tribes which dwell between the further side of the Adriatic and the pillars of Hercules, had all migrated in a body and were marching into Asia through the intervening Europe and were making the journey with all their household.' (Book X, p 248.) The language is that of hyperbole, but the use of the expression

c

'barbarian' accurately reflects the view taken of the westerners by the most polished circles of Byzantium.

The Princess was full of curiosity about the appearance of the barbarians and described their arms and armour in her narrative as occasion arose. The crossbow 'a bow of the barbarians quite unknown to the Greeks' is described in detail when the Princess finds it necessary to write of its use in warfare. Later, when hostilities were likely to break out between Alexius and Bohemund's Franks, she gives a very careful account of the armour of the latter. She says that Alexius exhorted his archers to shoot at the Franks' horses rather than their riders because their armour rendered them practically invulnerable. 'For the Frankish weapon of defence is this coat of mail, ring plaited into ring and the iron fabric is such excellent iron that it repels arrows and keeps the wearer's skin unhurt. An additional weapon of defence is a shield which is not round, but a long shield, very broad at the top and running out to a point, hollowed out slightly inside, but externally smooth and gleaming with a brilliant boss of molten brass' (Book XIII, ch VIII, p 341).

A generation after Hastings, then, the Norman knights were still armed as in 1066, for here are the very swallow-tailed long shields to be seen in the Bayeux Tapestry and the same kind of armour. Within forty years, after the First Crusade (1095–99), heraldic devices begin to appear. They are shown on seals as early as 1136, and between then and 1155 armorial seals are found in England, France, Germany, Spain and Italy. It seems, though, that heraldic devices were employed on shields even earlier than 1136. Geoffrey Plantaganet, son-in-law of Henry I, died in 1151. He was buried at Le Mans, in Normandy, and the museum there possesses an enamel portrait which shows him holding a decidedly heraldic shield—azure, four lions rampant or. This portrait was made not later than 1151 and his possession of the shield agrees with an account in a chronicle which states that Henry I, son and successor of William the Conqueror, when knighting Geoffrey in 1127, bestowed upon him a shield which bore painted lions. At the ceremony of knighting, the one who bestowed the accolade gave arms to the new-made knight, as can be seen in the Bayeux Tapestry where, at the conclusion of a campaign in France, William bestows arms on Harold. In the Tapestry scene no armorial bearings are even hinted at, whereas in the knighting of Geoffrey Plantaganet the enamel confirms the specific mention in the chronicle.

It could be that arms were first used on seals, or even in ornamental fashion, and subsequently adapted to meet the clamant need for distinction in warfare, though I think their use in warfare is more likely to have come first. Certainly during the twelfth century armour became ever more enveloping as the knights tried to guard against the type of accident which had killed Harold. More than a century later an arrow was the cause of Richard Coeur de Lion's death. Wearing only light armour, he had been reconnoitring a castle when he was wounded in the shoulder by an arrow, and later died as the result of unskilful handling by the leech.

It was during the time of Richard I that the heavy 'heaulme' or helmet which covered the face except for the small aperture of the visor came into fashion. So far from being easily thrown back, it was so cumbersome that it needed a squire to bear it and to assist the knight to put it on. It was donned only at the moment of going into battle. About the same period the surcoat began to be worn over the armour. Here was an opportunity for heraldry to be used to set forth the knight's arms.

Coming back to the question of how heraldry originated, we simply do not know if the idea was conceived by a single mind. By the time that men and women began to write about it, heraldry had been in active use for over 200 years. There was no one to report its arrival. Perhaps if there had been an Anna Comnena in France in 1150 we should have received a written account of the subject. As it is, all that we can do is to record the successive appearances of armorial bearings.

As to the place of origin, we shall not be wrong in assigning it to France. The language of heraldry is to this day French. An attempt about 1400 in England to substitute English terms for French, such as gold and silver for *or* and *argent,* failed. During the middle ages, Latin was the language of the Church and of most official writing, and French the spoken tongue of the gentle-folk, while the English language endured a difficult fate. Before the Norman Conquest it had developed the earliest of European literatures, and had become, to a large extent, the language of official documents and record keeping. The Normans by their conquest thrust English into the inferior linguistic position to which politically they assigned the conquered, though they could not prevent the bulk of the inhabitants from speaking their own language and were themselves forced to learn some English. Those who can see a consolation in every calamity may expatiate on the beneficial results of the freeing from grammatical bonds and the extensive borrowing of foreign words which undoubtedly occurred in English. At last, in the fourteenth century, English became again a literary language used by poets of renown, and the daily speech of all English folk.

Since the heraldic language is French, could the science of heraldry have originated in Normandy? The idea that the Normans were more civilised than the English whom they conquered has no more validity than had the assumed superiority of the conquerors. Superior in the planning of warfare and in building the Normans without question were; but they had no literature and no law, two fatal deficiencies for any people claiming to be cultured. They were also very clever and adaptive—one reason why they have been absorbed by the peoples of every country they conquered—and they were the first race in England to use surnames. Camden, in his famous *Remaines concerning Britain,* remarks that Edward the Confessor was 'all Frenchified' and, through his Norman favourites, introduced surnames into England. Some of the most notable Norman names like Curzon or Tremlett, Harcourt or Gorges, are derived from places in Normandy and were used there before their owners came to

England. As we noted in the Tapestry, there are rudiments of devices on a few Norman shields, and we know that the leaders of the First Crusade included several Normans. It could be, then, that heraldry began in Normandy and spread rapidly among the French, and so to the French-speaking seigneurs in other lands.

The earliest collections of armorial records are to be found among seals, and very large numbers of these are preserved in England, France and Germany, with smaller quantities in Spain and Italy. Next to seals as evidences of heraldry are the rolls of arms which were compiled by persons interested in heraldry but not necessarily professional heralds. The rolls in England date from the middle of the thirteenth century and are found up to 300 years later. They refer to some event, a tournament or a military expedition, at which many armigers were present. The compiler was interested in making a record of the arms, sometimes with written descriptions only, but more often with illustrations and names of bearers appended.

England is rich in collections of rolls of arms, followed by France; other countries have little in the way of rolls, but Germany possesses many richly-emblazoned painted books of armorial bearings. In England, a typical specimen is that called the Falkirk Roll, which gives the list of armigers who served under Edward I when he made his expedition against Wallace in 1298. The arms of 111 persons are described, all of them being of sufficient importance to have a banner borne before them. Many very important names are recorded : Percy, Wake, Martyn, Fitz-william, Hastings, Moulton, Despenser, Clifford, Basset, and De Vere. The account is divided into sections, those whose banners were in the vanguard, or which were borne in one of the other divisions of the army—the four battles as they were called. The medieval battle array presented a magnificent picture as the host came into view. The polished armour of the knights standing out against the dull jerkins of the majority of the men-at-arms or archers, with here and there along the line a brilliant splash of colour on the banners—all gave a special relevancy to the

Biblical phrase, 'terrible as an army with banners'. Such an awe-inspiring sight was granted to the Scots when they saw the great English host deploying in front of them before the battle of Bannockburn. The flower of English chivalry, some 400 nobles, was there, and even the bravest of the Scots must have felt some inward qualms as they realised that, laggard as Edward of Carnarvon might be, he had indeed mustered a kingdom's power. The king himself felt something of the sort for when he saw the Scots fall on their knees to ask God's blessing he thought that they were begging for mercy.

For the period 1308–14 which ended in Bannockburn, there is a roll of arms of the reign of Edward II which contains over 1,100 coats of arms. This roll begins with the king's arms and those of his principal nobles, after which it is divided by counties, though Durham and Monmouth are omitted. Omissions also occur in the counties listed, as many notable families are not included. This is easily understood as it would not have been practicable to have gone through each county and the roll was probably drawn up as a record of armed assemblies at which not every armiger from every county would have been present.

Dealing with the period of Edward I's wars in Scotland is the Roll of Caerlaverock, a poem describing the short siege of a fortalice in Dumfriesshire in 1300. Over 100 coats of arms are here described, of which eighty-eight were borne on banner as well as on shield. The Caerlaverock Roll is supposed to have been written about 1350, possibly by a herald who was in the train of Edward I during the expedition. The poem was written in old Norman French, and contains much more than the blazons of arms. It describes the attempt to take the castle and well illustrates the wasteful indiscipline of the medieval army. There is much in the poem reminiscent of Scott's story of the assault on Torquilstone Castle in *Ivanhoe;* the poet says of one knight that 'so stoutly was the gate of the castle assailed by him that never did smith with his hammer strike his iron as he and his did there'. One can almost hear the Black Knight hammering at Front de Boeuf's gate. There is, too, a very striking example of the skill of the archers; the Scot who shows a flag of truce has his hand pierced through to his face by an arrow. The roll also bears witness to the not infrequent disputes over the ownership of arms by knights who found themselves in possession of identical coats. Brian Fitz-alan and Hugh Pointz bore barry or and gules at Caerlaverock. In other instances the arms of persons whose descendants in the male line are still with us have altered over the centuries from what they were in 1300. One simple knight, Ralph de Mont-hermer, had married above him, a very great lady indeed, the Princess Joan, daughter of Edward I. She had been married previously to a De Clare, and through her he acquired the Clare earldoms of Gloucester and Hereford. At Caerlaverock, de Mon-thermer had a banner with the arms of Clare in right of his wife's first husband's earldoms, and on his shield bore his own coat of arms. Then again at Caerlaverock, John de Cromwell used his own arms, but we know that at other times he carried the insignia of his wife's family, the Vipoints.

Later rolls are concerned with the wars in France. Such is the list of the Calais Bannerets, 1345–48, which gives seventy-nine coats of arms for persons who had a banner borne at the siege of Calais. It is possible that this roll may have been copied with additions in the sixteenth century from a medieval manuscript. In another roll there is a list of 107 names of those who served with Henry V at Rouen in 1418. The arms are illustrated in colour.

In the collections of the Society of Genealogists in London there is a manuscript book of arms mentioned in different rolls in the period from Henry III to Edward II (1216–1327). It contains more than 6,500 entries of 2,085 coats used by 3,026 persons.

The production of rolls died out in the sixteenth century as the occasions for making them disappeared. Tournaments were on the way out and although there were many military expeditions they were conducted not by feudal contingents but by more modern-style armies.

The rolls are by no means confined to the arms of Englishmen only, unless the special occasion was one which concerned English knights alone. The arms of great potentates appear in some rolls, the sovereigns of Continental countries, and French and German coats of arms are also described. An instructive account of the manner in which a roll was compiled was given by Sir Robert Laton, a witness in the famous *Scrope v Grosvenor* dispute. In his evidence he said that Scrope had used the arms—azure a bend or—as long as he could remember and that he had been instructed by his father to compile a list of all the arms known to the latter, and to include Scrope in the collection. In this way many rolls must have been made, and from the class of those interested in compiling them the official heralds probably developed.

In all this consideration of the evidences of heraldry no mention has yet been made of records in book form. This is because it is not until 200 years after heraldry came into use that books about it began to appear. The first extant known work on heraldry is by an Italian lawyer whose book, *Tractatus de Insignis et Armis,* was published about 1358, not long after the author's death. Bartholus was a considerable jurist and has been called the father of private international law by Professor G. C. Cheshire. (*Private International Law,* 1949, p 30.) He lived from 1314 to about 1356, and was professor of law at Bologna, Pisa and Perugia in turn. He became *doctor legum* at Bologna in 1334, when he was in his twenty-first year. He served as an assessor to the podesta of Todi, then of Pisa, and became professor of civil law at Pisa when he was about twenty-four, and later at Perugia where, in 1348, he was given citizenship. In 1355, when the Holy Roman Emperor, Charles IV, spent a week at Pisa after having been crowned at Rome, Bartholus was sent to Pisa by Perugia as one of its envoys. From the emperor, Bartholus received many privileges, including a grant of arms which were those of the emperor as King of Bohemia with changed tinctures: or, a lion rampant with two tails gules.

On this subject of Bartholus I have drawn from the researches of a learned American scholar, Dr L. M. Mladen, whose paper, *Bartolus on the Right to Bear Arms*, was read at the Vth International Congress of Genealogy and Heraldry at Stockholm in 1960. Dr Mladen remarks of the grant of arms, not only to Bartholus but to others by the emperor at the same time: 'Charles (1316–78) was in all probability the first ruler ever to grant arms. To my knowledge, no earlier occurrence has been found.' Although Mladen considers that a writer on seals, Konrad von Mure (ca 1200–81), could theoretically be classed as the first writer to mention heraldic emblems, he is definite that Bartholus was the first to produce a theoretical treatise on heraldry.

Another writer, now dead, H. Stanford London, said of Bartholus: 'His tract has nothing to do with English heraldry except in so far as the uses and customs of heraldry in the fourteenth century were common to the whole of western Europe. Bartholus, however, enjoyed a high reputation in those days and his works and those of Francis de Foveis are quoted as authorities in nearly all the fifteenth-century treatises known to me.' Of Francis de Foveis, we can only add that he was a Frenchman who lived in the fourteenth century, that no copy of his treatise has yet been identified, but that his heraldic teachings have been incorporated in other works which will be noted below.

I am not here concerned with the doctrines of Bartholus on the right to bear arms as I have dealt with them at some length in my book, *The Story of Heraldry,* but only with the pedigree of heraldic writers. The first writer in England on the subject was John of Guildford, as he is commonly called. He wrote a *Tractatus de Armis*, or 'Treatise on Arms', usually described as by Johannes de Bado Aureo, which was produced about 1394. How did he obtain his copy of Bartholus, whom he quotes with approval? 'His collaborator, the Frenchman, Franciscus de Foveis, may have got it in France. Or the daughter of Charles IV, who became the good Queen Anne of Richard II, may have brought it with her from Bohemia.' (Dr Mladen.)

Next came a Welsh treatise based on John of Guildford, the *Llyfr Arfau*, or 'Book of Arms'. This has been printed in Professor Evan Jones' book, *Medieval Heraldry*, 1945. In this work, five treatises of arms were published (i) the *Llyfr Arfau*, (ii), the *Tractatus* of John de Guildford (iii) the Pakenham Tract compiled mainly from (ii) about 1449, (iv) a little *Tretis on Armes*, in English, also by John de Guildford and (v) Bartholus' *Tractatus de Insignis et Armis*.

Next there is *De Studia Militari* by Nicholas Upton. He was a canon of Salisbury Cathedral who dedicated his book to Humphrey, Duke of Gloucester (died in 1446), and the work must have been written about 1440.

John of Guildford's Treatise was printed in 1654 with Upton's *De Studio Militari* and with the *Aspilogia* of Sir Henry Spelmann, by Sir Edward Bysshe, Garter King of Arms, who edited and annotated all three works. The whole was in Latin and no English version of Upton's book has been published. A translation in manuscript was made by John Blount, an Oxford student, about 1500. Portions of this translation were published in 1931 by Dr F. P. Barnard of Oxford—*The Essential Portions of Nicholas Upton's De Studio Militari*.

The flood of writing on heraldry had begun, and many others now set themselves to put down their thoughts. The following treatises have been found in recent years; many others may exist and may yet be found. (i) The Dublin tract in the Genealogical Office, Dublin, about the middle or late fifteenth century, follows the same line as Upton and others of the earlier writers. (ii) The Ashmolean Tract, dated about the mid-fifteenth century in the Bodleian Mss. It has the idea that armorial ensigns were first used at the siege of Troy and then brought to Britain by the Trojan, Brutus. (iii) The Bradfer Lawrence Tract, of about 1445. (iv) Strangways' Book, about 1454, in the British Museum, by Richard Strangways of the Inner Temple, mostly heraldic memoranda. (v) The Heralds' Tract Ms in the College of Arms, about 1460, much the same as (iv). (vi) Patrick's Book, after 1461, found in Antwerp. (vii) The Wrythe-Strangways shields, about 1480, in Wrythe's Garter Book. (viii) The Peter Le Neve's shields, about 1480–1500. (ix) A poem in Lowland Scots written in 1494 by Adam Loutfut, Kintyre Pursuivant. This has been printed in 1869 in a volume of the Early English Text Society. (x) Povey's Tract, about 1550, in the College of Arms. (xi) Kimbey's Tract in Harleian Mss, about 1600.

Among the printed works is *The Boke of St Albans*, published in 1486. It is usually ascribed to a lady, Dame Julyana Bernes, or Berners, of whom very little is known save that she is reputed to have been Prioress of Sopwell, a nunnery near St Albans, in whose abbey the book was first printed and from which it takes its name. The work is in five sections : Treatises on Hawking, of Hunting, of Coat Armour, Fishing with an Angle, and Blazoning of Arms, these being then regarded as prime essentials in the education of a gentleman. The ascription of the authorship to a lady has not prevented some very ungallant criticisms of the 'Boke' on the part of crabbed, confined and constipated male critics, solely because the authoress followed out in her descriptions the heraldic practice of her times as regards the taking of coats of arms other than by grant from the Crown. Dame Julyana followed Upton's work on the whole.

In the sixteenth century, large folio works began to appear, similar to the 'big book of Harrowtry' of which Master Michael Mumblazen in Scott's *Kenilworth* was so fond. There were John Ferne's *Blazon of Gentrie* (1573), Gerard Leigh's *Accedenee of Armorie* (1591) and Guillim's *Heraldry* (1610) to be followed by many others, though not all the succeeding treatises even in the seventeenth century were as large.

The works mentioned above all have three features in common. None of them can provide any set clue as to the origin of heraldry. The writers just do not understand the changes in manners, clothes, and habits over the lapse of centuries. Just as painters for many ages persisted in representing characters of the past in clothes and surroundings identical with those of the artists' con-

temporaries, so heraldic writers assumed without question that
arms had existed from a remote period. To state that coat armour
began at the siege of Troy, approximately 1,000 BC, was almost
an advance in historical criticism compared with the views of
writers who thought arms coeval with the skin clothing of our
first parents on their expulsion from Eden. Owing to their naïve

Arms of the Grand Soldan

outlook, it was natural that heraldry should be extended in space
as in time; even the Sultan of the Turks (the Grand Soldan) was
assigned armorial bearings.

Secondly, these writers indulged in many quaint conceits, mentioning at times charges or practices in heraldry which probably
never existed outside their own minds. Much false natural history
was also found in heraldic works, as in all other medieval treatises.

Thirdly, despite all the errors and misunderstandings, these
writers up to the seventeenth century did have the advantage of

being able to see heraldry in practical use in the tourney, the fields and the streets; the procession of a great noble with his retainers or the funeral of a distinguished man provided ample opportunities to see heraldic devices borne as they were intended to be.

From the nineteenth century onward there is the application of historical science to the study of heraldry. Like all other historical subjects, from Biblical criticism to fashions in dress, heraldry has been given a thorough examination. Great writers have studied the science and art of heraldry, and the subject is now as clear, in the broad European outlines, and in the British Isles, as it is ever likely to be. The writings of Oswald Barron, of J. Woodward and G. Burnett, of Charles Boutell, of A. C. Fox-Davies, to mention only a few of the dead, have given an illumination to the study which has removed even from obscure corners the fanciful notions of the past. Today, the study of heraldry can be as clear and easy of comprehension for the student as were the insignia borne on the march or in the van of battle in medieval times. Heraldry was meant *ab initio* to be pellucidly clear. It is so again now for all who care to take the very little trouble its understanding requires.

CHAPTER 3

English Heraldry

THOUGH Englishmen do tend to regard heraldic systems other than their own as deviations from the true standard, there is no justification for such an attitude as heraldry has developed quite independently in different European countries, though retaining sufficient basic elements to enable anyone from another heraldic discipline to recognise and describe a coat of arms. If any country has the right to look on the heraldry of other lands as derived from its own, that country would be France, especially if the theory advanced in the last chapter is correct.

In its origins, English heraldry is derived from France, since it was the French-speaking seigneurs who introduced it into England in the twelfth century. Owing to the expansion of English political and economic power, English heraldry has been carried into a wider area than that of any other European country, Spain only excepted. In 1500, not even the most Chauvinistic patriot could have described English as a leading language in Europe. By 1600 the position was altering, but even in the seventeenth century the greatest English epic poet considered the choice—Latin or English—before helping to establish the ultimate supremacy of English by his decision to write in his native language. A language owes its standing among the multitude of tongues almost as much to the great poets and writers who use it as to the commercial and military successes of its native country.

Portuguese is not a language essential to the diplomat or business man, but it can claim at least one world poet. Camoens by his epic, *Os Lusiadas*, prevented the submergence of the Portuguese tongue by Spanish during the years of the Spanish captivity (1581–1640), when Portugal was a province ruled from Madrid, and for over 200 years translators have striven to reproduce in their own language the poetry of Camoens. Another country, Russia, enjoyed great political power for more than a century before it had any poetic voice. Carlyle, writing well before 1870, lamented that poor Italy was unrepresented at the councils of the nations, and yet she had Dante; whereas Russia, mighty in the extent of her empire, could not speak. Dostoievsky, Tolstoy, Turgenev and others have since redeemed that silence.

So it has happened that the enormous expansion of English commerce and political power over the last 400 years has carried with it some of England's less material assets, too. The English language has become the first in the world; its literature is now the property of the educated everywhere. The English Church is the only Protestant communion which has a world-wide extension of over 550 episcopal sees, including those bodies such as the American Episcopal Church, whose countries are outside the British Commonwealth but are in communion with Canterbury. The heraldic influence of London, the seat of the College of Arms, is now felt in the USA, Canada, Australia, New Zealand, South Africa, and wherever people of English descent have settled, grants of arms from the three Kings—Garter, Norroy and Clarenceux—have gone all over the world. Very many more English coats are in use without benefit from the College, a practice with a venerable tradition behind it. Scottish heraldry has also assumed world-wide proportions but, for other than purely numerical reasons, not to the same extent as its English equivalent.

What then are the characteristics of English heraldry? It is, I think, true to say that it is freer, both to the advantage and to the detriment of the users, than other national systems. Once a grant

of arms has been made, all the legitimate male descendants of the
grantee are entitled to use those arms. So, too, are female descendants in accordance with the law of arms, that is provided that
their husbands are armigerous and can display their wives' arms.
After the first generation of females, the use of the arms by their
descendants depends on the views held about quarterings. If an
eldest married daughter has no brothers, then she is an heraldic
heiress and her children can quarter their mother's arms. On the
European continent the practice of sixteen quarterings applies,
and every ancestor must be armigerous. This system, especially
when carried back another generation, giving thirty-two shields,
provides very impressive pedigrees, and bears eloquent testimony
to the aristocratic grandeur of a family.

English heraldry is free of the meticulous registration and recording which is the mark of the Scots heraldic system. Many
people contrast Scottish heraldry to its disadvantage with the
English, overlooking the fact that the loose English system has
laid itself open to abuses of a very serious nature. Certainly it
seems right that a grant once made should continue *ad infinitum.*
Of course, there are grants in Scots heraldry, but after a generation recourse must be had to matriculation, otherwise the arms
may not continue to be used. This is the law and full account
will be given in the next chapter of the legalistic nature of Scots
heraldry. Owing to circumstances which no one could foresee
400 or 500 years ago, the checks which would have prevented
abuses in the English system have gradually fallen into disuse.
First of these is the system of cadency which has, with two exceptions, disappeared from English heraldry. It was explained in
the preceding chapter how the use of arms arose for practical
purposes and without official regulation. Control by the Crown
through the heralds came later. In France the heralds, who were
members of the king's household, were formed into a College in
1407. In 1484, Richard III of England did the same, and thus
began the English College of Arms, although many of the heraldic
offices had existed for generations as dependent upon the royal

household. Not only kings but great nobles also had their private heralds, though in England these did not survive the fall of the feudal nobility. From early times some means of differencing arms were used to distinguish the cadet from the senior lines. This is the origin of cadency, and it might have been expected that the consolidation of the royal heralds into the College would have given precision to the method of denoting cadency. Such was not the case. It is as well to hear on this subject the views of an English and a Scottish author.

The Rev John Woodward in his *Treatise on Heraldry* (1892) p 396, wrote: 'Before armorial bearings had been for a century in general use it was found necessary to distinguish by their variations, not only different families but different members or branches of the same family. It came to be understood that the head of the house could alone use the pure unaltered coat. Even the heir apparent, or heir presumptive, had no right to use the ancestral coat without some variation, in common with other cadets he had to bear it with a *difference*, or *brisure*. This was early an unwritten but generally accepted law. The obligation of cadet lines to difference their arms was recognised over nearly the whole of civilised Europe in the fourteenth century; and when, later, the obligation seemed in danger of being forgotten, it was made the subject of direct legislation.'

Equally definite is the view of Lt-Col Robert Gayre of Gayre and Nigg in *Heraldic Cadency* (1961), p 19; 'Under the Law of Arms no two men can have the same coat of arms within the same armorial jurisdiction. Consequently, merely to have descent from an armigerous ancestor does not confer *his* arms upon anyone excepting the *chief of the line*, and any other coat must bear its brisure.'

How then has it happened in England that cadency has been almost abandoned? The explanation, I think, is that the wearing of armour began to decline in the sixteenth century, so that identification of persons became much less necessary. Floriated and over elaborate armorial bearings then became possible. The older

D

modes of differencing—change of tincture, addition of charges, the label, use of the canton, quarter, escutcheon, bordure etc— began to be abandoned, and there was evolved a system of marks of cadency designed to denote the order of birth of brothers, and supposed to be charged in the next generation by other minute differences. This method would have proved equal to differencing the arms of quintuplets or sextuplets; it was probably invented to deal with families in days long before birth control was practised, when one child followed another each year and unfortunate women often bore a dozen or more children before succumbing. The marks of cadency in English heraldry as they are set out in *Burke's General Armory* smell of the same cycle which produced the Petrasancta system of delineating arms. Neither of these methods has any connection with the practical use of arms in warfare.

The marks of cadency soon fell out of use, if they were ever much employed. Very occasionally a coat of arms is seen in England bearing eg, a crescent, as in the case of Earl Stanhope which shows that he is derived from a younger son of an Earl of Chesterfield. The crescent is still shown in illustrations of Stanhope arms even though Earl Stanhope succeeded to the earldom of Chesterfield in 1952 and thus became the head of the family. This is one of the two exceptions previously mentioned as to the disuse of cadency. Thus while we can agree in theory with the two writers, Woodward and Gayre, in English practice any man descended from a grantee of arms is entitled to the arms of the family and can use them. The question is should he difference the arms by his own ingenuity? I see no reason against it, but every argument for it, though I would suggest that in differencing he should not use the cadency marks which are to hand, but one of the older ways described in detail by Woodward or Gayre.

The second exception as to cadency in England is in connection with the arms of the royal family. No member of the royal house can bear arms until authorised to do so by the reigning sovereign.

The reason for this is that the English royal arms are not personal or family arms, but arms of a dominion or sovereignty. Richard I was the first King of England to use a coat of arms and, under his successors of the Plantaganet dynasty, these arms became those of the Sovereign of England, ie, of England. When the Tudors displaced the Plantaganets the three lions remained the royal arms. Similarly with the Stuarts and the Hanoverians, the shield was shown quarterly, as it is now, with the arms of France, later of Scotland and Ireland, but the arms of England remained the same, despite changes of dynasty. Thus the royal arms are borne whole and entire only by the reigning sovereign, and not by any other until authorised by that sovereign.

The arms then assigned to the royal cadet are always marked with a label. The use of the label, with varying number of points, was fairly common in the middle ages, but as far as England is concerned is now used only by the royal family. To take some modern examples; Princess Margaret, Countess of Snowdon, has a label of three points, argent the centre point charged with a thistle slipped and leaved proper and each of the other points with a Tudor rose.

For the son or daughter of a sovereign, the label has three points; a grandson's label has five points. Thus the late Duke of Kent, who was killed in 1942, bore a label of three points argent, each point charged with an anchor azure. His son, the present duke, has a label of five points argent, the centre point and two outer points charged with an anchor azure, and the two inner points with a St George's Cross.

The Duke of Gloucester has a label of three points argent, the first and third points charged with a St George's Cross and the centre point with a lion passant guardant gules. The Duke of Windsor bears a label of three points argent, the centre point charged with an Imperial crown proper. This differs, of course, from his label when he was Prince of Wales.

The arms of the Queen Mother have no label as she was the consort of the sovereign, although when King George VI had been Duke of York the label of his arms would have appeared on the royal arms as borne by his wife.

The Duke of Edinburgh does not bear the royal arms, and therefore has no label. And although three lions appear in the first quarter of his shield they are passant, not guardant as in the royal arms of England. The ground of the shield is or, not gules, and it is semée of hearts gules. It has, therefore, only a heraldic reminiscence to the arms of England. Very different was the procedure for the duke's ancestor and predecessor, the Prince Consort. 'On the marriage of the Queen to the Prince Consort there was made to him a grant of the Royal Arms of the United Kingdom with the difference of a label argent on the central point a cross of St. George; to be borne in the first and fourth quarters, with the arms of Saxony in the second and third. Her Majesty the Queen has told us in her "Life of the Prince Consort" that she herself discovered the precedent for this arrangement (of which the then Garter was ignorant or unmindful) in the grant made to Prince Leopold of Saxe-Coburg on the occasion of his marriage with the Princess Charlotte, daughter of George IV' (Woodward, *op cit*, p 424).

This latter arrangement was certainly a strange one. By the use of the English royal arms as quarters, the shield would appear to be that of a person who had inherited these arms, ie, a son of a marriage between an heraldic heiress and an armigerous husband. It is a sign of greater heraldic knowledge that this curious inversion has not been followed for the present Prince Consort. Prince Albert of Saxe-Coburg had arms in which the quartered arms of England appeared as 1 and 4, his paternal arms as 2 and 3; the supporters were lion and unicorn, and six crests were shown without a helmet.

The Prince of Wales has a label of three points argent. Prince Andrew has a three-point label with an anchor on the centre point. Princess Anne bears a three-point label with a cross on the outer points and on the centre point a heart.

When a cadency mark is used in English heraldry other than

royal, it can be perpetuated for many generations. If a cadet line which bears the cadency mark becomes settled in another country, the cadency mark will be treated as if it were an integral part of the arms, eg, in Denmark, where no cadency rules are applied.

Probably a cadency system more akin to that of Scotland would now be applied in England if the two traditional means of regulating arms-bearing had not broken down. These methods were those of the Visitations and of the Court of Chivalry. The latter is still in existence, as indeed it existed before the Visitations began, but as the Visitations ceased completely 300 years ago and will not be resumed, they can be dealt with before the Court is described.

The bearing of arms has been shown to be a matter within the discretion and the needs of the user. Frequent cases are known of people, strangers in blood, who used the same arms. Disputes as to the right to bear identical arms were frequent and are often mentioned in medieval records. Such disputes were referred, sometimes but not always, to the Crown for settlement. This implies that just as the bearing of titles was a matter within the jurisdiction of the sovereign, so, too, the bearing of arms came within the royal purview. It was a very natural and proper recourse to apply to the Crown for elucidation and resolution of the difficulty. As time passed, the royal power as the Fountain of Honour became more exact, especially under the Tudors who had reduced the overbearing authority of the nobles. A considerable step in the direction of royal control of arms had been made when the College of Arms was founded in 1484, but as this had been the work of the usurper Richard III, the College fell into some disfavour under the first of the Tudors, Henry VII. No doubt the fact that the Duke of Norfolk, the head of the College as Earl Marshal, had been killed at Bosworth along with his master, also contributed to prejudice against the College.

Under the charter of King Richard which incorporated the College—*Literae de incorporatione heraldorum*—a building was assigned for the use of the heralds, called Cold Harbour or Arbor,

formerly Poulteney's Inn, in the city of London, in the parish of
All Saints the Little. This grant was annulled under Henry VII,
and during his reign and that of Henry VIII the heralds petitioned in vain for a new grant. In the meantime they retired, in
the words of the Rev Mark Noble, the historian of the College,
to a cell of the priory of Rouncevaux in Navarre, which was
situated at Charing Cross, upon part of the site of Northumber-
land House. When the heralds moved there, it was occupied by
an English order of monks, the foreign order having been suppressed by Henry V.[1] The site was eventually granted by Edward
VI to Sir Thomas Cawarden. The heralds were there merely on
sufferance, and although they obtained from Edward VI a fresh
charter of incorporation which reaffirmed their privileges it was
not until the reign of Mary I that they were granted a messuage
called Derby House, 'situated in the parish of St Benedict and St
Peter within the city of London'. (Robson, *British Herald*, 1830,
p 36.) Derby House was totally destroyed in the Great Fire of
London in 1666 and, until the College was rebuilt, the heralds
had temporary accommodation in Whitehall, and later in the
palace of Westminster. The rebuilt College was finished in 1683,
and Robson, writing in 1830, describes the College as consisting
of an extensive range of quadrangular buildings 'one of the hand-
somest and best edifices in London'. It has continued for upwards
of 300 years on this site, which must now have an enormous
financial value, a relic, along with a neighbouring church or two
and St Paul's Cathedral, of the old style of the city, though dominated today by the vast box-like edifices of modern business.

On 18 July 1955 the College celebrated its 400th anniversary,
this being the date when Mary I and her husband, Philip II of
Spain, gave a charter of renewal to the College officials. The
formal celebrations came a year later on 11 May 1956 when the

---

[1] It appears that the cell at Charing Cross was used only for chapter
meetings, as were the houses of the kings of arms during this period when
the College had no permanent home (see—*Heralds of England*, 1967, Sir
Anthony Wagner, Garter King of Arms).

then American ambassador, Mr Winthrop Aldrich, opened with a gold key the beautiful eighteenth-century gates of wrought iron which now adorn the forecourt of the College. They came from Goodrich Court in Herefordshire, which had been demolished after the war, and had been presented to the College by an American benefactor, Mr Blevins Davis. The ambassador remarked, 'It is here, in a treasury of family records, that the lines of descent of so many of us, in both our countries, come together and mark out our common heritage.' (*The Times*, 11 May 1956.) Mr Davis paid £2,500 for the gates, and another £2,500 was spent on the cost of adaptations, painting and installation. Altogether, at this time of restoration of war-damaged buildings, nearly £20,000 was spent on restoring the College premises, most of this sum having been raised by public subscription.

The public esteem in which their twentieth-century successors were to be held would perhaps have been a little consolation to the Tudor heralds in their difficulties, and certainly it seems more than a little unfair that the College should have, in effect, been punished for receiving its charter and building from Richard III. More so, because Henry VIII had no scruples about using the heralds to further royal control of arms. In 1529-30, the first commission was issued by the Crown under the great seal to the officers of arms authorising them to visit particular counties of England with the object of registering arms of the nobility and gentry of those parts, including arms of institutions, and to control the use of arms, disallowing arms in cases where the user had no right to them.

The Visitations were held during the period from 1530 to 1686, and no further commissions were issued to the officers of arms after the abdication of James II. It is thought that the monarchs who succeeded James did not wish unnecessarily to ruffle the susceptibilities of the predominantly Tory gentry of England, a reasonable assumption since three of the succeeding sovereigns were of foreign birth—William III a Dutchman, George I and II Germans—and hardly the best judges of English customs. And by the time that George III, who was born in England, came to the throne in 1760, the custom had been forgotten.

Still, during a period of nearly 160 years the forty counties of England were covered by the officers and some measure of visitation was also given to the twelve Welsh counties. Wales is joined with England heraldically as in other administrative matters, and it was the custom in former days to appoint a Welshman or Welsh-speaking expert as assistant to the College in order to deal with Welsh pedigrees and armorial problems. This practice, after a long lapse, has now been revived, and one of the greatest living experts on Welsh genealogy, Major Francis Jones, is the present Welsh Herald Extraordinary. This title is given from time to time to persons learned in heraldry, who are termed 'Extraordinary' in that they are additional to the establishment of the College of Arms which is limited to thirteen officers (see end of chapter). Before leaving the subject of Welsh heraldry, it should be mentioned that reference in some pedigrees, mostly of the eighteenth century, to Welsh heralds in no way suggests a body of officers of arms as with the English College or the Court of the Lord Lyon, but refers to someone at the College in other times who was dealing with Welsh families and their arms. In former times, when an English herald made a Visitation in Wales it was the practice to appoint a Welsh deputy. Lewis Dwnn was probably the most celebrated of these and the pedigrees recorded by him in his Visitations are generally considered to be accurate. There were other Welsh officers who served as members or deputies of the College. Among them were Thomas Chaloner of Chester and Capt Robert Chaloner, who became Lancaster Herald in 1665. Griffith Hughes, who lived about 1639, described himself as 'deputy to the office of Arms for North Wales'. George Owen became Norroy King of Arms in 1658. David Edwardes was described as Herald for the Principality of Wales, being appointed in 1684 as deputy to Clarenceux.

The position of Wales as the fourth country and nation in the United Kingdom is not reflected in the royal arms and never has been, for the good heraldic reason that the royal arms are those of kingdoms. Wales is a principality, not a kingdom. For this reason also, there is no order of chivalry for Wales, like the Thistle for Scotland. There is, however, a royal badge for Wales, the design of which is the Red Dragon of Wales. By order of the Queen in the Privy Council, on 11 March 1953, the badge is enclosed in

The badge of Wales

a scroll which bears the words: *Y ddraig goch ddyry gychwyn*—'The Welsh dragon gives the lead'. The wording is in green lettering on a white background, and the design is surmounted by a royal crown. This new badge is used on all government publications relating to Wales, and on all the stationery of government departments in Wales. It can also be used throughout the country as a flag. The colourful Welsh banner, with the red dragon on a white and green background, has for years been flying over many Welsh buildings including some of the old historic castles such as Conway. I have even seen it over a Welsh gentleman's house in Perthshire, in Scotland!

Returning to the Visitations, it does not appear that anything but a rough system was used in carrying them out. The difficulties of travel in the England of the seventeenth century were very great. Even the main roads were little better than tracks, such as now lead to remote farmhouses. Consequently the counties easily accessible from London were more regularly visited. Kent had five Visitations, in 1530, 1574, 1592, 1619 and 1663; Essex in 1552, 1558, 1570, 1612, 1634 and 1664–8. Westmorland, on the other hand, visited in 1530, had to wait until 1615 for its next inspection. Durham was lucky to have four Visitations, while Cumberland and Cornwall each had three only. Gradually, with the progress of the Visitations, pedigrees of families were built up, especially as regards the longer established gentry, so that over the period of 160 years we can trace the growth of the family records. A family like the Hookes of Gloucestershire, for 550 years in possession of the same property, figure in every Visitation of their county, and the heralds' entries grow from skeletal beginnings to entries bearing more resemblance to pedigrees.

Had the Visitations continued to our own time, the heraldic position in England would, so far as the majority of armigerous persons are concerned, be quite regular, as over a period of four and a half centuries most coats of arms would have been brought within the purview of the heralds. It was not to be. The Visitations ceased nearly 300 years ago, and the officers could then only wait for people to visit them to record their arms or take out grants. For the second weapon of the English heralds had also failed, although it had a fairly active life for fifty years after the last Visitation had been conducted.

This second means of regulating the use of arms was through the Court of Chivalry. This was the Court of the High Constable and of the Earl Marshal and, as its name implies, it dealt with matters relating to knights and gentlemen. It is a mistake to regard it as the medieval equivalent and original form of the courts martial of the present day. Undoubtedly there were courts martial for the better maintenance of order and discipline in the English armies, such as those which fought in France and Scotland in the thirteenth to fifteenth centuries, but these courts were not identical with the Court of Chivalry. Even when they were held under the presidency of the Constable and the Marshal, it does not follow that these two high officers of state were actually present. Every English army had its constable and marshal for the necessary discipline of the soldiers, and since the two great officers could not possibly be present on every military expedition, a constable and a marshal were appointed for particular campaigns.

The office of Lord High Constable was held in the family of the De Bohuns, Earls of Essex, for several generations. Eventually it passed to the Staffords, Dukes of Buckingham, but the last duke of this line lost his life through the machinations of Cardinal Wolsey. It was then decided that such an important key position as commander-in-chief of the forces, which that of the Constable had been, ought not to be left in the permanent control of a subject. From that time the office has been in abeyance, except for short periods, as at a coronation, when it is granted to a distinguished nobleman. The Earl Marshal remained to sit alone in the Court as president. The records of the Court are preserved in any detail only for the seventeenth and eighteenth centuries, and it is only on the cases reported during those periods that judgment can be passed. There were, as one would expect, many disputes about arms, but also a great number which involved the status of a gentleman. Someone had called into question a man's right to style himself 'gentleman'; or his right to bear arms had been queried, such cases being brought by the officers of arms, though not by them only. There can be no doubt that the Court imposed penalties and gave orders; it had all the legal status and authority of a court, not of the Common Law in which it had not originated, but of the old Civilians' Law. It was of like origin and nature with other courts which either perished in the reforms of the

Commonwealth period or dragged on a not wholly satisfactory existence until the next reforming era, in the reign of Queen Victoria.

Not surprisingly, the Court of Chivalry also aroused great opposition, especially among the new classes of the well-to-do who became prominent in the England of the sixteenth to eighteenth centuries. The medieval chivalry with whom arms-bearing began did, in fact, originate their own arms but, proud as they were, they bowed to the decisions of the Sovereign as given through his Constable and Marshal. When arms-bearing ceased to be the prerogative of knights in armour and was spread abroad among the generality of the citizens, new conceptions of the value of coats of arms appeared. The knights had first used arms for their utilitarian value, and from this there followed naturally the idea that arms were a necessary appurtenance of the knightly class of gentlemen. The newly emerging classes from Tudor times onward seized upon the converse of the idea—to them arms spelt gentility. Consequently they tended to assume arms without bothering to sue for them, and even had they petitioned the heralds they might not always have obtained them. The grant of arms by Dethick, then Garter, to John Shakespeare at the suit of the latter's son, William, was not favourably viewed in certain quarters, and there are verses of the period critical of players who are made esquires. Dethick, like many of the Tudor heralds, was venal and spent a short period in prison, though not in connection with the Shakespearean grant. Incidentally, the arms which he granted to the poet—or on a bend sable a spear of the first steeled argent—could well have belonged, for their simplicity, to an ancient house. In all probability there had not been an official record of a Shakespeare coat before 1596, the date of the draft of the arms grant. The arms of the baronetcy family of Shakespeare, which are modern, show differencing marks, which inevitably clutter the shield with charges.

Many other rising or already risen men in Tudor and Stuart times did not have the temerity or luck of Shakespeare. Hence they devised arms for themselves, or more often simply assumed those of some armigerous family. This is by now a fine old tradition in English life, still busily practised at the present time. Occasionally it happens that the arms assumed as being those of an armigerous family have themselves been assumed without any proper warrant. A common and perfectly understandable practice has been for schools and colleges to bear arms of their founder, or of the person in whose memory they were founded. The Visitations brought to light many such cases of arms borne without proper authority, and their records often read like the correspondence I used to receive when editing *Burke's Peerage*. Such as: 'My grandfather used a seal with our arms upon it,' or 'We have always understood that we were connected with the family of Lord Dynevor,' and so on. In many of the Visitations, lists are given of persons who were forced to disclaim arms, and there must have been many others who were not detected.

At length, when the Civil War began in 1642, the Court of Chivalry sat no more until after the Restoration. It was abolished along with the High Commission and the Court of the Star Chamber. The House of Commons was careful to appoint a commission to deal with the use and abuse of arms; probably most members bore arms. Certainly all the signatories to the death warrant of Charles I sealed it with their own arms. After Charles II's restoration, the Court of Chivalry was brought back, and sat at fairly frequent intervals until 1737. Then it ceased to sit and for over 200 years there was no control over the use of arms in England and Wales. Inevitably, such a state of heraldic anarchy would produce a huge number of misappropriated arms. It has, of course, always been open to would-be armigers to petition the College to grant them arms, but the charges for this may have deterred many—£76 prewar, now about £130–£140. Obviously, it was much cheaper and easier to look up one's name in some heraldic list and take the arms there described. When *Burke's General Armory* first appeared in 1842 it made the assumption easier, for it is a much more comprehensive work than any previous collection and gives over 100,000 coats of arms. A popular superstition holds that there is a coat of arms to every surname—whether this idea came from the habit of assuming arms or simply prompted it, I do not know, but it is certainly widespread. Rather than merely to take someone else's coat, I think it is far more reputable to devise a new coat; at least that is not stealing someone else's property, especially as the goods may have passed through other hands before reaching market overt! Of actual devising of new arms there has, I should say, been very little—indicative of a decided lack of imagination.

In 1954 the Court of Chivalry was revived, a feat which could not be paralleled in any other country in the world except the Vatican State, and that after all is only the tiny temporal appendage of a spiritual power. The details of this sitting were reported verbatim in a publication of the Heraldry Society in 1955, *The High Court of Chivalry*, and I have described and commented upon the matter in my work *Teach Yourself Heraldry* (1957). Very briefly, the Court was revived to deal with a test case, that of *The Mayor and Aldermen and Citizens of the City of Manchester v The Manchester Palace of Varieties Ltd*. The defendant had used the arms of the plaintiffs on their drop curtain and on their seal. The Court sat under the presidency of the Earl Marshal, with Lord Goddard, then Lord Chief Justice, as his Surrogate or Deputy. Lord Goddard made his own court available for the hearing instead of using the court of the Earl Marshal at the College of Arms, but he did not, of course, sit as Lord Chief Justice, or wear his normal judicial robes. He was dressed, instead, as a Doctor of Civil Law. The hearing was short and the judgment was read on 21 January 1955. It was given against the defendants. The Surrogate ruled that they had no right to use the arms of Manchester City, which had been granted by Queen Victoria; they were ordered to give up their use and to pay the costs of the action (£300). The position of the Court was confirmed, that it existed and had jurisdiction. The whole of the judgment should be read by those who are interested in the

chaotic condition of English heraldry, but one passage is of particular relevance in the present context. Lord Goddard stated :
'If therefore it is laid down as a rule of this court, as I would very respectfully suggest to His Grace the Earl Marshal it should be, that leave must be obtained before any proceedings are instituted, it would I think prevent frivolous actions, and if this Court is to sit again it should be convened only where there is some really substantial reason for the exercise of its jurisdiction. Moreover, should there be any indication of a considerable desire to institute proceedings now that this Court has been revived I am firmly of the opinion that it should be put upon a statutory basis defining its jurisdiction and the sanctions it can impose.'

There the matter has been left. Soon after the hearing of the case the City of London put its heraldic house in order by recording at the College of Arms its crest and supporters. As Fox-Davies pointed out, (*A Complete Guide to Heraldry*, 1961, pp 329–30) the arms of the City of London were recorded in the College without a crest, as at that time in the sixteenth century there was no crest. An arrangement known as a fan was then placed above the shield with part of the arms, to be used on the city seal. From this fan developed a wing with rays, ie, a dragon's wing charged with a cross. The supporters were originally two lions but these were dropped after the seventeenth century in favour of the familiar dragons. The entire heraldic achievement of the City has now been regularised by recording in the College.

How many others have followed the example of the City of London? Only the College of Arms could tell us. It has not done so and is unlikely to. My thought is that, after the initial surprise at the revival of the Court, very little effect has been produced among families or individuals who are using arms unrecorded. With municipalities or institutions, it may be otherwise. There are always persons at hand to advise that an assumed coat is 'put right'. Unfortunately, when arms are corrected by being recorded, something is nearly always left out of the revised shield which had important local associations. This was the real point at the centre of the dispute some years back over the arms of Berwick on Tweed. The proposed revision of this coat by the College of Arms was correct enough heraldically, of course, but had insufficient association with the old history of the burgh. The subsequently matriculated coat from Lyon Office had just that appeal and was thus acceptable to the citizens. Similarly, the town of Aldershot, in Hampshire, formerly bore a home-made coat of arms, which, when 'put right' at the College lost some of its quite harmless allusions. (See Note 1 at end of chapter.)

Nothing has yet been done to implement the Surrogate's suggestions, and as one cannot envisage the revival of the Visitations the only means of checking the disorders of English heraldic usage is by means of the Court of Chivalry. For thirteen years a Conservative government was in power, for nine years after the Surrogate's judgement, ample time in which to have put forward a private member's bill for which a presumably sympathetic Conservative administration would surely have made time. Had this been done the English College would have possessed the same strong position as the Lord Lyon in Scotland. (See next chapter.) As it is, the Court of Chivalry is one of those weapons which the possessors can use as a vague menace but are afraid to put to real and extensive use. No one would advise the officers of arms to disregard the counsel of the Lord Chief Justice, yet without frequent sittings of the Court it will be impossible to stop the misuse of arms in England. Probably the real objection to seeking the confirmation of the Court by an Act of Parliament is the harassing fear that Parliament might insist on an investigating committee, leading to public control over the College.

It cannot be said that Parliament has done much so far to assist in the regulation of armorial bearings in England. In 1803 a statute of 43 George III, c 161, imposed an assessed tax on the use of armorial bearings on carriages, seals, plate etc. In 1869 the Revenue Act, s.19, ordained that the term 'armorial bearings' should include for the purposes of tax not only arms which were recorded with the College of Arms, but all arms, ie, those also which were self-assumed. It must be admitted that this was a direct encouragement to anyone who wanted to assume arms for himself without bothering the College. The dues exacted under the Acts were slight, about two to three guineas a year, but there was difficulty in collecting the money and the tax was repealed by the Finance Act, 1944, s.6. The existence of the tax was generally known and is the origin of the idea, quite prevalent in England, that payment of the licence money guaranteed the validity of the arms; also that failure to pay meant that the right to use the arms had lapsed. These views are completely wrong; the sections of the Acts were merely concerned with payment but, by exacting the licence money on any arms, whether recorded or self-assumed, the British Parliament certainly contributed very substantially to heraldic lawlessness in England and Wales.

There the matter can be left and the rest of this chapter devoted to consideration of various features in English heraldry. And here I hope I am not inspired by merely nationalistic considerations in preferring an English coat to that of a Continental for seemly setting out of the charges. The figures used in the different European countries often seem to me ungainly and too large for the shield. The same preference extends to Scottish and Irish—I cannot write of 'British heraldry' because there is no such creature.

Taking the different parts of the coat of arms in turn, we can say that the charges are divided into ordinaries such as the chevron, fesse, chief etc, illustrations of which abound in books on English heraldry, and then into the charges which might perhaps be called extraordinary. Many of the latter are frequently used in heraldry—items such as eagles, lions, and other animals— but this does not give them a place in the honourable ordinaries. The reason is that the latter usually occupy or delimit a definite part of the shield, which a charge such as an animal or tree cannot do. As I am not here engaged in setting out the principles of blazoning, I will not enter upon explanations of marshalling,

E

dimidiation or impaling and the like. Book after book comes from
the press on this subject and my own *Teach Yourself Heraldry*
contains a full account of this aspect of the subject. My larger
work, *The Genealogist's Encyclopedia*, also goes into detail on
the matter. Here we are more concerned with the special features
of English heraldry.

A coat of arms should always be represented with a helmet,
though most peerage books contain examples in which the helmet
is absent. The crest is then shown hovering in the air above the
coronet, in case of a peer, or just over the shield, for a commoner.
A particularly awkward specimen of this was seen in the illustration of Earl Wavell's arms in *Burke's Peerage* in the first post-
war edition. The drawing came from the College but was
decidedly amateurish in style, especially when compared with the
magnificent drawing from the same source of the arms of
Viscount Montgomery. On this subject Lord Lyon (Sir Thomas
Innes) was quoted in *The Times* of 5 March 1960 as saying,
'Unfortunately so many people have the complex that Scottish
coats of arms must be better if they are made in the south of
England. They pay five times the price and often get something
wrong.'

There are rules for the manner in which helmets should be
shown, to differentiate that of an esquire, a knight, a peer or a
king. That the heraldic purist, Fox-Davies, should have thought
disparagingly of these rules is sufficient indication of their late
development.

The lambrequin, or mantling, which hangs from the helmet
and curls around the shield is usually shown in a very pleasing
form in modern English drawings, in which there has been a great
revival of artistic skill. They now show bold outlines and are
generally very well executed.

Reference has been made several times to crests. They were of
later development than coats of arms and are not essential to the
latter. Some families still do not possess them, though all modern
grants include the crest. The origin of crests is veiled in the same

mystery as so much that is connected with heraldry. It is thought that they may have originated at tournaments, in the manner of the German *helmschau* in which there was a display of helms and coat armour as a means of showing that the participants were noble. Readers of Scott's novel, *The Antiquary*, will remember the story of the three brothers (The Fortunes of Martin Waldeck) who obtained arms and nobility from their king, only to find themselves rigorously excluded from the tournament. The scene was laid in Germany, but without recourse to romantic tales we need only recall the many cases cited by Colonel Gayre in his work, *The Nature of Arms*, to know that burgher, peasant or bourgeois arms, though true arms, did not make their owners the equals of the greater armigers. Probably then, even in England, the crest was at first the sign of higher rank, but any such differ-entiation ended in the sixteenth and seventeenth centuries when the English heralds were anxious to grant crests to all who pos-sessed arms. The charge in Tudor and Stuart money values was £5, and from this business activity arose the present practice of always granting the crest as part of the coat of arms. Perhaps it was because of the assiduous pushing of the crest by erstwhile heralds in the Visitations that the word has come to assume such importance with the public. I have known would-be entrants to *Burke's* pages who strenuously claimed possession of a crest but, when asked about their coat of arms, looked dubious and said they knew nothing about it. As for the frequent misuse of the word 'crest' instead of the proper 'coat of arms' in newspapers and periodicals, anyone who set out to correct every instance of this would have a time-consuming hobby. A good deal of harm has also been done by the incorrect use of *Fairbairn's Book of Crests*, which has appeared in several editions and is often sold at second-hand at enormously enhanced charges. In this work only name, crest and motto appear, so that the user ignorant of heraldry could be excused for thinking that these items are all that matter.

A great deal of misunderstanding exists on the subject of

mottoes. They are not part of a coat of arms, but the standard practice in making a grant is to include the motto with the arms blazon. The motto is the private property of the individual and can be changed as often as he wishes. Anyone who has inherited high-sounding sentiments, 'Death before dishonour', 'All for the King', etc, can easily substitute something more in accordance with his own views. Mottoes are often supposed to refer to an historic event in the remote past, and ideas of this nature are no doubt very useful in novels. The hero learns as a small boy of his family motto, and then later, in dramatic circumstances, lives up to it. A few very old mottoes did originate as war cries, but the origin of the majority is far more prosaic. It would indeed be enlightening to know the reason for mottoes like the *Che sara sara* of the Russells; or who first thought of 'Touch not the cat bot a glove' for Macpherson and other Highland chiefs. '*Dieu et mon droit*', the royal motto, began as a war cry used by Richard Coeur de Lion in battle against the French king. *Pro rege dimico*, the motto of the Dymokes who are the hereditary Champions of England, is very appropriate, and like many mottoes is a play on the surname.

Another delusion similar to that concerning family mottoes is the belief that everything in a coat of arms refers either to a specific happening in the life of an ancestor, or to a particular virtue. The best thing to do with this idea is to discard it completely—there are plenty of genuine augmentations to a coat of arms without dragging in legendary or mythical occurrences. An augmentation when genuine is usually well documented, though there have been augmentations which went unrecorded save in family tradition. Several augmentations as well as grants can be substantiated from the time of Charles II's restoration, equal in romantic value to anything that Harrison Ainsworth could have written. The history of England's wars over the last 300 years could almost be chronicled from augmentations in the arms of distinguished British admirals and generals. One of the most astonishing heraldic displays is that in the arms of Viscount

Gough, the heroic general who won his fame on battlefield after battlefield in Spain, in China and in India. All honour to his memory, but the result in terms of the heraldry of the nineteenth century, when heraldic art had reached its nadir, is terrible to behold. The shield of the Goughs is covered with the record of their ancestor's distinctions, so that the original arms are well nigh obliterated. Similar horrors have been perpetrated in the arms of Nelson by attempts to signify the battle of the Nile in heraldic style. A second crest for Nelson is described as being 'upon waves of the sea, the stern of a Spanish man of war, all proper, thereon inscribed San Joseff with the motto above, "Faith and Works" '. This is not to say that I am opposed to traditions as such. On the contrary. We often hear it said that for such and such a matter there is no documentary evidence, only tradition, and this, if it is reliable, can often provide sounder basis for proof than documents of mendacious character. In the very darkest period of English history, the 180 years from the official Roman withdrawal up to the mission of St Augustine, we have only one document, a sermon or moralizing work by St Gildas. This, from its very nature, tells us little, and to supplement it we can have recourse to tradition as recorded much later by the Venerable Bede, a careful writer who is unlikely to have written down as fact anything which he did not think had really happened. The evidence of archaeology is also now available, and shows that very few of the Romano-British cities were taken by storm. On the other hand, the Roman villas were clearly deserted and not made their places of residence by the incoming Saxons, whereas the cities were inhabited, albeit after a period of desertion. Negative evidence perhaps, but it does seem to bear out the tradition recorded in Bede that the British, if not exterminated, did flee into the west.

Irish traditional lore is particularly valuable, and by this I do not mean the Noachian pedigrees of Hart's famous collection. These are, in fact, not at all traditional but the work of the early Irish chroniclers who, like their brethren in other European lands, liked to tie their rulers' pedigrees on to the Old Testament genealogies. Disregarding the Biblical link-up, the Irish pedigrees back to 400 AD are valid enough to satisfy scholarly examination. Even long before this the lists of names of kings are probably correct, for why should anyone want to invent them? Again, the ancient traditions of the Irish hold that their first settlers came from Spain. Why should this be wrong? We know a little about the migrations of peoples in the world of pre-history, before Caesar, Tacitus, Strabo were able to lift the curtain of darkness. Much more extensive and hazardous migrations took place in the Pacific —as witness the voyages of the Maoris to New Zealand—than any from Spain. Why then be scornful of tradition in regard to heraldic matters? Because we are dealing here with tradition which is generally not old and derives from ages when the ruling caste was literate and even cultured. How then can we credit an Elizabethan tradition when it appears in the family of a new-made Tudor grandee? They had no need to rely on memory which always weakens with the development of facility in writing. Ability to take notes, minutes and memoranda destroys the ability to recall sentences in detail. Moreover, the links between the Elizabethan noble and his predecessors of the middle ages were rarely more than extremely tenuous. Attempts to connect by means of so-called tradition are therefore suspect from the beginning. Besides, I am sure that family traditions have grown up in unconscious imitation of incidents in the narratives of Sir Walter Scott and other novelists.

Coming, then, to the subject of supporters, these are the prerogative in modern English heraldry of peers of the realm, of Knights of the Garter, or Knights Grand Cross of the other orders. In Scotland, the position is quite different and many families have supporters which are outside the classes given above. It was formerly so in England and traces of the use of supporters by families of landed gentry are to be found. There is a famous case, that of the Chetwynd-Stapyltons who supplied more than one Knight of the Garter in medieval times. The use of supporters in this family may have arisen from the privilege possessed by the

Garter knights. The fact remains that this family has borne supporters to its arms since the seventeenth century. In their pedigree
roll Sir Miles Stapleton, who lived about 1660, is shown with
two talbots (ie, large dogs) argent as supporters. In Wighill
church, in Yorkshire, where the family formerly had property,
the monument of Robert Stapilton who died 11 March 1635
again has the same supporters. Sir William Dugdale refers in his
Visitation of Yorkshire to the Stapylton supporters. It is thus clear
that for 300 years the Stapyltons used supporters, from the time
when the Garter order was founded (1348) and when one of the
family was a founder knight. After so prolonged a usage it seems
most unfair for the arms now to be shown minus supporters, and
I took special pleasure in including in one of my books a full
drawing of the Chetwynd-Stapylton arms showing the supporters.

Sir William Dugdale had a much more reasonable view of the
use of supporters than is now the established practice. He said of
Foljambe of Steveton that 'this family have for many ages used
their arms with supporters' and he so recorded them.

Another instance of the use of supporters among the English
gentry is that of the Fountaines of Narford, in Norfolk, where two
griffins are sometimes used, although here the support for the
usage is not strong. Sir Andrew Fountaine Kt, of Narford, born in
1676, was described as 'a distinguished antiquary and one of the
most celebrated connoisseurs of his time . . . he became Warden
of the Mint, 1727, upon the death of Sir Isaac Newton, and was
also Vice-Chamberlain to Queen Caroline, and proxy for Prince
William, then a child, at the installation of the Knights of the
Bath, for which he received a grant of supporters to his arms'.
(*Burke's Landed Gentry, 1952*.) He died without issue in 1753
and the present family descend from his sister, whose grandson
assumed by Act of Parliament the name and arms of Fountaine.
In this case, then, the descent is in the female line, at two removes,
and collaterally, so that there is not a continuance over three
centuries as with the Stapyltons in the use of the arms. Still, the
old adage that Parliament can do anything except change the

sexes, could be held to apply. For the grandson, whose name was Brigg, took the name and arms of Fountaine, not by royal licence through the College of Arms, but through Parliament.

William Speke of Jordans, near Ilminster in Somerset, was granted an augmentation to his arms and an additional crest in 1867 and, for his life, supporters of a crocodile on the dexter and a hippopotamus on the sinister. These honours were in recognition of the achievements of his son, John Hanning Speke, the discoverer of the sources of the Nile who died prematurely in 1864 without mark of royal favour. The limitation of the grant to last only for the life of the grantee was made in accordance with the modern English practice as regards supporters. The illustration of the Speke arms with supporters continues in *Burke's Landed Gentry*, but in the 1952 edition I added the words 'Arms of William Speke of Jordans (1798–1887)', with a note to the effect that the supporters were a grant for life only. The augmentation of the coat of arms continues in perpetuity.

When Sir Winston Churchill was made a Knight of the Garter he was entitled to supporters but did not take them out, so that his arms as a member of the order appear without supporters.

The denial of supporters in modern times, save to peers and certain classes of knights, is an indication of that hardening of the heraldic arteries which occurs, on occasion, in the otherwise fairly easy English system.

Badges are a feature peculiar to English heraldry. The origin of heraldic badges is much disputed, and the question of their antiquity cannot easily be settled. They exist now, and have existed for several centuries, in English heraldry as an heraldic device distinct from the coat of arms. They appear to have begun their history, heraldically-speaking, in the time of Edward III, and were often used as signs of adherence to a great lord. The followers of the Earl of Warwick, for example, bore on their clothes the ancient device or cognizance of the bear and ragged staff. With the disappearance of retainers in the Tudor period, badges became much more a matter for the royal house, though some ancient families have preserved their use of badges. Even now one occasionally hears of the grant of a badge—which I think, is carrying heraldic interest rather too far—though if one's family anciently bore a badge, it is understandable that one might wish to keep it up. So far as royalty was concerned, badges were very variable. In parts of Westminster Abbey the white hart badge of Richard II is to be seen and was peculiar to that king, whereas his grandfather, Edward III, had borne different badges at different times, a trunk of a tree, or sunbeams issuing from clouds. These emblems were also used by Richard II and, in addition to the white hart, he used a white falcon as a badge. Henry IV used a white swan and a white antelope. Henry V had beside these, a fire-beacon as device. Most people know of the royal roses, the white rose of York and the red rose of Lancaster. They know from Shakespeare of the wild boar cognizance of Richard III. The Tudor rose was a combination of the rival roses, because Henry VII's marriage with the Princess Elizabeth of York united the two houses. Today, the badge worn on the uniforms of the Yeomen of the Guard is the rose of England, joined with the thistle of Scotland and the shamrock of Ireland. Reference has been made earlier to the badge of Wales.

Along with badges, standards are granted and these occur in modern arms grants. The arrangement shows the arms on the standard next to the staff, the badge being depicted on the rest of the surface. In former times banners and standards were used for practical purposes in warfare. Many heraldic banners existed and quite a substantial proportion survive. The British national flag, the Union Jack, is a combination of three heraldic flags, these being the Cross of St George for England, of St Andrew for Scotland, and of St Patrick for Ireland. Over many English churches can be seen the Cross of St George, a red cross on a white background with, perhaps, in the top right-hand quarter, the arms of the diocese to which the church belongs, and a most attractive sight it is to see this ancient banner flying over a church tower itself perhaps a thousand years old. The arms of a knight were borne on the pennons, or small swallow-tail flags, attached to his lance and when he had performed some particularly brave exploit, it often happened that the forked ends of the pennon were cut off, so that there remained a banneret, or diminutive banner. The bearer was then known as a knight banneret, a term which is not to be confused with the word 'baronet', meaning what is, in effect, an hereditary knighthood. It was the famous antiquary, Sir Robert Cotton, who suggested to James I the founding of an order of bannerets, based on his reading in old chronicles. This gave rise to the order of baronets, but baronet is probably a misunderstanding or mispronunciation of banneret.

One use of heraldic banners in the British Isles is in connection with the office of high sheriff of a county. This functionary must have an armorial banner which can be displayed when he is discharging his duties and flown over the public building where he is received. It can also be beautifully worked for hanging from the instruments of the trumpeters who herald the approach of the judge on occasions such as the opening of the county assizes, at which the sheriff must be present.

Irish Heraldry

It is not out of place to deal here with this part of the subject as Irish heraldry follows the lines of English heraldry, because of England's rule over Ireland during the centuries when heraldry arose and flourished. There have, however, been significant differences in administration.

The early history of heraldic organisation in Ireland is obscure. Few English kings took much interest in the country, and between Henry II and Richard II, a period of 200 years, none of them visited the island, though King John as a prince made an unfortunate Irish tour. When Richard II went to Ireland he endeavoured to effect many reforms but as his reign ended in tragedy, his good intentions were largely frustrated. As early as 1382 in his reign we find mention of an Ireland King of Arms. The first holder of the office was Chandos, who had been herald to the famous knight, Sir John Chandos. On the latter's death he came into the royal service, and according to the chronicler Froissart, he was the senior of the English Kings of Arms. He died about 1385. The duty of Ireland King of Arms was to administer the whole dominion of Ireland in matters heraldic, but although there were seven holders of the office, none of them had much to do with Ireland. They were looked on as members of the English College and apparently lived in England. The last Ireland King died in 1487, when the title lapsed. In 1553, Edward VI created a new King under the title of Ulster, to have control of the whole of Ireland and to live in Ireland. This office still exists but is now united with that of Norroy King. Edward VI noted in his diary under 2 Feb. 1553 'There was a King of Arms made for Ireland, whose name was Ulster and his province was all Ireland, and he was the fourth King of Arms, and the first Herald of Ireland'. The reason why a provincial name was used instead of that of the island itself is not clear. When the Irish Free State was set up 1921–22, the Ulster Office in Dublin Castle, where the Ulster King worked, was reserved as a Crown Office and the then Ulster, Sir Nevile Wilkinson, was to hold office for life. He died in 1940. An arrangement was then made by which the Ulster Office with its records should be taken over by the Irish government. Photostat copies of the records were made and sent to the College of Arms. The Irish government appointed a Chief Herald of Ireland and Ulster Office became known as the Genealogical Office, Dublin Castle. The first Chief Herald was a distinguished scholar, Dr Edward MacLysaght, who is in charge of the Irish Manuscripts Commission. He was succeeded by Mr G. Slevin. Meanwhile, the Office of Ulster King was combined with that of Norroy, whose jurisdiction now takes in the six northern counties of Ireland, that is of Ulster, which is still part of the United Kingdom. The Chief Herald conducts his office in very much the same way as his Ulster predecessor, except that he has twenty-six counties instead of thirty-two for his parish. Both of the heraldic authorities, in Ulster and in the Republic, recognise each other's grants of arms, and as the working of the Office in Dublin continues on the same lines, it is convenient to describe the Ulster set-up, noting any essential differences. There were, of course, other officers on the old Ulster establishment—the Athlone Pursuivant, two heralds of the Order of St. Patrick, under the titles of Dublin and Cork, and a Cork Pursuivant of the order—but these posts no longer exist.

During the 400 years' existence of his office, the Ulster King was the senior member of the staff of the Lord Lieutenant of Ireland and the only permanent member. His duties in this respect consisted in ordering state ceremonies and in officiating at proclamations, and the tenure of the office continued unbroken even in the worst periods of Irish history. Cromwell made Richard Carney Ulster, evidence of the care with which the Puritan gentry regulated matters armorial. This attitude helps to explain the domination of the English revolution by the gentry and their suppression of any truly democratic movements like those of the Levellers or the Diggers. Richard Carney held office until the Restoration, when he was replaced by Richard St George, of a family which has had five Kings of Arms among its members. When St George resigned in 1683, Carney returned to office, holding the position jointly with George Wallis. He was knighted in 1684, and his son, also Richard, succeeded as Ulster in 1692. Sir Nevile Wilkinson was appointed in 1908 and continued until his death in 1940. Thomas Ulick Sadleir was Deputy Ulster until 1943, when the Chief Herald took over. With this continuity of 390 years it is not surprising that a very large volume of records has been built up in Dublin Castle, invaluable to the genealogist as well as the herald. The Chief Heralds appointed by the Irish government are carrying on the good work. Among other labours, they are endeavouring to clarify the history and present positions of the chiefs of the Irish clans, of whom there are about seventy.

Irish heraldry has followed the same lines as in England. It was not possible to do much in the way of Visitations, since Irish tracks were even worse than the alleged roads in England. Only three Visitations are recorded; Dublin County (1606), Dublin City (1607) and Wexford County (1618). There was no Court of Chivalry, although the Ulster King would have had the power of the Crown to decide disputed matters. To counterbalance the lack of inspection, Ulster had authority to confirm arms which the claimant's family could show to have been used for three generations. Irish records have always been somewhat defective owing to the many rebellions and periods of disorder. Even that arch legitimist of heraldry, Fox-Davies, was constrained to say of the Irish practice, 'In Ireland there still exists the unique opportunity of obtaining a confirmation of arms upon mere proof of use. . . . The present regulation is that user must be proved for at least three generations and be proved also to have existed for 100 years.' (*Heraldry Explained*, 1925, p 24.) Sir Bernard Burke, who was Ulster King of Arms for nearly forty years, was the son of John Burke, the founder of the *Peerage*, the *Landed Gentry* and many other works which bear his name. In the introduction to the *General Armory*, Sir Bernard mentions that a confirmation at Ulster Office was accompanied by the addition of some slight heraldic difference mark.

In Ireland, as in England, heraldic funerals were the rule for the gentry. The Irish heralds used to deposit in their records a certificate that they had attended a funeral, setting out the arms used for the deceased. Unfortunately, this useful practice ceased with the seventeenth century.

Anyone who wishes to study good examples of Irish coats of arms will do well to look at the examples of blazons given in the 1958 edition of *Burke's Landed Gentry of Ireland*. This work gives expression to the genealogical and heraldic history of every stratum among the gentle families of Ireland, from the original Celtic pedigrees of the ancient kings and princes through the different sections of the invaders of the country.

It has been mentioned that people of English descent who live

outside England can be said to come under the jurisdiction of
the College of Arms, and those Canadians, Australians and New
Zealanders who are of English ancestry should apply to the
English College for a grant of arms. Similarly, before the removal
of Ulster King from Dublin, all persons of Irish descent could
apply to him for arms. Now that two separate heraldic jurisdictions exist for the two political sections of Ireland, the best advice
is for those of Ulster ancestry to apply to Norroy and Ulster King
in London, and for the remainder to contact the Chief Herald
of Ireland.

The College of Arms

In general, under the arrangements of the old British Empire,
anyone who was not specifically Scottish or Irish came under the
rule, heraldically, of the College of Arms. Sometimes there were
exceptions, as with the Maltese nobility whose position had been
recognised by the British government and whose hereditary
honours were regulated by the Committee of Privileges in Malta.

The Channel Islands and the Isle of Man came under the rule
of London. In Man, there was not a native development of
heraldry, and the few landed families therefore recorded their
arms with the College. In the Channel Islands there has been
much opposition to College rule. The argument of the old families
there is that the Channel Islands were part of the former Duchy
of Normandy, and that as such they were outside the jurisdiction
of the English College, coming under the direct rule of the
Crown. The Channel Islands are, indeed, a relic of the Duchy of
Normandy, and when the title to the latter was formally given
up by the English king in 1259, the islands were reserved to him.
As late as 1953 the Ecrehous and the Minquiers rocks were the
subject of a case between England and France, heard before the
International Court at the Hague, which adjudged the islets to
belong to England, or rather to the Channel Islands, because they
lay near them. The Channel Islanders tend to regard themselves
as conquerors of England and certainly not as colonies of the

latter. Heraldically, there is more than a little to be said for this view. Practices of very old date, such as the use of supporters by the De Sausmarez family of Guernsey, have not been accepted by the College.

The establishment of the College of Arms consists of the Earl Marshal at the head, with thirteen officers under him. The office of Earl Marshal is hereditary in the family of the Duke of Norfolk and passes with the dukedom. This has been the case over the past 300 years.

There are three Kings of Arms—Garter, Clarenceux, Norroy and Ulster. Garter deals with the armorial bearings of peers and baronets, and is deputy to the Earl Marshal. Clarenceux is responsible for matters heraldic in southern England, Norroy for the north of England, beyond the Trent, being in fact 'Nord Roy'. Then there are six heralds—Windsor, Chester, Lancaster, Richmond, Somerset and York—and four Pursuivants—Rouge Croix, Blue Mantle, Rouge Dragon, and Portcullis. These attractively picturesque titles are derived in many cases from geographical sources, and some originated in the chivalrous reign of Edward III. It was Henry V who instituted the office of Garter for the service of the Order of the Garter, and for this reason it has precedence over the older offices of Clarenceux and Norroy. He also instituted Rouge Croix. Henry VIII created Somerset Herald, while Rouge Dragon and Portcullis were made by Henry VII. There were many other heraldic offices, like that of Ireland; or of Guienne, connected with the former English possessions in France, which have died out. A full list with the holders' names is given in the 1952 edition of *Landed Gentry*.

The salaries of the thirteen members of the College are small by any standards, even those of the Tudor period, and ludicrous in modern times. *In toto*, they amount to £300, no more, for the entire thirteen. There is, however, the very long-standing practice by which the officers are able to charge fees for their services. It happens that no one can set up in practice as a herald at the College without at least a reasonable private income. Even the uniform, including the picturesque tabard or sleeveless coat and the hat, must be purchased by each new pursuivant. He may be able to buy the outfit of a predecessor, if their sizes agree, at a cheaper rate than would be needed for new clothes. Thus far the situation of the fledgling pursuivant resembles that of a newly-called barrister, but his finances can soon improve. Every pursuivant and herald must take a tour as duty officer, during which time any inquirer at the College who has no other herald in mind, will be directed to the duty officer. A millionaire, either British or American, can by this arrangement become the client of a fairly new officer. Practices can and do grow, depending largely upon the skill and diligence of the particular officer, and it is unlikely that any herald who has attained a fair degree of celebrity has gone financially unrewarded.

NOTE 1: Arms of Aldershot. This item cannot be better described than in the words of Colonel Howard Cole. In his book, *The Story of Aldershot* (pp 201–04) he says: 'Until 1923 the arms of the urban district council had been unofficial. The design which had been adopted in the 'nineties on the formation of the council had been based on the name Aldershot and could almost be classified as a rebus or pun on the name of the town. These arms were composed of a shield upon which was an alder tree in green and brown on a scarlet background below three piles each of six round shot in gold on a dark blue background, thus linking the town's name with this symbolism, the alder tree, and the shot, representative of the military association of the town'. In 1923 an official coat of arms was granted when Aldershot became a borough and received its charter. The family of Tichborne had a connection of 200 years with the manor of Aldershot, and the arms granted to the new borough by the College of Arms were based on the Tichborne coat with the 'addition of special quarterings representative of the bishopric of Winchester and the military association of the borough'. The arms as now borne are: quarterly 1, gules a gold mitre; 2 and 3, vaire; 4, gules two crossed swords. Crest: in a mural crown, a hind's head charged on the neck with a spur rowel all proper.

NOTE 2: The Queen's Beasts. The Queen's Beasts were commissioned in 1952 by the Minister of Works, Sir David Eccles, to form part of the decorations for the Coronation of Her Majesty, Queen Elizabeth II. The inspiration for the ten beasts came from ten heraldic animals at Hampton Court, restored early in the present century from originals made for Henry VIII. The sculptor was James Woodford, RA, and the work was carried out in collaboration with the chief architect of the Ministry, Mr Eric Bedford, CVO, ARIBA. The figures were placed at the approach annexe to Westminster Abbey, through which the queen went before and after her coronation. Each of the beasts was six feet high, made of plaster, and supporting a shield upon which was emblazoned a heraldi● badge or a coat of arms. Replicas of the plaster models have been carved in Portland stone and now stand on the terrace of the Palm Houses in Kew Gardens. The original ten Queen's Beasts are in the Great Hall at Hampton Court Palace.

The Queen's Beasts thus described are a selection of thirty devices or badges inherited by Her Majesty from her ancestors. They are :

(1) The Lion of England, with the present royal arms on the shield.

(2) The Griffin of Edward III, with a shield of the royal livery colours, on which is the Round Tower of Windsor Castle, the badge of the House of Windsor.

(3) The Falcon of the Plantaganets, a device much used by Edward III and Edward IV.

(4) The Black Bull of Clarence, derived from Lionel, Duke of Clarence, third son of Edward III.

(5) The White Lion of Mortimer, which was inherited by Edward IV through his grandmother, the heiress of the Mortimers, the Earls of March.

(6) The Yale of Beaufort. This is a mythical creature, of very rare occurrence in heraldry; so much so that Burke did not include it in the glossary to his *Armory*. The Yale is coloured argent (silver) with spots or (gold); it is maned, tufted, hoofed, horned and tusked or. The shield was divided in white and blue, these being the Beaufort colours, and thereon is a portcullis crowned. The history of the yale device is of great interest in the tortuous claim to the throne of Henry Tudor, Earl of Richmond, afterwards Henry VII. The Lady Margaret Beaufort, King Henry's mother, used two yales as her supporters; her father, Sir John Beaufort, grandson of John of Gaunt, was created Duke of Somerset and Earl of Kendal. He used as one of his supporters the yale which had been used by John, Duke of Bedford, a son of Henry IV, who had been also Earl of Kendal. This earldom lapsed in 1435 when the duke died, and so was available for John Beaufort, Earl of Somerset, when he was made Duke of Somerset in 1443. The word 'yale' had been given in the form *eale* by that father of so much false natural history, the elder Pliny, and then taken as a rather bad pun on Kend-eale (Kendal). A unique feature of the yale as represented by artists is its ability to swivel its horns at will, so that one horn points forward and the other backward.

(7) The White Greyhound of Richmond and

(8) The Red Dragon of Wales were both closely associated with Henry VII who used them as supporters, sometimes in pairs.

(9) The Unicorn of Scotland.

(10) The White Horse of Hanover came into the royal heraldry when the Elector of Hanover became King of Great Britain and Ireland as George I. The royal arms from that date, 1714, until 1837, when Queen Victoria succeeded to the throne, bore the arms of Hanover in the fourth quarter of the shield. In the base of the arms of Hanover was the white horse running on a field gules (red). A very ancient emblem of Kent is a white horse on its hind legs or rampant, a device which antedates heraldry by about 500 years and is traditionally associated with the arrival of our Saxon ancestors, led by Hengist and Horsa, in Kent in the fifth century.

A very useful book on the subject of the Queen's Beasts is one written under that title by the late H. Stanford London, a very fine heraldic scholar but of a vitriolic temperament akin to that of the celebrated Horace Round. In this work is included a genealogical chart which shows the relationship of the users of the Queen's Beasts, and also demonstrates the futility of trying to understand the Wars of the Roses and the succession of the Tudor dynasty without the aid of genealogy.

CHAPTER 4

Heraldry in Scotland

SCOTTISH heraldry has several most interesting features. It
is entirely distinct in administration from the English system,
much more exact, and it is deeply grounded in Scots law. Further-
more, certain heraldic practices abandoned elsewhere still exist
and flourish in Scotland.

At the heart of the Scottish system is the position of the Scottish
heraldic executive, the Lord Lyon King of Arms, who is responsible for all matters of heraldry in the northern kingdom. He is
quite unlike the Garter King with whom he is sometimes compared. The Lord Lyon is not the deputy of an Earl Marshal or
any other great officer of state because he is himself a great
officer. In the old kingdom of Scotland he was a Privy Counsellor,
an Officer of State and a Minister of the Crown with a place in
the Scots Parliament. The style of Right Honourable by which
he has been designated since 1554 derives from his status as a
Scottish Privy Counsellor.

The origin of this very exalted office is traced back to times far
antedating the rise of heraldry. The Lyon was, in the beginning,
the chief sennachie of the royal line of Scotland whose duty it
was as the king's bard to recite the pedigree of the king in Gaelic
at the coronation. The monarch was regarded as the head of the
chief clan and thus as father of the nation. The sennachie was
clad in a red robe on these occasions when he was styled the

Official Inaugurator of the King. The names of the early holders of this important position are unknown. From 1452 we have the names of the successive Lords Lyon; in 1318 there is the first mention of a Lyon as having been knighted, but clearly the office goes right back to ancient times when the Celtic kingdom was in being. Continuity of custom has been preserved; not only does Lyon still wear his red robe on official occasions, but he is the judge of genealogies in Scotland and to him is committed the whole heraldic jurisdiction there. Since 1542, no King of Scots has granted a coat of arms or an augmentation save through 'our Lyon', as he is called in the royal warrants so issued.

The heraldic establishment is: three heralds—Albany, Marchmont and Rothesay; and three pursuivants—Unicorn, Carrick and Dingwall or Kintyre. There are also two pursuivants extraordinary, Linlithgow and Falkland. These gentlemen are members of the Queen's household in Scotland and act as distinguished messengers on solemn occasions, as well as engaging in heraldic practice like their English equivalents.

One of the greatest differences between English and Scots heraldic practice is that in Scotland there can be no argument as to the legality of anyone's arms. The address of the Lord Lyon, 'At his Court', is to be taken literally. He is a judge of the Court of Session, of which his court is an integral part. How has this happened?

In 1663 the style of Lord Lyon was formally recognised in an Act of the Scots Parliament. In 1672 the same parliament ratified the 'style, title, liberties, pre-eminencies, jurisdiction . . . of old used and wont, or which did ever pertain to the said office at anytime bygone'. This Act of 1672 did more. It set a period of three months within which arms could be recorded in Lyon register, after which arms not so entered would be illegal. With the Act behind him, Lyon can control the use of arms in Scotland. In virtue of his authority he can deface arms on monuments or in windows, or require their removal. He can bring proceedings against any who refuse to obey his orders, and has power to fine or imprison. Nor are these powers unused. Proceedings have been instituted in this century against those who failed to obey the law and they would no doubt be taken again if the need arose. In 1867 the Lyon Court Act of the United Kingdom Parliament confirmed yet again the style and position of the Lord Lyon.

In Scotland, then, there is never the difficulty, as elsewhere, of being unaware if one has the right to bear arms. Either the arms have been matriculated, ie, recorded in Lyon office, or not. If not, then they cannot be used, and the person in question does not possess arms. The rule of Scottish heraldry is that a grant of arms or a matriculation applies to one person and that person's eldest son. Everyone else must matriculate. It may be supposed that this exact attention would mean a shield cluttered up with constantly increasing additions at each matriculation. This is not so. The principle already mentioned, that only one person can bear the undifferenced arms, is here adhered to, but this does not mean a series of cadency marks upon cadency marks, growing ever smaller, but merely that the main coat is differenced for each cadet. A good example of several matriculations over a few generations can be seen in the article 'Pirie Gordon of Buthlaw', in *Burkes' Landed Gentry 1937*.

Scottish heraldry is closely connected with the clan system of Scotland, which is based on the theory that all who bear the name are of the same blood as the chief of the name. All Mackintoshes are, therefore, akin to the Mackintosh, the chief of the Clan Chattan, all MacMillans to their chief and so on. I do not think that this theory can be substantiated, at least not for the larger clans. Under the old feudal system there were always persons, both individually and in bands, who wished to place themselves under the protection of some lord. This happened quite often in the Highlands where clan warfare was frequent. There are historical events which support this view. For instance, in 1396 there was the famous battle on the North Inch at Perth, fought between two powerful clans which sought to dominate the High-lands. The defeated association broke up and disappears from history, but some of the members must have sought shelter under what were at first alien clan headships.

Whatever the historicity behind the theory of clanship, anyone can see the strength which it would exercise and still does exercise today all over the world. It is a sentiment the reverse of class consciousness and snobbery, for it destroys at one stroke the theory of upper and lower classes. When Sir Walter Scott spoke of the countess in her castle and the milkmaid in her cottage, he knew that there could be a connection between them in blood and ties of kinship. As a matter of daily observance, there is not among the Scots the tiresome and unpleasant snobbery about occupations which is so rampant elsewhere. Provided the occupation is not disreputable, the main consideration is that the man concerned should be good at his job.

Within the clan system there is, of course, a great deal of blood relationship. At the head of the clan is the eponym or chief, whose pedigree is traced in the direct line with the cadet lines branching off. Over the ages, as many as a dozen or more lines can arise and be in existence now. It can at once be seen that this clan con-ception lends itself to the Scottish heraldic system. Clearly, the chief only can have the undifferenced arms; after that the cadet lines which are established will bear differenced arms. In its turn, the need to matriculate in order to have lawful arms will streng-then the clan concept.

The clan is associated with the Highlands and with the Celtic race, though even some of the Highland clans are not of Celtic origin. Thus, Frazer is Norman and Gunn is Norse. In process of time, these leaders have become clan chiefs and their families and followers form the main body of clansmen. The concept has spread to the Lowlands, where it is strong in the Border country.

The Scottish clan system is crowned by the royal house so that the sovereign is the chief of chiefs, and thus chief of the whole

nation. This goes far to explain the long-standing attachment of
the Scottish clans to the House of Stuart. When the last male
Stuart, the Cardinal of York who styled himself Henry IX, died,
he left his royal jewels to the Prince Regent, thus constituting the
latter his Tanastair, or successor. The arrangement has enabled
the most ardent Jacobites to enjoy the best of both loyalties, that
of service to the House of Windsor, while retaining a sentimental
attachment to the Stuarts. I have known Scottish officers who
have served with distinction in the British forces yet who, in
writing of the British Army during the 1745 Rebellion, have
referred to it as the Hanoverian Army. References to James VIII,
meaning the Old Pretender, are very common among modern
Jacobites, though I do not recollect Charles III or Henry IX
being mentioned, except for the latter's assumption of the title
of king, *voluntate Dei non hominum,* as he stated on a medal
which he had struck. In passing, one can remember Dr Samuel
Johnson's remark in the middle of the eighteenth century that
if the return of the Stuarts could have been effected by a vote
without any further trouble, they would have been brought back
and the House of Hanover sent packing. Next to this it is
interesting to note the view taken of the whole matter by another
English writer, a century later than Johnson :

It was in the reign of George II, 1745, that the
Pretender did his last mischief, and made his last appearance. Being an old man by that time, he and the Jacobites
—as his friends were called—put forward his son, Charles
Edward, known as the Young Pretender. The Highlanders
of Scotland, an extremely troublesome and wrong-headed
race on the subject of the Stuarts, espoused his cause, and
he joined them, and there was a Scottish rebellion to make
him king, in which many gallant and devoted gentlemen
lost their lives. It was a hard matter for Charles Edward
to escape abroad again, with a high price on his head; but
the Scottish people were extraordinarily faithful to him,
and, after undergoing many romantic adventures, not
unlike those of Charles II, he escaped to France. A number

of charming stories and delightful songs arose out of the
Jacobite feelings, and belong to the Jacobite times. Other-
wise I think the Stuarts were a public nuisance altogether'.
(*A Child's History of England*, 1867–8, by Charles
Dickens.)

I think these two quotations fairly represent English feelings
on the subject. No one in their senses would claim that the
Dickensian view is historically accurate, but both Johnson and
Dickens are right in recognising the attraction of the romantic
Stuarts and their appeal to poetic feeling and the sense of the
picturesque, even though at the same time English practicality
refused to do anything for them and regarded them as simply
a nuisance. Perhaps the scholars who wrote *1066 and All That*
summed up the English outlook when they said that the Cavaliers
were wrong but romantic and the Roundheads right but re-
pulsive.

I have made this apparent excursion because I think it helps
to illumine the differences between English and Scottish heraldry.
The attachment of the Scots to the clan tradition carried with it
support for the chief of chiefs, the clan king, and this clan structure is very faithfully reflected in the Scots system of recording
and matriculating arms. Here it should in fairness be mentioned
that by no means all the Scots were Jacobites in 1745. The armed
force of the Highlands was reckoned then at about 24,000 men,
but Prince Charles Edward never had more than 6,000 or 7,000
clansmen in his army. At Culloden, there were at least as many
Scots as English troops opposed to him. The dour covenanting
tradition in the Lowlands prevented a whole-hearted rising in his
favour.

The Scottish heraldic system does also show the much more
legalistic or juridicial Scots mind. Scots law is nearer than English
to Roman law, though English law has, of course, been influenced
by the Roman model. I am, however, far from sharing the popular Scottish view that their legal system is better than the English.
Some practices such as the 'not proven' verdict in murder trials

appear harsh, while the famous claim that Scots law does not burden itself with a coroner is really a play on words. In Scotland, as in England, a death which is unusual or likely to excite suspicion is officially investigated.

When it comes to the heraldic system, however, I do not merely admit but positively acclaim the value of the Scots system. In describing Irish heraldry, I mentioned that there is record of only three Visitations in contrast to the many that took place in England. In Scotland, there were no Visitations as such, although in the statutes of the Scots Parliament the Lyon and his officers were given the power to 'visit the whole arms used in Scotland, and to matriculate the same in their Registers, to fine in £100 all who have unjustly usurped arms, to escheat all such goods and geir as shall have the unwarrantable arms engraven on them'. The above is a quotation from an Act of the Scots Parliament in 1592, (quoted by Lord Lyon, Sir Thomas Innes of Learney, in *Scots Heraldry*, 1956, p 77). It would have been impossible to have carried out a series of Visitations as in England, especially through the Highlands where no roads existed before 1715. The statute of 1592 referred to other earlier Acts which have not survived but it is clear that, from an early period, the Scots had taken the commonsense attitude that, as control by Visitation in the English sense was impossible, the best means of controlling arms was by passing an Act on the subject. The 1592 Act stated that 'the usurpation of arms by any of His Majesty's lieges, without the authority of Lyon King of Arms' was illegal.

The second English remedy for checking abuses in arms-bearing is also found in the Lyon Court which, being an integral part of the Court of Session, could no more fall into desuetude than the rest of that court. As I have shown in the previous chapter, the Court of Chivalry is definitely an existing court having the necessary jurisdiction. It fell into a suspended state of being because of the conflict in England between Common Law and Equity, and for an even more stringent reason, the English habit of allowing an institution to go on with the same name but different functions. There are few instances in England of an outright abolition having been carried out. It happened with the Court of the Star Chamber, but even then much of the practice of this court, as with libel, was saved and taken over by the Common Law courts. The modern division of the High Court in England—Probate, Divorce and Admiralty—has been formed from old courts, the Church courts which administered wills and dealt with matrimonial offences (though they could not grant divorces), and the court of the Lord High Admiral. Now had the Court of Chivalry been functioning in the nineteenth century when the changes were made, it would quite possibly have been incorporated as a division of the High Court. Because the court had been obnoxious to many persons in the seventeenth and eighteenth centuries, it was allowed to drop into oblivion. It still existed, and has been revived, but it is something of an anachronism, the only survivor in England of the courts of the Old Civil Law (*Juris Civilis*) of the middle ages. Had a statute of the sixteenth or seventeenth century existed, setting out the court's powers, it might very well have functioned into the last century and been modernised and saved like the other courts upon whose functions our present High Court divisions are based.

In Scotland, the wise precaution was taken from an early period of legislating in support of the Lyon. In 1672, the statute which is usually quoted in this connection reiterated the terms of that of 1592 but also set up a public register of all arms and bearings in Scotland. There had been from 1617 a Register of Sasines which required the registration of transfers of land, and this system is now being extended to cover all England.

A year and a day were allowed for those using arms to bring to Lyon office their claims for bearings, with the various gradations of descent from the head of the family. The arms would then be duly entered in the register after Lyon was satisfied of their genuineness, with such corrections or differences as he found necessary. Anyone who used unrecorded arms after the time allowed would be subject to the penalties of the law, fine and/or imprisonment and confiscation of the moveable property on which the arms were shown.

The period allowed was insufficient and it was not until 1677 that the time of gratuitous registration was ended. During these five years 'the heralds scoured Scotland, rectifying heraldic errors and "casting down" unwarrantable arms'. (Sir Thomas Innes of Learney, *op cit*, p 79.) I am bound to think, however, that not all Scotland was covered by this once-for-all Visitation. Some parts were not only difficult of access but also hazardous to traverse, even in the Lowlands where the Covenanters were very active. Yet when all allowance has been made, not many arms were left without attention from Lyon office by 1677. The register in which the arms were entered had by 1956 come to fill thirty-nine large parchment volumes—a magnificent record indeed. With hardly any exceptions, the control of succeeding Lords Lyon has been powerfully exercised. In 1867, the Act of the United Kingdom Parliament mentioned above substituted payment of a salary to the Lyon for the previous arrangement by which the officers had been paid out of the profits of their office, like their brethren in England. This followed the recommendation of a royal commission in 1822. From the time of this reform, fees on the registration of arms and fines for breach of the regulations were paid into the national exchequer, and there is little doubt that a similar reform could advantageously be effected in England. As evidence of the strict control exercised by Lyon, in 1927 a number of bogus civic arms were removed from the Scottish national war memorial in Edinburgh Castle, as mentioned by Sir Thomas Innes.

The Scottish system works very simply. Arms are either granted or matriculated, and in the former case the grantee has recognition from the Crown that he and his family have noble status. Should the grantee's wife possess arms, these may be shown by impalement, with the husband's arms being in the dexter side of the shield, the wife's in the sinister. The English practice of placing the arms of an heraldic heiress in the centre of the husband's shield in an inescutcheon is not favoured in Scotland, but as a general rue the arms of an heiress are shown by impalement. The eldest son of the grantee, the heir in each generation, succeeds to the undifferenced arms, but during his father's lifetime bears a label of three points on the arms, the grandson, who is second heir, using a five-point label. This is the same system as used in the British royal family, but in Scotland it is used for all families which are armigerous.

Daughters, while unmarried, can bear their father's arms undifferenced upon a lozenge. Where younger sons are concerned, they must matriculate the arms in Lyon register, when a difference mark will be added to them to denote the son's position in the family.

I have previously mentioned that persons of Scottish descent who live outside Scotland can and should apply to Lyon in matters heraldic. Many of them do, and if they live in a British dominion where there is no heraldic jurisdiction, their course is easy. If they are not British subjects, or are domiciled in another heraldic jurisdiction, as in England, they can still qualify for matriculation in Lyon register, if they can prove descent from a Scottish armigerous ancestor. In some cases of Scottish descent, the petitioner could obtain from Lord Lyon a grant of arms to the ancestor and then rematriculate so as to bear the undifferenced arms.

The use of arms in Scotland has been widespread for centuries, indeed by a statute of 1400, landowners were required to take out arms. In former times in England the use of arms by tradesmen was perfectly normal, eg, Robert Southey's family, though armigerous, was engaged in retail trade. So the Scots burgesses and merchants bore arms and displayed them over the premises in which they carried on their trade, while on their gravestones both trade and arms descriptions appeared. The only persons unlikely to be granted arms in Scotland were those engaged in occupations, such as bookmaking, which were not regarded as altogether respectable.

Scotland is in many respects an heraldic museum and this is due to its staunch adherence to the old feudal ideas. It is particularly so with changes of name, or the use of territorial designations, these being regarded as part of the name. Just as a peer continues to be known, eg, as Lord Morton of Henryton though he may not own any territory in Henryton, so a Scottish territorial designation continues although the bearer of the name does not own the land. The designation is used as a means of distinguishing between cadet branches of a family, and examples like Macpherson of Cluny Macpherson, Cheyne-Macpherson of Dalchully, Macpherson of Banchor etc are to be found in hundreds in books which record Scottish pedigrees, such as *Burke's Landed Gentry* or *Burke's Peerage*. It is wrong to put a comma between the surname and the designation, because the latter is part of the former, nor is there any need of either 'Mr' or 'Esquire' when writing to a Scots laird, the correct term by which to describe a Highland or Lowland chief.

Then there are the old feudal baronies, eg, Gayre of Gayre and Nigg, Baron of Lochoshire, or Sir Thomas Urquhart of Cromarty, Baron of Cromarty, translator of *Rabelais*. These baronies are not identical with those of barons who form the lowest rank in the peerage and who are termed 'lords of Parliament' by the Scots. Feudal baronies do not exist in England any more. When Sir Alec Douglas-Home disclaimed all his peerages there were said to be six in all; one of them at least must have been a feudal barony as there were not six peerages entered in *Burke* or *Debrett*. Strictly, a feudal barony, not being a peerage in the more restricted modern sense, would not debar its holder from sitting in the House of Commons, but the legal advisers of Sir Alec were probably wise in arranging for a disclaimer of all dignities which bore any resemblance to a peerage. The feudal baron is well represented in literature by the Baron of Bradwardine in *Waverley*, and by Mr Vere, Baron of Ellieslaw, in *The Black Dwarf*. Another instance of a feudal barony is that of Dunvegan. This property and title belong to the chief of the Macleods, and the present head of this clan is a lady, Flora, Mrs Macleod of Macleod, 28th Chief. Under an entail (tailzie, in Scots) of the last century, the succession passed in the event of failure of the issue of the 24th Chief to the eldest daughter of the last chief and her issue. Mrs Macleod had married Hubert Walter, but in 1934 took the name of Flora, Mrs Macleod of Macleod and Dunvegan. She matriculated arms with supporters at Lyon office in 1935, and a crest in 1943. The Scottish practice in these matters does not prevent a woman from possessing a crest, providing that she is representative of the name.[1]

One of the most important decisions taken by a Lord Lyon was in 1672, when Sir Charles Erskine of Cambo, 1st Bart, gave a ruling in the matter of the headship of the Clan Chattan (pronounced Hattan), a confederacy of the clans, which had been the winner in the battle of the North Inch in 1396. The chief of the Clan Mackintosh was then acknowledged as the chief of the Clan Chattan, a position which had been claimed by the Macpherson of Cluny. This decision of 1672 by the Lyon cannot be reversed, and to this day the Mackintosh of Mackintosh is the chief of Clan Chattan. Yet even now, after a lapse of three centuries, we find Macphersons who regard the question as still open.

An expression which puzzles those who have not been diligent in reading Sir Walter Scott, is the term 'of that ilk'. It means simply that the name of the baronial estate and of the family are identical, eg, Swinton of that ilk—Swinton of Swinton. A crest or coronet often appears in the arms of these lesser barons.

Anyone travelling in Scotland will find plenty of heraldic memorials on which to exercise his knowledge of the science, and he will certainly be delighted by the abundance of heraldic stained

---

[1] A crest was granted to Mrs Douglas of Brigton as she had become representer of the family and barons of Brigton, since it has been held by Lyon that any woman who succeeds to the representation of her house and family inherits the crest as well as the shield of arms, but the style of shield for any female is a lozenge. No helmet is given to a woman but *qua* feudal baroness of Brigton, a chapeau is accorded to the lady representer.

glass in the churches, as with the stonework on castles, mansions and public buildings. Of written heraldic records, there are some armorials similar to the rolls of arms which have been mentioned in connection with English heraldry. Among these, the earliest are two of foreign origin, the *Armorial de Gelre* dated 1369–88, preserved in the Royal Library of Brussels, and the *Armorial de Berry*. The latter was compiled about 1445 by Gilles le Bouvier, who was appointed Berry, Roi d'Armes de France. He travelled in several European countries and included many Scottish arms in his record. He described and illustrated the arms of fifteen earls, 101 barons and nine others. Then there is the *Armorial de l'Europe*, prepared for the Duke of Burgundy by the herald of the Golden Fleece, and which also includes descriptions of Scottish arms. The earliest Scottish armorial dates from about 1508–19, and was the work of the several occupants of the office of Lyon up to Sir Robert Forman 1555–67. It is known as the Forman-Workman Manuscript. After this, in 1542, is the Register of Sir David Lindsay of the Mount, who was a poet and Lord Lyon from 1542–55. He was placed as Lyon by Sir Walter Scott in *Marmion* much earlier than he was in history, an anachronism. Some other Scottish armorials exist up to the end of the seventeenth century. The English armorials begin much earlier, from 1250.

Turning to Scottish heraldic practice in regard to the different components of a coat of arms, it is not hard to understand why there are many differences from the present English system. It is mainly due to the persistence of the feudal system in Scotland, with emphasis on the clan. This has led to the preservation of much that was formerly found in England. The use of supporters is an instance. The confinement of these to peers and certain knights prevents recognition of the distinctions in families like the Stapyltons, mentioned in the last chapter, and even the purist Fox-Davies mentions supporters as having been used by the Hoghtons of Hoghton, (two bulls argent), Tichborne of Tichborne (two lions guardant gules) and Scrope of Danby (two

choughs). Families of this calibre are ranked, in England, among
the landed gentry or squirearchy, whereas in Scotland they would
certainly be the equivalent of the minor barons. As such there
would be no difficulty about their supporters. 'In Scotland not
only peers, but the heirs of the many minor barons, or "Lairds",
who were liable to be called to Parliament prior to 1592, and
chiefs of clans and "old families", and certain knights, are entitled
as of right to obtain grants of supporters from the Lord Lyon.'
(Sir Thomas Innes of Learney, *op cit*, p 130.) So we find supporters for Swinton of that ilk and for Barclay Grahame of
Morphie, the latter family being headed in 1952 by a lady. Incidentally, many Scottish families have as their suporters two
savages wreathed about the middle and the head with laurel, and
armed with clubs, such figures typifying no doubt the fierce
ancient inhabitants of Caledonia.

Although the English practice of placing the arms of an heiress
wife on an inescutcheon is not followed in Scotland, the inescutcheon is used as a means of expressing heraldically such matters
as feudal lordships or augmentations. Arms which are included as
a rule as quarterings may thus be shown as inescutcheons, which
serve to draw attention to their importance. The inescutcheon is
also used by a man who is married to a peeress in her own right,
and who may show her arms on an inescutcheon, or escutcheon of
pretence as it is also called, ensigned with her coronet. Mottoes
are usually placed above the heraldic achievement in Scottish
arms, unless the position is specifically mentioned. When there
are two mottoes, one is placed below the arms. Mottoes are
always registered with the arms, and although I do not think they
are technically part of the coat of arms, any more than in England,
they are much less variable. Many Scottish mottoes do genu-
inely go back to an old clan or family slogan or war cry.

The slogan, or slughorn, is restricted to the chief or head of
the family, and here again we see an example of the continuance
of feudal habits into modern life. Similarly with the use of
heraldic flags. Probably many more banners are used in Scotland

than in England, and wherever a chief has retained the ancestral castle, it is most appropriate that he should display his banner above the roof of the clan centre. The banner is a square flag on which the shield of arms should appear, but not the crest, motto or supporters. The full achievement is shown on a flag known as the ensign, which is rectangular. Standards are long, narrow flags with the swallow-tail ends which we associate with pennons (see Chapter 3 on English heraldry). Rules exist specifying the length of standards for the different ranks, from sovereign to knight or feudal baron. Guidons, displaying crest or badge only, are one-third shorter than standards, pennons are half the size of guidons. There is also the pinsel, a triangular-shaped flag, on which is displayed a chief's or baron's title with a coronet or cap above it. I quote again from Sir Thomas Innes, because the pinsel is peculiar to Scotland and so typical of the feudal past. 'This flag is used by a chief's tosheador, or local commander, exercising his authority in his chief's absence. Given only to chiefs, or very special chieftain-barons for practical use' (p 45 *op cit*).

Badges in Scotland, as in England, are often identical with the crest, and were meant to be worn by the clansmen or the following (ie, retainers) of a baron. The difference between the use of badges in the two countries is that whereas in England, apart from royal badges, they are now rarely used, in Scotland the clan badge is very frequently in use by clansmen and clanswomen.

The order of Scottish baronets, those of Nova Scotia, bear a special badge, the cross of St Andrew with an inescutcheon of the royal arms of Scotland. This can also be borne as a canton on the shield.

The 'compartment' is used to support the supporters, and is usually rock or earth, though occasionally the make-up or other feature of the compartment is specified in the grant. This practice is very advisable because a compartment which is solid-looking can never degenerate into the dreadful thing humorously but not too inaccurately described as a gas-bracket in English Victorian heraldry.

One of the most distinctive and interesting features in Scottish armory is the tressure. The second quarter of the royal arms is blazoned as: or a lion rampant gules within a double tressure flory counterflory of the last. The tressure is a diminutive of the orle. The latter is defined as an inner border which does not touch the extremities of the shield, the field being seen within and round it on both sides. The appearance of the orle can be described as that of an escutcheon which is voided. The tressure is half the size of the orle. The tressure flory has fleurs-de-lis on the two lines at intervals. In tressure flory counter flory, each alternate fleur-de-lis points to the centre of the field.

The tressure is the royal tressure and cannot be borne by a person other than a member of the royal family without permission from the sovereign. Such grants rank among augmentations. Many of the old families in Scotland bear the tressure which they claim by right of descent in the female line from the Scots royal house, but more probably there was a grant, in the fairly remote past, of the tressure as an augmentation.

Why should the Scottish royal arms bear the distinctive heraldic device of the kings of France? An obvious answer would be because of the Auld Alliance between Scotland and France against England but, as usual, awkward historical facts stand in the way of such a reasonable explanation. Alliance against England came in the fourteenth century, whereas a device on the shield of Alexander III of Scotland (1249–85) shows what is apparently a double tressure flory counter flory.

The tressure has been known to be decorated with crescents and demi-fleurs-de-lis (arms of the Earl of Aboyne) and, in another case, with thistles and roses alternating with the fleurs-de-lis (Gordons, Earls of Aberdeen.) Most ordinaries are enclosed by the tressure, but the chief and the canton cover its top.

Last among the heraldic survivals in Scotland is the existence of private heralds among Scottish noble families, whereas for several centuries in England only the royal household has had its own heralds. The Countess of Erroll is the Hereditary High Constable of Scotland and her private herald is known as Slains Pursuivant.

CHAPTER 5

Corporate Bodies I
Military, Territorial and Civic Arms

BEFORE going on to the heraldry of countries outside the British Isles, it is, perhaps, desirable to describe the present position of arms of bodies as distinct from those of individuals. By such bodies I mean municipal arms primarily, but there are also very many others which use arms. These include schools, colleges, universities, professional associations and societies, and commercial undertakings, at least in Great Britain and the countries connected with her. There are also the arms of states, not those long-established countries which generally use the arms of their royal families but the many new states which have become independent in the last twenty years. In addition, there are many instances of the use of badges, in some cases full coats of arms, by military and naval units.

An interesting point about the arms of corporate bodies is that they do not cause any stirring of democratic feeling, whereas grants of arms to individuals seem often to do so. In several countries, including Sweden and Denmark, although arms are not now granted to individuals, many such grants are made to towns and other bodies.

Units of the Armed Forces

That modern heraldy should be used in connection with units of the armed forces is evocative of the days of chivalry. Then knights met in single combat and the issue was decided in favour of individual bravery and skill. With the advent of mass destruction by machinery, chivalry passed out of warfare. The enormous interest with which the careers of air 'aces' in the 1914–18 war were followed was a flicker of the old romance of war in bygone days, and even the rigid discipline of the Germans permitted this sentiment to flourish. The greatest hero of their air force, the 'Red' Baron von Richthofen, was allowed to put his ancestral arms upon his 'plane.

Even the magnificent heroism displayed by the Royal Air Force in the 1939–45 war became almost impersonal; perhaps where so much bravery was to be found, it was hard to signalise even the most outstanding. One feature from the chivalric past was, however, carried over into modern warfare, and that was the use of heraldry. All branches of the British forces had their emblems, and these were under the care of members of the College of Arms. The badges of the Navy, for instance, (in 1961) came under Somerset Herald; Garter King of Arms was inspector of Army badges, and Clarenceux King of Arms was inspector of RAF badges. These appointments were held under the Admiralty, the War Office and the Air Ministry, and were quite apart from the officers' positions in the College.

Only a few units received coats of arms; for the most part, the heraldic devices in use in modern armies are badges. In modern warfare the necessity of denying information to the enemy makes it essential for all clear signs which mark vehicles or disclose unit identities to be removed. How then was one formation to be distinguished from another, unless some other divisional signs were invented? So it was in the 1914–18 war that there was a great development in devising signs which did not disclose the identity of the unit by specific words. In the 1939–45 war there was a much greater extension of the use of such signs, many of which became familiar to the general public. The Crusaders' Cross of the 8th Army, the rising Phoenix of South-east Asia Command, the Bellerophon astride a winged Pegasus, these and very many more became known far and wide outside the formation which had adopted the design in the first instance. However well known they were, they did not immediately disclose the identity of a regiment or other smaller unit. Lt-Col Howard N. Cole, who has written on military heraldry and who is the president of the Military Heraldry Society, lists over 500 army signs of the British and Allied HQ commands and formations. He says that 'the choice of signs was left to each formation and this soon led to a wider meaning. It built up the *esprit de corps* of the corps and divisions.' The signs were in six categories, heraldic, (mostly crosses or national emblems), symbolic, territorial, national, animal and geometric. Soon the problem of security presented itself again. The wearing of the signs on battledress made them familiar to the public and from this there could have been a leakage of information to the enemy. Often the signs could not be used, especially when operations were pending. Only a minority of formations continued with the same design.

In the case of the Royal Air Force, the use of badges followed on the same lines as for the Army and the Navy. A former Garter King of Arms, the late Sir Gerald Woods Wollaston, has clarified this matter of military badges. People sometimes refer to the crest of a regiment or an Air Force squadron, but this is a misnomer.

> 'As long ago as the eighteenth century', wrote Sir Gerald 'it was laid down by royal warrant that no regiment might bear on its colours the arms or crest of its colonel. Before that time, regiments were generally raised, and for the most part supported, by the officers who commanded them, who assumed a proprietary right over them; and it was the custom for such commanding officer to place his arms or crest on their colours and accoutre-

ments. But by the time the above quoted royal warrant was issued, it had become established that regiments are the King's regiments and that any badges borne on their colours must be royal badges, or badges sanctioned by the sovereign, and not the property of an individual. This rule against displaying arms and crests of individuals and corporations has since been generally enforced in regimental colours though, of course, it is permissible to take some charge from the arms and adopt it as a badge. When Air Force badges were instituted a similar rule was laid down for the same reason.

'Badges, not crests, are used by the armed forces of the Crown. Every ship in the Navy has its own badge, every regiment has a badge in the centre of its colours, indicative of the regiment, and every Air Force unit also has its badge. . . . Air Force badges are generally designed to bear some allusion to the service, or associations, of the units to which they are assigned, and many of them are happy adaptations of symbols and heraldic charges which are both decorative and allusive. All such badges receive the sanction of the sovereign before they are issued and received. In this connection a further point of interest may be mentioned. There have long existed in heraldry different types of crowns, or coronets, associated with the services or with various aspects of civil life. The Naval Crown consists of the stern and sails of ships alternating. The Mural Crown resembles the turreted top of a tower. The Eastern Crown is ornamented with triangular spikes. The Celestial Crown has these spikes terminating in stars. These are generally granted with armorial bearings to persons distinguished in those walks of life to which they specially refer.

'The Kings of Arms have recently decided to add to these a new crown indicative of association with the air, to be called an Astral Crown, and to consist of wings and stars alternating. Such a crown has been sanctioned by the King for No. 1 Flying Training School, and it will be available to be granted with armorial bearings to distinguished officers in the Royal Air Force, and to persons or corporations especially connected with aviation, whether military or civil.'

The above is from a privately circulated paper written, obviously before 1952. Much of it has also by now acquired an historical interest, as many squadrons and regiments ceased to exist following reforms in dcfcncc arrangements made by recent British governments. No 500 (County of Kent) Auxiliary Squadron bore as its badge the age-old symbol of the White Horse of Kent, the true antiquity of which is unknown but which goes back at least to the time, 1,400 years ago, when there existed the old English kingdom of Kent. The Electors of Hanover who succeeded to the British throne in 1714 bore in their arms the White Horse of Hanover, and it is tempting to think that the device of the Kentish white horse, which is shown upright in the 500 Squadron badge, was brought to England by the first English settlers from the Continent. Most of the Air Force, Army or Navy badges have been borne across the world in the many campaigns in which the British forces have been engaged. With the cutting down of the services, many devices have acquired a purely historical interest, as with that of 500 Squadron which is now disbanded.

Territorial Coats of Arms

Great care has been taken in the preparation of many of these modern territorial arms, and some examples will illuminate the practice and procedure involved. The Federation of Rhodesia and Nyasaland, ie, the great Central African Federation set up in 1953, lasted only a few years, but its coat of arms, approved by Queen Elizabeth II on 22 July 1954, was a beautiful piece of heraldry. The description was as follows. Arms: per fesse azure and sable in chief a sun rising or and in base six palets wavy argent over all a fesse dovetailed counter dovetailed of the last thereon a lion passant gules. Crest: an eagle reguardant wings extended or perched upon and grasping in the talons a fish argent. Supporters: dexter, a sable antelope, sinister a leopard both proper. Motto: *Magni esse mereamur*. This beautiful and elaborate piece of work was a highly skilful combination of the most characteristic elements in the arms of the three colonies which were to be united in the Federation. From the arms of Nyasaland were taken the sun in the chief of the Federation shield and the sinister supporter, the leopard, which in the Nyasaland coat was the principal charge. The arms of Nyasaland were bold and simple : argent on a rock issuant from the base a leopard statant proper, on a chief wavy sable the rising sun or. (Granted by royal warrant, May 1914.) Motto : *Lux in tenebris*. The dexter supporter came from the arms of Southern Rhodesia, which also suplied the lion passant on the fesse in the centre of the Federation shield.

The arms of Southern Rhodesia convey allusion to its mines, its wildlife, association through its founder and pioneers with England and Scotland, and finally to the mysterious ruins of Zimbabwe. Thus : vert a pick on a chief argent a lion passant gules between two thistles leaved and slipped proper. Crest : representation of the bird carved in soapstone and discovered at Great Zimbabwe (otherwise the Great Zimbabwe Bird) gold. Supporters : on either side a sable antelope proper. Motto : *Sit nomine digna*.

The third constituent of the Federation, Northern Rhodesia, supplied one of the most striking heraldic features prepared in the College of Arms in this century. The Northern Rhodesian coat is described thus : sable six palets wavy argent on a chief azure an eagle reguardant wings expanded or holding in the talons a fish of the second (royal warrant, 16 August 1939, after a long and very thorough working-out in Rhodesia). The significance of the coat of arms is explained when it is understood that the arms represent a fish eagle flying with its prey over the Victoria Falls. Dr Livingstone's discovery of the Falls put Central Africa on the map, and he was the forerunner of the present European settlement and African development. The sea, or river eagle is common throughout Africa, and enhances every river scene in Northern Rhodesia as it perches by the banks, or flies gloriously high overhead, occasionally uttering its strange wailing note. The white (argent) palets represent the water and the black (sable) the rocks over which it falls. It was from the Northern Rhodesian coat that the Federation derived the base of its own shield and its crest. The representation of the Victoria Falls demonstrates how well the old science of heraldry can be used to display modern ideas or objects in the medieval manner.

Now that independence has been given to the greater part of the old British Empire, there are all over the world coats of arms granted by the College of Arms to states which are now completely free and independent. As recently as 1953 a chart in common circulation showed forty examples of the use of heraldry in badges, armorial bearings and flags of the British colonies, protectorates and territories. These ranged from Aden to Uganda in alphabetical order; physically, they covered British-controlled areas in Asia, the West Indies, South America, the Pacific, the Mediterranean and Africa. In another illustration made in the reign of George VI, and after the end of the war in 1945, thirty-two coats of arms were shown of 'His Majesty's Dominions beyond the Seas'. In the latter example (which came from a most unlikely place, an illustration set up by London Transport on main Underground stations like Piccadilly) only full coats of arms are shown, whereas in the former instances not all the cases were of full coats of arms; many were badges only, and three— Brunei, Federation of Malaya, and Tonga—were flags, albeit heraldic. Some of the armorial bearings in these two lists overlap but for the most part they are distinct, since in the old Empire there was a constitutional distinction between a dominion and a colony or protectorate. Allowing for the overlapping of some half-dozen cases, there are over sixty armorial bearings or heraldic badges which emanated from the College of Arms and which belong to territories in six continents—North and South America, Africa, Asia, Europe and Australasia. Some which appertained to the territories of the new African states may have been modified or even abrogated by the present rulers, but those which belong to the great dominions of Canada and Australia are still existing. Unless a coat of arms granted by the College has been definitely renounced by the new independent African or Asian government, it will even in an altered form bear witness to the world-wide jurisdiction of the College of Arms. Only the former Spanish kings of arms, in the American dominions of their monarchy, could have had such extensive heraldic sway. Incidentally, an overseas country seeking a coat of arms would usually apply to the College of Arms, and not to either Lyon or Dublin Castle.

Many very interesting examples of the ability of this ancient science to interpret modern life are shown in these territorial coats of arms. Bermuda's coat has a ship being dashed against the rocks, an allusion to its discovery when an English ship was driven on to its shore, the island being 'the still vexed Bermoothes' mentioned by Shakespeare. Many overseas possessions also have ships in their arms. In those of Sierra Leone, a native on the shore is seen welcoming the vessel, while the Falkland Islands have a rather overloaded achievement whereon a sheep in chief surmounts waves of the sea, bearing an old-style sailing ship, allusions to the main occupation of the islanders and to the discovery of the island in the sixteenth century. St. Helena's rocky coast is well brought out on its arms, and both Fiji and Jamaica have supporters in the form of figures of natives, the Jamaicans being the now-extinct original inhabitants. Canada's arms are a quarterly coat with the heraldic emblems of England, Scotland, Ireland and France, the country having been colonised by people from these four lands; in the base is the maple leaf, the symbol of Canada. Nova Scotia has the St Andrew's cross or saltire and upon the centre of this an inescutcheon of the royal arms of Scotland, because the original colony was founded by financial contributions from the Scottish order of baronets under Charles I. As to the Canadian provinces, each is distinctive, with an allusion to origin, products or natural conditions. Thus Alberta has the Rockies in the background, with the rolling prairie and wheat fields in the lower part of the shield. British Columbia bears in chief the British flag, waves of the sea as ground of the shield, with the setting sun in base (see Chapter 11). Ceylon's coat has an elephant between two groves of palm. New South Wales has a kangaroo as one of its supporters. One of the most interesting examples of the adaptation mentioned above occurs in the arms of the Republic of South Africa. Formerly the Union of South Africa and part of the British Empire and Common-wealth, it was granted in 1910 a quarterly coat of arms which showed the ensigns of the four provinces of the Union—Cape of Good Hope, Natal, Orange Free State and Transvaal. There are supporters and a crest, the latter a lion holding a bundle of staves in its dexter paw. When South Africa left the Common-wealth in 1961, the crest and motto—*Ex unitate vires*—appeared on the new rand notes. The crest was also adopted as the emblem of the South African Navy and appears on the naval flag. The arms as granted in 1910 were confirmed in 1963 by the South African Bureau of Heraldry and appear on the State President's official sashes of office; they are also, it seems, used as the state emblem of Parliament, on staff and mace.

South Africa, like Ireland, is a republic which has a proper regard for heraldic matters. If used at all heraldic emblems should be used properly and in order that this should be so, an Act was passed in 1962 (No. 8 of that year) by the Republic, to 'make provision for the establishment of a bureau of heraldry and a heraldry council; for the grant, registration and protection of coats of arms, badges and other emblems; and for other matters incidental thereto; and to amend the Protection of Names, Uni-forms and Badges Act 1935'. Under the provisions of the Act, a Bureau of Heraldry was set up for the registration of coats of arms etc, and a state herald was appointed as head of the bureau. There was also established a heraldry council which consists of the state herald and at least seven other members to be appointed by the Minister. One of the members of the council is Dr C. Pama, the well-known heraldic writer, whose book,

Lions and Virgins (1965), traces developments in the use of arms in southern Africa from 1487 to the present day. Two examples given by Dr Pama well illustrate the manner in which the extension of European colonisation has brought heraldic connections into the most unlikely places. In the fifteenth century, Portuguese explorers and navigators opened the way round the Cape of Good Hope to India. In their passage past the African coasts they set up crosses to mark important points. At first these were of wood but later more durable material was used. Diego Cão erected a marble *padrao* (stone pillar) in 1483 on the southern bank of the great Congo river, 'which was subsequently called Ponta do Padrao. It was the first of eleven *padraos* now known to have existed along the coast of Africa.' (Pama, *op cit*, p 3.) Cão's fourth *padrao* was erected at Swakopmund and was still standing in good condition in 1899, when the Germans who were then the possessors of South-west Africa removed it to Berlin, in whose university it now is. In 1487, Bartholomew Dias put up a *padrao* at False Island, or Kwaaihook, and fragments of this were found in 1938 during excavations of the site. These fragments are now in the University of the Witwatersrand. The *padraos* bore the arms of the king under whose patronage the voyage was undertaken, and so the first heraldry in southern Africa displayed the royal arms of Portugal. Pietermaritzburg, the capital of Natal, has on the bottom knob of its civic mace the arms of the city of Lincoln in England in enamel and at the rear the letter 'P'. The main body of the mace has fleur-de-lis indicative of the city of Lincoln, and refers to the close association between the two cities.

The Origin of Municipal Arms

The use of seals by official bodies such as the English boroughs is traceable to the late twelfth century. Thus municipal heraldry appeared very little later than that of individuals, and developed greatly in England and in Scotland during the thirteenth and fourteenth centuries. Apart from the usefulness of a device on

a seal in preventing forgery or making it more difficult, the use
of arms by corporate concerns was a natural development from
the thought of an institution or community as a person. The
abstract conception of an association or assembly of persons as
a *persona* was derived from several sources; the language and
practice of the Church, the terminology of the law and the thinking of civilised communities. Thus Plato represents the Laws of
Athens as personified and speaking to Socrates. From the earliest
days of Christianity, in the pages of the New Testament, the
Church is referred to as the Bride of Christ. Deeply imbedded
now in the law of civilised countries is the conception of the
corporation as a legal entity. Yet despite the use of abstractions
in the medieval terminology and the growth of the idea of a
corporate personality, it was not until the nineteenth century
that a corporation came within the scope of the criminal law
(*scolicet* in England), and could be brought to book and made
responsible for its errors. It was held formerly, the conception
being based on Roman law, that as a corporation had no actual
existence but was an abstract conception it could have no will.
Even if the imaginary existence of a corporation were to be
extended so that it could be regarded as possessing an imaginary
will, it was still thought that a crime would be *ultra vires* the
corporation. As a corporation had no physical body it could not
suffer punishment. An English advocate in the seventeenth
century remarked triumphantly, 'Can you hang a corporation's
common seal?' The proliferation of municipal arms in the middle
ages shows, therefore, that the acceptance of the idea of a corporate body was ahead of legal theory.

Arms of office also appeared, such as those for bishoprics and
abbacies. Sir Bernard Burke, writing of the arms of bishops says:
'An archbishop or a bishop impales the arms of his see with his
family arms, being, if I may so express it, married to the church,
the arms of the see on the dexter side, and his family arms on
the sinister, but if he be maried he does not carry his wife's arms
on his shield.' (*The General Armory*, Introduction, pp x-xi, where

Burke is, of course, referring to Protestant bishops who are permitted to marry, though his remarks as to the arrangements of personal arms with those of the see apply equally to the arms of medieval or Catholic bishops.)

The heraldry of civic bodies was usually differentiated from that of individuals by being much more involved. It was essential for the medieval leader to be easily recognised when he was in full armour, which is why a simple coat is generally an ancient coat. In many cases also, a family coat contained a pun on the surname. The armorial bearings of cities could be much more intricate, and there was no need of a canting allusion as the name of the place would appear on the seal of the institution. One writer succinctly describes the classes of municipal arms: 'The designs on the majority of early town seals fall into four categories: royal and seignorial emblems; religious emblems, especially the image or symbol of the town's patron saint; castles, representative of and sometimes faithfully illustrating the stronghold in association with which the town had grown in prosperity; and ships denoting martime interests.' (C. W. Scott-Giles, *Civic Heraldry of England and Wales*, p 1, 1933.) From these beginnings there came an enormous development in the use of heraldry by institutions, and particularly in arms of office.

The Development of Civic Arms

The assumption of arms by cities and towns was a practice which occurred all over western Europe. 'Today . . . we demand that civic arms be officially administered and granted to new towns or to such towns hitherto without them. The middle ages knew no such scruples and just as the nobles for a long time themselves settled what symbols to put on their armorial bearings, the towns did the same', is the opinion set forth in a work by a Czechoslovak heraldist which all western students should welcome. (*European Civic Coats of Arms*, by Jiri Louda, 1966, pp 12–13.) This work contains 320 coloured illustrations of civic arms, from Aachen in the Federal German Republic to Zwichau in the German Demo-

cratic Republic, and takes in many countries as far apart as
Yugoslavia and Finland.

The view that towns took the arms which pleased them is undoubtedly correct, and even in England the question of validity
in the use of civic arms has by no means yet been resolved. To
quote one example alone, the arms of the city of Chester in the
county of Cheshire, were not granted until 1580, but arms were
in use as early as 1324. Many other illuminating examples of
heraldic usage can be gathered from towns in Cheshire. In 1949
a firm of refrigerator makers whose works were located at Crewe,
in that county, produced a tastefully-illustrated book entitled *The
Arms of Cheshire*. A note at the beginning of the book stated that
the project had been sponsored by the parent company in
America and paid for in dollars, though execution of the scheme
was purely in the English manner. After a brief account of
Cheshire, (the arms of the Earls of Chester from the Norman
Conquest are given in this section, though the earlier of these
worthies lived before arms were invented), there are separate
accounts of each Cheshire borough with an illustration of its
arms in colour. The truly armigerous later Earls of Chester had
three golden sheaves of wheat on a blue background for their
arms, and many of the Cheshire boroughs adopted these into
their own coats.

From this interesting little study it emerges that the arms of
Birkenhead were granted in 1878, those of Stockport in 1932, and
those of Altrincham in 1937. In the last instance there had been
in use an older coat, which was simply the arms of the Masseys.
In several towns the arms of an historic and formerly prominent
family have been used as a basis of the arms granted. Stalybridge
uses in its coat argent a chevron engrailed gules, borne by the
Staveleys, and there are allusions to the families of Dukinfield of
Asheton, and the Earldom of Chester. The Dukinfields have given
their arms and crest to the borough of Dukinfield's coat of arms,
while the feathers of the Prince of Wales, as Earl of Chester, also
contribute to the crest.

Congleton uses the arms of the Vintners' Company—'and how they came to be appropriated by the borough is lost in decent obscurity'. The arms are described as claimed and used. Crewe has 'no armorial bearings, but carries a device which consists of an escutcheon quarterly of four with a canal boat in one quarter, a stage coach in another, a pack horse in a third and a pillion in the last. The helmet is surmounted by a locomotive and tender.' Whoever devised these arms did so in the proper heraldic manner, and the result is certainly no worse than the overcrowded coats of Gough or Nelson and the vast elaboration in that of Herschel. 'Macclesfield has no coat of arms but for some time the Corporation has used a handsome device consisting of a lion rampant, guardant bearing a wheatsheaf.' This is considered by some people as a badge.

The little work just mentioned would seem to indicate that twenty years ago the position regarding civic arms outlined by an authority in 1933 had not altered much. 'A distinction has been drawn between genuine coats of arms—that is, those granted by the Kings of Arms, who have jurisdiction over armorial matters in England and Wales—and devices adopted by local authorities without reference to the Heralds' College. The latter sometimes have the form and appearance of arms, but are in fact only unauthorised local insignia. They largely outnumber true coats of arms, and because they have not the status of arms, and are not recorded at the Heralds' College, have generally been neglected by students of heraldry. Nevertheless, many of them are of great interest for their references to the history and character of the county or town which they represent, and for this reason, and also because they may in time be recast in heraldic forms and established as true coats of arms, I have judged them well worthy of inclusion in this book. Of some 580 local authorities whose insignia are here recorded, approximately 320 are using devices of local adoption.' (*Civic Heraldry of England and Wales*, by C. W. Scott-Giles, 1933, pp vii-viii.)

It is unlikely that the state of affairs described in 1933 has

H

altered very much in the past thirty-seven years. From time to time one reads of a town taking out a grant of arms. The town of Sawbridgeworth, in Hertfordshire, received such a grant in 1962; in 1949 Maidstone, in Kent, added supporters and crest to its shield. One of the supporters was an iguanodon, the oldest known inhabitant of the county. According to a report of 28 July 1955 in *The Times*, Manchester proposed to modify its coat of arms, presumably by a new grant. Whether this was ever done, I do not know, but that such a step could even be contemplated seven months after the revived Court of Chivalry had decided in favour of the City (see Chapter 3, pp 62-3) shows the difficulty in England of bringing heraldic offenders onto the right path. The chairman of the Manchester Town Hall Committee, ran *The Times* report, 'informed the city council yesterday that the change would help to overcome considerable trouble in preventing the widespread use of the coat of arms. It would make out-of-date the one at present being used by certain organisations. Last December, the Court of Chivalry found in favour of the corporation on a complaint that Manchester Palace of Varieties Ltd had displayed the corporation's coat of arms.'

Very different, as indicated in Chapter 4, is the position in Scotland because of the judicial status and powers of the Lord Lyon. 'When the Public Register of All Arms and Bearings was instituted a special division was set apart for the arms of Corporations, and in 1680 the Royal Burgh of Jedburgh was compelled not only to register arms but to discontinue a shield which it had invented in 1650. All the Burghs were enjoined to obey the Statutes, and most of those which then had arms did so. Of course there were several who neglected to obey the Statute. In 1732, the City of Edinburgh itself was prosecuted, and registered its arms, and in 1909 Dunfermline obtempered (ie, obeyed) the law after the Lord Advocate had instructed prosecution of the Town Council. The arms of Scottish Burghs are ensigned with a "burghal coronet" a mural crown proper. During the years 1916–30 practically every corporate body in Scotland, municipal or commercial, known to be using arms was on instructions of HM Treasury, compelled to obtemper the law.' (*Scots Heraldry* 1956, pp 223-25.)

From civic arms, it is not perhaps too far a step to those of trade associations and professional bodies. Before me as I write I have illustrations for the arms granted to the Birmingham Chamber of Commerce (*The Times*, 30 Dec. 1959); to the British Institute of Management, after an application had been made by Lord Verulam on behalf of the council of the Institute (*The Times*, 25 Feb. 1960); also to the city of Hampton, in Virginia. The crest of the arms for the last depicts a Chesapeake Bay crab holding the Mercury space capsule. The Langley Research Centre of the National Aeronautics and Space Administration is at Hampton.

CHAPTER 6

Corporate Bodies II
Arms of Institutions

Ecclesiastical Heraldry

ECCLESIASTICAL heraldry flourished all over western Christendom. In England the ruthless destruction of the monasteries removed a great many evidences of arms as used by abbots; after the Reformation the arms of Popes and cardinals did not appear in England as they would in Catholic countries. To replace them, the royal arms were set up, and are still to be seen in many Anglican churches. These displays afford excellent opportunities to study the arms of our royal house as used in former times. The principal or only work on ecclesiastical heraldry in English is by Dr John Woodward, and this draws mainly on Continental sources for examples. For more modern treatment it is best to consult *Coutumes et Droit Héraldiques de L'Église* by Mgr Bruno Bernard Heim.

One point of particular interest in connection with church heraldry is the portrayal of arms as borne by an ecclesiastic with a helmet and crest. Many writers contend that this is wrong. Certainly it seems most inappropriate and I do not think that, in modern illustrations, an ecclesiastic would have his arms shown in this manner. In the case of a bishop a mitre surmounts the shield, for a clergyman below this rank the ecclesiastical hat is shown. The latter is a flat hat with hanging tassels, which varies in colour according to the communion to which the clergyman belongs. I recall an occasion of more than slight difficulty in which the arms of a Presbyterian clergyman were drawn with the scarlet hat appropriate to a Roman Catholic priest. Many examples can be quoted of the use of full heraldic achievements by ecclesiastics. This includes not only helmets and crests but coronets also, though forbidden by church law. The prohibitions quoted by Mgr Heim are numerous and completely definite. '*Aux ecclésiastiques, le métier des armes était et reste toujours rigoureusement interdit, (op cit,* p 29). He cites in support many decrees of Popes and councils, of which one is sufficient. '*Clerici arma portantes et usurarii excommunicantur!*' (Decretals of Pope Gregory IX, Lib. III Tit. I. Cap. II. Friedberg II 449.) Yet a large number of historical incidents, from Bishop Odo's participation at Hastings onwards, demonstrate that priests and bishops disobeyed the church's ruling. In the same way tournaments continued to be held though often condemned in church councils. Those interested in campaigns against nuclear weapons may care to be reminded that the medieval church condemned the crossbow as a weapon unfit for use by Christians, at least against other Christians.

There is no good reason why arms of office should not be used by ecclesiastics, and some of the episcopal arms which remain in the Church of England are of great beauty. One of the loveliest is that of the see of Chichester, in Sussex, which has the field in azure (blue) with Our Lord in glory seated on a throne proper, vested argent, girdled or, His dexter arm raised in the act of benediction. Issuant from His mouth fesseways towards the sinister a sword proper. The whole is between two golden candlesticks with candles illuminated proper.

This blazon is an allusion to the scene in the book of Revelation, ch 1, in which Christ appears to St John between the seven golden candlesticks. As far back as 1245 these arms were used on the seals of the bishops of Chichester, but by some weird metamorphosis they were transformed to read : 'azure a Presbyter John sitting on a tombstone right hand extended, all or, with a a linen mitre on his head and in his mouth a sword proper.' Just why the Presbyter, or Prester John, should have been chosen for the arms of Chichester, and sitting on a tombstone, no one could understand. The blazon is now correctly shown and described in *Crockford's Clerical Directory*.

Arms of Schools and Colleges

As soon as educational bodies, particularly the universities, gained a strong position, they used arms. One of the most natural ways in which a school or college took arms was to assume those of its founder, or of the person in memory of whom it was founded, and so it was that the public schools of Harrow and Mill Hill originally used the arms of their respective founders. Keble College, Oxford, uses the arms of John Keble's family, which, in turn, had used the arms of a family of the same name, that of Henry Keybell, Lord Mayor of London in 1510. Even without this doubly incorrect usage, the arms of Oxford colleges are sometimes remarkable in perpetuating the armorial bearings of persons who died before these devices were invented. A well-written and well-illustrated account of the *Arms and Blazons of the Colleges of Oxford*, by F. P. Barnard and J. Shepard (1929), gives some curious details in this connection. The arms of the University of Oxford are based on those of St Edmund the Martyr, the king of East Anglia, who was killed by the Danes in the ninth century : azure three open crowns two and one or. With the addition of an open book, they form the shield of the university and have been, say the authors, 'in use since the middle of the fifteenth century'. University College bears azure a cross patonce between five martlets or, the arms attributed to Edward the Confessor, King and Saint. University College was supposed to have been founded by King Alfred the Great in 872, and the arms of Alfred would have passed to his descendant, the Confessor. None of these kings, St Edmund the

Martyr, Alfred or Edward bore coat armour. The alleged Confessor arms have achieved great celebrity by being used not only by an Oxford college but also by the City of Westminster, the See of Westminster in its short life (1540–50), by Westminster School, and by King Richard II, whose devotion to the Confessor led him to impale the supposed arms with his own royal coat. It is even possible that Richard's devotion caused the invention of the Confessor's arms. As already mentioned, the medieval rolls of arms contain numerous coats of arms ascribed to various personages of note who either lived before coat armour was invented or in areas where it was not used. King Richard may simply have wanted to use the Confessor's arms, whereupon they were piously invented, or he may have seen them in a roll, perhaps near those of Alexander the Great or the Moslem Caliph, and thought he would like to use them. We shall never know how the arms came to be invented.

The arms of Exeter College are given in the Visitation of Oxford in 1574 as those of Sir Richard Hankeford, or Hauckford. The college was founded by Walter de Stapledon, Bishop of Exeter, and the arms are those of the Stapledon family of Devonshire. At the end of the fourteenth century Sir Richard Hankeford married the heiress of the Stapledons, and henceforth the arms were known as those of Hankeford. This was an example of a practice quite common in other instances, where a (presumably) non-armigerous husband assumed the arms of his wife without changing his surname to hers. The arms of St John's College are those of Sir Thomas White, sometime Lord Mayor of London and founder of the college.

By contrast with some of these cases is the achievement of the famous Rugby School: azure on a fesse engrailed between three griffins' heads erased or a fleur-de-lis of the first between two roses gules barbed and seeded proper a bordure of the second. Crest: a lion's gamb erased or charged with two roses in pale as in the arms and holding a branch of dates the fruit gold in pods argent the stalk and leaves vert. This extraordinarily complex crest shows clearly that the arms are a fairly modern coat, in addition to which no arms are given for the school in *Burke's General Armory*, whereas any in use when the last edition of that book was issued in 1884 would certainly have been mentioned.

The 'Big Five' Banks

In another very different sphere of interest, that of the 'Big Five' Banks, the growth of their armorial bearings illustrates the manner in which the heraldry of an individual or a city has in course of centuries become the property of great financial concerns of world-wide scope. The five banks concerned all obtained arms in the present century. I deal with them in the chronological order of their grants.

(1) Westminster Bank Ltd (now known as the National Westminster Bank Group) bears arms—azure semèe of roses argent, barbed and seeded proper, a fesse wavy also argent, in the quarter, a portcullis or. (Granted 22 May 1928.) The portcullis and the roses, the familiar badges of Henry VII, are derived from the arms of the royal City of Westminster. The wave (ie, fesse wavy) is the common heraldic representation of water, and refers to the Thames as represented in the arms of the County of London. The allusion is a play on the names 'London' and 'County' in the bank's former title. The present Westminster Bank has been formed from much smaller banks whose history began in the time of James II (1685–88) and has extended over fourteen reigns. The bank has produced a pedigree-like document to illustrate its development. It is not surprising that the arms of the Westminster Bank refer to some of its major constituent areas.

(2) Barclay's Bank Ltd. The grant of arms here, made on 18 October 1937, is of a shield only—argent an eagle displayed sable charged on the body and on each wing with a ducal coronet of the field. As the last is white (argent), the eagle is often shown by Barclays, on notepaper for instance, without a shield.

The origin of the eagle is of great interest. In 1728 Joseph Freame, the senior partner in a banking business which had been carried on in Lombard Street since 1692 or earlier, bought the premises (now 56 Lombard Street) with the sign of the Black Spread Eagle, and the firm moved in. Joseph Freame's sister Sarah married James Barclay and her husband was admitted to the partnership. In the course of years, the business expanded and additional properties were acquired. The bank eventually adopted as its official address, 54 Lombard Street, which is now the head office, but the sign of that house, the Bible, was thought by the devout Quaker partners to be inappropriate for commerce, so they kept to the Black Spread Eagle. When Barclay's Bank Ltd sought a grant of arms, it naturally wished to retain the eagle, but because other ancient and royal houses bore an eagle in different forms the College of Arms decided that the eagle must be differenced. This was done appropriately by charging him with three silver crowns; 43 and 55 Lombard Street, which are now part of the head-office site, had in former days borne the signs respectively of the Three Crowns and the Three Kings.

In this instance we have the derivation of the arms from the shop and house signs which were so prominent a feature of City life in earlier centuries. At the head-office of Barclay's the eagle is on a field of gold and bears no crowns, but is shown facing left on one side, right on the other; the signs displayed outside the bank's branches are usually of the arms.

(3) Midland Bank Ltd. This bank represented an amalgamation of other banks in the Midlands and in London. For many years it had used a shield only, and in this device were included elements from the arms of the cities of London and Birmingham. The use of this emblem began after 1899, when the London and Midland Bank, as it then was, absorbed the City Bank. In 1952 a grant was obtained from the College. The arms are—quarterly 1 and 4, azure a bend of lozenges conjoined or; 2 and 3, per pale indented of the last and gules over all a cross also gules thereon in chief a sword erect proper hilt and pomel of the

second and in fesse a mural crown between four ermine spots gold. Crest: issuant from a mural crown proper a dragon's wing gules bezantee. Supporters: dexter, a dragon, sinister, a griffin argent, each collared and with chain reflexed over the back or. Badge: within a circlet of bezants a griffin segreant or. Motto: *Vis unita fortior*. The red cross and the sword are from the arms of the City of London and the quarterings are from those of Birmingham, whence also are derived the crown and the ermine spots. Of the supporters, the dragon is from the arms of the City of London and the griffin is the traditional guardian of treasure, as in the famous Old English poem of Beowulf. On the crest, the dragon's wing again is from the City of London, but for the Midland Bank it is marked with gold bezants, representing gold coins, which took their name from the capital of the Eastern Roman Empire, Byzantium or Constantinople. The badge, with griffin and bezants, likewise represents the banking service.

(4) National Provincial Bank Ltd was granted arms on 19 December 1952. They are: per chevron azure bezantee and or in base a representation of the Bishop's Gate anciently in the City of London ensigned with an urn supported by two squirrels all in stonework proper.

Here again is the reference to bezants, and as they are fifteen in number and as the arms contain the device of the Bishop's Gate, this is a neat way of representing the address of the head office of the Bank, 15 Bishopsgate in the City of London. The squirrels were suggested by the College of Arms as denoting thrift and foresight. The urn which the squirrels support is actually a flower pot, the topicality of which is that the Flower Pot Inn stood originally on the site of the present entrance to the City office.

The Bishop's Gate was taken down nearly 200 years ago. The date of erection of the first gate on the site is unknown, but in the thirteenth century its maintenance and defence were the responsibility of the German Merchants of the Steel Yard, members of the Hanseatic League who had been settled in London since the tenth century. There are records of the gate having been repaired or rebuilt in 1282 and 1479. In 1551, according to Stow's *Survey of London*, the 'Haunce Merchants, having prepared stone for that purpose caused a new gate to be framed, there to have been set up, but then their liberties, through suite of our English merchants, were seized into the King's hands, and so the work was stayed and the old gate yet remaineth'. This gate was taken down in 1731; the last gate was built on the site in 1735 and was removed in 1760.

(5) Lloyd's Bank Ltd had its arms granted on 17 February 1956. The arms are : azure five bezants in chevron between two chevronels and three cocks argent wattled crested and tufted argent respectant and supporting between a sword erect also gules the blade enfiled by a mural crown gold. The supporters are : on the dexter a horse reguardant sable knotted about the girths with a riband and ends flowing to the dexter argent, and on the sinister a goat reguardant argent armed unguled and gorged with an Eastern Crown or. There is also a badge : a bezant charged with a horse forcene to the sinister reguardant sable knoted about the girths with a riband the ends flowing to the dexter argent.

The shield of Lloyd's Bank is derived from the arms of the family of Lloyd of Dolobran in Montgomeryshire, one of the old banking families in Britain. The Lloyds have their pedigree for the past 600 years in *Burke's Landed Gentry*; a cadet of the family is Lord Lloyd of Dolobran. To the shield of the Lloyds have been added five bezants, to indicate the nature of the family business. Of the supporters the goat on the sinister is derived from the Lloyd family crest; the black horse was the sign under which Humphrey Stokes, a goldsmith, traded in Lombard Street in the latter half of the seventeenth century. The sword and Mural Crown in the crest refer to the Bank's connection with the City of London. The griffin is the traditional guardian of treasure, as already noted; the unicorn is one of the old house signs which hung in the seventeenth century on the site of the Bank's present head office. The motto, *Esto vigilans*, is that of the Lloyd family.

Bank devices in the form of armorial bearings may well be said to be international. Apart from the 'Big Five' in Britain whose offices are found in many overseas centres, other banks of decidedly international character also have coats of arms. Taking British examples only, these include the Bank of London and South America, whose shield has the motif of the sword of the City of London and also of a sixteenth-century ship; the Chartered Bank, whose quartered shield recalls some British colonies and spheres of influence; the British Bank of the Middle East, with palm trees as supporters; and the National and Grindlays.

Public Corporations

Another example of the use of heraldry in connection with a very modern creation occurs in the arms of the United Kingdom Atomic Energy Authority. The arms are : on a field sable semèe with argent roundels a pile gules and or dancetty. Supporters : pantheons with collar and chained to earth gules with hooves or each pantheon bearing fifteen stars. The crest is a sun with rays enclosing a shield or bordure gules thereon a martlet sable. All these items have a precise significance in relation to atomic energy. The pile is an ancient heraldic charge which has proved most useful in blazoning this coat, and here provides an excellent pun, in the best heraldic manner, on the uranium pile. The pantheons are mythical creatures, like the wyvern and griffin, of the kind so often used in heraldry. Shown with collars and chained to earth, they signify the might of the atomic power harnessed and obedient to the service of man. Of the fifteen stars, thirteen are six-pointed, amounting to a total of ninety-two points, the number given to uranium in the catalogue of chemical elements. Finally, the martlet in the crest is from the arms of Lord Rutherford, the pioneer of atomic fission. The black (sable) ground of the shield represents the graphited core of an atomic pile, and the silver roundels the 'cans' of uranium placed in the core. On the pile the alternate gold (or) and red (gules) lines symbolise the dancing heat and power of an atomic pile. The motto of the Authority is *Maxima e minimis*.

Company Arms

From the arms granted to a public corporation it is not such a great step to the granting of arms to a public company or group of companies. The Save & Prosper Group Ltd is concerned with unit trusts, or mutual funds as they are known in the United States and, prior to a change of name in 1962, was known as the Bank Insurance Trust Corporation Ltd. In 1960 the company obtained a grant of arms : or semèe of hexagons gules voided of the field over all three keys fessewise in pale wards to the dexter sable. For the crest : on a wreath or and sable a rising sun or charged with three keys erect in fessewards to the sinister sable as the same are in the margin hereof more plainly depicted. 'And by the authority aforesaid I the said Garter do by these presents further grant and assign unto the Bank Insurance Trust Corporation Ltd the supporters following that is to say— on either side a lion triple queued and grasping in the interior paw a key erect wards inwards sable as the same are also in the margin hereof more plainly depicted the whole to be borne and used for ever hereafter by Bank Insurance Trust Corporation Limited on seals or otherwise according to the Law of Arms.'

In this description of arms I have given the actual wording from the grant. The full text has a preamble which is worthy of study as an example of the application of archaic language and (apparently) archaic procedure.

> 'To All and Singular to whom these presents shall come the Honourable George Rothe Bellew, Knight Commander of the Royal Victorian Order, Garter Principal King of Arms, Sir John Dunamace Heaton Armstrong, Knight Member of the Royal Victorian Order, Clarenceux King

of Arms and Aubrey John Toppin, Esquire, Member of the
Royal Victorian Order, Norroy and Ulster King of Arms
send Greeting. Whereas Arthur Horace Reid, Esq, Commander of the Most Excellent Order of the British
Empire, Chairman of the Board of Directors of the Bank
Insurance Trust Corporation Ltd, hath represented unto
the Most Noble Bernard Marmaduke Duke of Norfolk,
Knight of the Most Noble Order of the Garter, Knight
Grand Cross of the Royal Victorian Order, Earl Marshal
and Hereditary Marshal of England and one of Her
Majesty's Most Honourable Privy Council that a Company known as Trust of Insurance Shares Limited was
duly incorporated under the Companies Act 1929 on the
Twenty-Eighth day of May 1934 and that by a Resolution passed as a Special Resolution on the Third day of
May 1945 the name of the said Company was changed
to Bank Insurance Trust Corporation Limited. That the
Board of Directors of the said Corporation is desirous that
the Common Seal of Bank Insurance Trust Corporation
Limited should contain fit and proper Armorial Bearings
and he therefore as Chairman of the said Board hath requested the favour of His Grace's Warrant for Our granting and assigning such Armorial Bearings and in the same
Patent such Supporters as may be proper to be borne and
used by Bank Insurance Trust Corporation Limited on
seals or otherwise according to the Law of Arms. *And
Forasmuch* as the Said Earl Marshal did by Warrant under
his hand and Seal bearing date the Nineteenth day of
February last authorise and direct Us to grant and assign
such Armorial Bearings and such Supporters accordingly
Know Ye Therefore that the said Garter, Clarenceux and
Norroy and Ulster in pursuance of His Grace's Warrant
and by virtue of the Letters Patent of Our several Offices
to each of us respectively granted do by these Presents
grant and assign unto Bank Insurance Trust Corporation
Limited their Arms following that is to say.'

Then comes the grant of arms quoted above. After the grant
comes the sealing and signing by the three Kings of Arms.

'In Witness whereof We the said Garter, Clarenceux
and Norroy and Ulster Kings of Arms have to these

Presents subscribed Our names and affixed the Seals of Our several Offices this Fifteenth day of July in the Ninth year of the reign of Our Sovereign Lady Elizabeth the Second by the Grace of God of the United Kingdom of Great Britain and Northern Ireland and of Her other Realms and Territories Queen, Head of the Commonwealth, Defender of the Faith and in the year of Our Lord One thousand nine hundred and sixty.'

Surely a very skilful adaptation of ancient language to the requirements of a modern organisation which was quite unknown in the days of chivalry. The keys on the shield represent security and the honeycomb effect is to represent the individual saving cells, (ie, the hexagons).

The Nationalised Industries

The heraldry of great public concerns also takes in the nationalised industries which are so much a feature in post-war Britain. The National Coal Board has arms approved in 1949, these being: per fesse argent and sable three fusils conjoined in fesse countercharged. The supporters are on either side a lion sable charged on the shoulder with a sun in splendour or. The motto is: *E tenebis lux*. The significance of the device consists in the symbolism of the raising of coal from beneath the surface of the ground, the black triangles representing the coal. The supporters represent the Lion of Britain, and are appropriately coloured black; the charge of the sun on each shoulder signifies the products of coal—heat, light, energy and power.

The arms of the Gas Council are shown with a sable shield, symbolising coal, and the flames which come out of the background represent gas. A bordure runs round the shield inside having twelve annulets gules, to represent the twelve area boards. The supporters are two owls, the emblems of Minerva, the goddess of Counsel. The crest is a dragon holding a torch to signify the Council's interest in education and research. The motto is: *In libertate consilium*.

It was for long the practice of British railway companies to use insignia of an heraldic or semi-heraldic nature, which in many cases was derived from the arms of the cities which the railways served. A very strange usage occurred in the carriages of the Pullman cars, where the royal arms were used, but with a difference. Whereas the correct quarterings are: 1 and 4 England, 2 Scotland and 3 Ireland; in the Pullman form, they are, or were, 1 England, 2 Scotland, 3 Ireland and 4 Wales. The last has never been given heraldic recognition in the royal coat because this shows arms of kingdoms, and Wales is a principality not a kingdom. Altering the royal arms without permission is a form of high treason!

A new departure in grants to business concerns came in the grant in 1956 of arms to Urwick Orr & Partners Ltd, who are management consultants and representative of a large and growing profession. In making this first grant of arms to a firm of management consultants, the College of Arms set a new precedent, and it is to be hoped that other companies of similar high standing will also apply for arms.

CHAPTER 7

Heraldry in America

O N St Patrick's Day, 17 March 1961, there took place at
the White House in Washington an event which must be
unique in heraldic history, the grant of a coat of arms by a
government to the head of another independent sovereign government. The Irish Ambassador in Washington, Dr T. J. Kiernan,
on behalf of the government of the Irish Republic presented to
President John Kennedy a grant of a coat of arms and a
genealogical chart showing the historical background of the
Kennedys in Ireland. The official Irish account was as follows:
'The documents which were prepared on parchment by the Chief
Herald of Ireland at the Genealogical Office in Dublin Castle,
were flown to the United States by Irish International Airlines'
Boeing jetliner. The specially-made box containing the documents
was lined with Irish poplin of a similar shade to the azure of the
Arms of Ireland. A harp in gold thread was embroidered on the
poplin lining inside the lid. The coat of arms is based on the
traditional arms of the O'Kennedy of Ormonde, with a recollec-
tion of the Fitzgerald of Desmond arms. The crest shows an
armed left arm holding a bundle of four arrows between two
olive branches, which is intended to be symbolic of President
Kennedy's office and is a play on the theme adverted to by him in
his first State of the Union address to Congress as representing his
approach to his own office.'

The heraldic description of his arms is : sable three helmets in profile or, within a bordure per saltire, gules and ermine. Crest : between two olive branches a cubit sinister arm in armour erect, the hand holding a sheaf of four arrows, points upwards, all proper. There is no motto.

There are frequent bestowals by one head of state upon another of orders and decorations. Nearly every state visit to Britain, or visit by Queen Elizabeth II or Prince Philip to another country, produces an exchange of these symbols. The grant of amorial bearings, however, differs *sui generis* from the gift of an order. It is tantamount to the creation of nobility, since armigers are the lowest, or first, tier in the patrician structure.

The grant of arms from the Irish Republic does not refer to a banner, but an armiger is usually thought to be entitled to one and, in due course, an armorial banner was produced for the late President. This was made for the occasion when the late Senator Robert F. Kennedy carried the armorial banner of his murdered brother to the top of the 13,900-ft high Mount Kennedy, in the Yukon Territory of Canada, a mountain named by the Canadian government in memory of the president. The time chosen for Senator Kennedy to climb the mountain was dictated by weather conditions and the banner had to be prepared at short notice. The maker, Mr Walter Angst, said that he made it by hand during the night of 13 March 1965. It measured about 25 inches square, and consisted of a piece of black cotton material, with a long white streamer sewn on to the top. The design was painted directly on to the material with textile paint thickened with oil colours, and ironed in to make it colour-fast. The cloth was later secured to a piece of dowel with shoe laces. The design showed the shield of the Kennedy arms, without the crest. The maker added the long white streamer which he called a *schwenkel* (from High German *schwenken*, to wave about) and on this he put a badge as charge, the latter being part of the Kennedy crest.

The grant of the Kennedy arms illustrates the difficulties inherent in American armory. There is no official source of arms grants in the USA, probably because of the reaction against hereditary titles which showed itself so strongly when the American Constitution was prepared. No American citizen is allowed to bear a title, though this does not preclude an American lady from becoming titled in right of her marriage to a foreigner, and there has been no lack of American princesses, duchesses, countesses and so forth. An American man may also be created a knight of a chivalric order, of the British Empire, or of the Elephant, but he never becomes 'Sir', and is listed as 'Hon KBE', etc.

Yet heraldic devices flourish in the United States. Large numbers of them are derived from the operations of firms which offer coats of arms, both description and picture, to anyone who sends in the required number of dollars. This practice is justified on the erroneous theory that for every name there is a coat of arms, a theory perhaps devised by the simple and utilised by the business-minded (I think this is the most careful description) for the benefit of the ignorant seeker of arms on the cheap. Arms, too, to which one cannot possibly be entitled, except in perhaps one case in 10,000, where, by mere luck, the buyer has secured arms of a family of identical name with which he happens to be connected. This business of purveying arms for money is not confined to America and is now flourishing on a vast scale in England and in Ireland. It is unlikely to arise in Scotland where, as we have seen, it would be illegal. The sources from which the sellers of arms draw their information are works like *Burke's General Armory*, *Fairbairn's Book of Crests* and, for the European continent, *Riestap's Armorial General*. The sale of coat armour cannot commend itself to anyone who understands the subject.

Very many American students of heraldry have come to the subject after trying to trace their own ancestry. Americans of English, Welsh, Scottish or Irish descent are interested in the place whence their immigrant ancestor was derived, and when

Arms of the late President Eisenhower

this has been discovered clearly the next stage is the affiliation of the first American ancestor to the original stock in the British Isles. Sometimes this is fairly easy. At other times the man who emigrated from England forgot or simply did not bother to record his place of origin. Sometimes not even his place of embarkation is known; a line of American settlers is traced in America but the date the family began in the American colonies may not be known. In many cases only the port of embarkation in Britain is recorded. A person who sailed from Plymouth could have been a West Country Englishman, but if he sailed from London, the difficulty of tracing his place of origin is obviously much greater. When the 1939 edition of *Burke's Landed Gentry* with its 500-page supplement on American families of British descent was being prepared, about 3,000 family trees were sent in to the editors, out of which some 1,600 were eventually included in the volume. Probably a majority of the families could supply only very vague indication as to place of origin in the British Isles. A case in point, that of Corey or Corry, shows an imigrant ancestor sailing from London, there being two families of the same name settled in England for some centuries, one family in Cornwall, the other in East Anglia. Separated by the width of England, these two families are said in some pedigrees to be connected, the East Anglian being a branch of the Cornish stock. The reason advanced for the supposed connection is that both families used the same arms—and this apparently at a period before arms were commonly assumed, as they are now merely because of the possession of the same surname.

In cases such as the above, the inquirer is bound to consider the question : has he the right to bear arms? Having come thus far in his studies, he is not going to be interested in the tactics— savouring of *suppressio veri suggestio falsi*—of the heraldic merchants. If he can establish his connection with an English, Welsh or Irish armigerous family, then by the fortunate indulgence accorded by English and Irish heraldic science, he, too, will be armigerous. If he finds himself descended from a Scottish armiger

he cannot, of course, bear the undifferenced coat, but he may
have a glow of satisfaction in knowing that his ancestors were
removed from the common mass of humanity. In addition, an
American of Scottish descent can apply to the Lord Lyon in
Edinburgh for matriculation of his arms.

Without offering any discouragement to researchers, the number of those who by their studies can connect themselves with
an armigerous ancestor is bound to be in the minority. Also
there are many cases in which a probable connection exists, as
with the numerous Hyde family in the USA, which is very likely
a branch of the Hydes, Earls of Clarendon. There are also American families of ancient English descent who are no longer represented in England because on this side of the Atlantic they have
become extinct, or—a fate far worse—gone down in the social
scale. There are far more Normans in America than in England!

When all allowance has been made for near-misses as regards
connection with an armigerous stock, the number of would-be
arms bearers in America is great. What, then, are they to do?
Leaving out of account two classes already mentioned at opposite
ends of the heraldic spectrum—those who belong to a British
armigerous house, Throckmorton, for instance, or Gravenor (the
US equivalent of Grosvenor), and those who are willing to pur-
chase arms from one of the business organisations already mentioned—there are three ways of meeting the difficulty.

The first is the assumption of a coat of arms to please oneself.
After genuine research has failed to find an English or British
forbear, the searcher can hardly with honesty take up the coat
of arms of a family merely because it bears the same surname as
himself. Let us consider, for example, a case in which the name
of Nation has been borne in the USA since about 1700, but where
the identity of the first settler in America is not clearly established.
In England there was a family of Nation living in Somerset.
The surname is unusual and there may well be a connection but
proof is wanting. A time-honoured practice would be for the
American family to use a coat of arms which, while resembling

that of the Somersetshire family, would not be the same. No one could object to this as it follows the usage of the English heralds. The present Shakespeare baronet's family originated in Warwickshire, not too far from the district in which lived the poet's forbears, but the baronet's arms are sufficiently differenced from those of John and William Shakespeare. As there is no official heraldic jurisdiction in the USA there can be no serious objection to this course of action. The American family then has a coat of arms as a distinguishing mark, without suffering the charge of having adopted the arms of another and unconnected family. If it is felt that the American ought not to use the arms of an English family, even when differenced, without even a probable connection, then an entirely new coat could be devised. Heraldry has kept up with changing times, adopting new meanings for its ancient charges, as with the pile, or taking into its artistry and nomenclature objects which would have been as wholly unreal to the medieval practitioner as the yale is to us.

The second course is for the US citizen to apply to one of the three heraldic jurisdictions of the British Isles for a straight arms grant. This alternative is widely adopted. A vague understanding of the high prestige of a grant with the seal of a King of Arms pendant to it has percolated into quarters in America where one would hardly have expected to find it. I remember one American aspirant after honours who asked me some searching questions about his family history in the hope, I think, of finding that he was connected with a noble British family. His great-grandfather was traced in the Northern Ireland records, but the trail was lost there as he was probably an indigent settler from Scotland. Disappointed in the quest, the inquirer then went on to ask about coats of arms, of which he had evidently heard something. After being introduced to a member of the College of Arms, my American really became enthusiastic, purchased enough English pounds to pay for a grant, and sent the necessary sterling to the surprised herald before the latter could even begin a rudimentary sketch of arms. Thereafter for nearly a year I received plaintive and impatient notes, asking where were the bearings?

This is one of the best ways of obtaining arms, though by no means the cheapest, and many Americans have adopted this course. Nor is it only to heralds in the British Isles that application may be made. There are, I am told, fourteen states of the USA which were formerly Spanish territory, and Americans living in these states may obtain coats of arms from Madrid. My informant added that the heraldic authorities in Scotland and Ireland are willing to recognise and register these grants, but London (ie, the College of Arms) will not. He added 'London claims exclusive armorial jurisdiction over all the American United States, even over people whose ancestors did not come from the British Isles!' I would not vouch for the last statement and would think that only people of Spanish ancestry could have applied to Madrid for grants of arms. In this connection there appeared in *The Augustan*, the bi-monthly magazine of the American genealogical and heraldic body, the Augustan Society, a very interesting account of a Spanish grant to an American. On 6 June 1967 arms were granted to Senor Don Estille Carl Reece, of Odessa, Texas, by Don Vicente de Cadenas Y Vicent, de Gaztañaga y Nogues, Cronista Rey de Armas. The certification of arms passed the Seal of the Ministry of Justice in Madrid on 7 June 1967. The certification was recorded in Protocolo 2–1967, Folios 153–4. The time required for the certification to be completed was eight months. The blazon was: *en campo de azur, una espada, de plata, encabado de oro, presta en barra y alterada, resaltado de una faja, de plata y surmontado en el canton diestro del jefo, de una estrella de cinco puntas, de plata. Va timbrado el Escuda de Armas de un capelo, de su color, con pluma de azur sobre en ramo de laurel de sinople frutado de oro.*

The arms of Rodney E. Hartwell, President and Fellow of the Augustan Society, have been certified by the Cronista Rey de Armas, Madrid, as follows: sable a stag's head affrontée argent, antlers or and surmounted by a cross patée, extended and sharpened in its lower arm or. The helmet in profile, bordure and grills or, crest a stag gules antlers or and with wings sable. Motto : *Sicut ante pro rege.*

Adoption of this course means that the citizen of an independent state petitions the head of another state for a grant of arms which, in effect, is a species of nobility. It seems to many Americans a strange thing to do, and the solution would be the establishment of an official American heraldic body. It is most unlikely that the US government would ever agree to this, even though so many Americans of the front rank have been armigerous. The Washingtons of Virginia were of old English stock and bore arms : argent two bars gules, in chief three mullets of the second, the crest an eagle which supplied the model for the arms, the flag and the national emblem of the USA.

Consequently, the only way in which an American college of arms can be set up is through the agency of persons, themselves well versed in heraldry, who have sufficient standing and authority to ensure respect for their judgments. The New England Historic Genealogical Society of Boston has a Committee on Heraldry which, over the years from 1928, has issued rolls of arms in which have been entered the arms of those who have submitted their claims to the committee. Not since the sixteenth century has a roll of arms been made in England, a fact which makes the revival of this heraldic practice in America all the more remarkable. The chairman of the committee, Robert Dickson Weston, said in the introduction to the second roll : 'There is certainly no legal reason, perhaps no reason at all, why an American gentleman should not assume *in more majorum* any new coat that pleases his fancy, but he should not assume an old coat, for if he does, he is very likely denying his own forefathers and he surely is affirming what he has no sufficient reason to believe is true.' Very clearly put, and the committee's views were broadened in the course of their work, so that not only have British-derived arms been registered but also continental European arms; besides which the committee has assisted inquirers in devising

new coats of arms, though these are for the most part the devices
of schools, colleges and other corporate bodies.

The first roll contained an introduction by the well-known
American scholar, G. Andrews Moriarty. In this he pointed out
many features of early, and not so early, heraldic practice—the
grant of arms by nobles to their retainers or others, the assumption
by a man of the arms of his wife, the taking of arms, or part of
a coat of arms, out of compliment to the principal family in a
county, the looseness in the supervision of arms, and summed up
a reasonable position, 'Taking into consideration the early history
of coat armour there seems to be no reason in this country at
least, why anyone provided he observes the simple rules of blazon
and does not appropriate the arms of another, may not assume
and use any coat he desires.'

There can be no doubt that in medieval times great nobles
conferred arms. Nicholas Upton writing about 1440 refers to
arms granted by others besides the sovereign. Some instances of
such grants are given by the present Garter King of Arms, Sir
Anthony Wagner, in his work, *Heralds of England, a History of
the Office and College of Arms*, 1967. These grants were either
of a coat based on, or derived from the arms of the grantor, or
else of a crest or some portion of the grantor's armorial bearings;
eg, John Touchet, Lord Audley, in 1404 gave arms based on
Touchet and Audley to the brothers John and Thomas Macworth.
In the beginning of the fourteenth century one of the Laceys,
Earls of Lincoln, gave one of the Scrope family the right to
place on a canton in his arms a purple lion, such right being
limited to Scrope's life. Thomas Holland, son of the Earl of
Kent, in 1371 granted his crest with a difference to Sir Richard
Waldegrave, as an hereditary possession.

At first, the committee would not register a coat unless it had
been granted or confirmed by the College of Arms. This attitude
was found to be far too rigid and the committee then came to
agree that coats should be registered which had been used from
time immemorial, or which had been brought to America by an

immigrant, as well as arms granted by the College or other heraldic body. In the third roll (1936) the committee stated that it was 'fully in sympathy with the statements made by Oswald Barron, the foremost living authority on heraldry : "A coat is not held from the Crown, but it is a piece of personal property, the right to which depends simply upon user and the right as against others upon prior assumption." '

Much good work has been done by the committee. Several hundreds of arms have now been recorded and published in the successive rolls. Each coat is illustrated with shield or lozenge only (for ladies) without crest or supporters. Most of the arms are old, and therefore simple and clear. They are numbered in the rolls usually with the name and some details about the first user.

In my book, *The Story of Heraldry*, I described this American endeavour as an American College of Arms. It was therefore natural that I should welcome the appearance in 1967 of a body which actually calls itself the American College of Arms. This came to my attention through the magazine of the Augustan Society (vol x, no 5). I quote from the statements issued by this body : 'A College of Arms should have been established in the United States and in the sovereign nations of Central and South America soon after their independence was gained. . . . Heraldry is in constant use in America today. Our currency is imprinted with the arms of the United States and the Treasury department, the vehicles we drive are adorned with the arms or crests of the manufacturers, and the Department of the Army has established a Heraldry Section which designs arms and insignias for every division and branch of our military services plus many arms of various departments of government. We live with heraldry constantly but have never had a heraldic authority in America until the summer of 1966. In 1966, with co-operation from the City of Baltimore, the State of Maryland and the Federal Government, the first College of Arms in the United States was established. Four heralds established the American College of Heraldry and

Arms Incorporated, which they divided into two distinct divisions, whose names and arms are registered and protected by an instrumentality of the US Government.'

The two divisions are defined by the founders as (1) The American College of Arms, and (2) The College of Arms of the United States. The address of both divisions is : Herald's Mews on Longdock, Harbourmaster's Building, Baltimore, Maryland 21202, USA. The reason for the two divisions of the new body is explained by the heralds :

(1) The American College of Arms is concerned with individuals. It will register any legitimate existing arms. More important, it will grant arms. 'Non-armorial persons may apply for a grant of arms if said petitioner can prove through just documentation his genealogy to the progenitor in America. (As Americans who pride ourselves in freedom, we the Heralds of the American College of Arms will not deny a grant of arms to any citizen of the United States who can qualify under the genealogical qualifications. Whether your progenitor came to America in 1607 or in 1927 is of no consequence !')

(2) The College of Arms of the United States is meant to deal with arms, crests, standard, devices, symbols and designs for all manner of corporate bodies. It will grant, matriculate and patent under the laws of trademark these insignia but it will not grant or assign them to individuals. 'It should be further stated that the American College of Arms will register existing arms and grant new arms to citizens from Central and South America with the permission of their respective governments. Such foreign nationals wishing arms or registration from British, Danish, French and Netherlands Colonies or Commonwealths must apply to the respective College of Arms in their jurisdiction. The American College of Arms will not grant arms to national groups which are so represented.'

This is a very fair beginning to an enterprise to which those interested in heraldry must wish every success. The choice of Maryland as a centre is appropriate. Maryland declared its independence one day before the other twelve colonies, on 3 July 1776. The arms of the original proprietors, the Lords Baltimore, have been used as the seal and flag of Maryland for over 300 years. They are: paly of six or and sable a bend counter-charged, quartering, the arms of Crosland of Crosland in York-shire the heiress of whom had married the 1st Lord Baltimore. The Crosland arms were: quarterly argent and gules a cross botonée counterchanged.

In thus supporting a useful experiment, the State of Maryland has followed a tradition which goes back to the times immedi-ately following the Revolution. In 1790, on 14 December, the State Legislature passed an Act by which it granted to Charles Ridgely Carnan the use of the coat of arms of the Ridgely family and the right to change his surname from Carnan to Ridgely. The provisions of the Act are as follows: 'Be it enacted by the General Assembly of Maryland that it shall and may be lawful for the said Charles Ridgely Carnan, and his said son Charles, and for each of them to take upon himself and themselves the name and surname of Charles Ridgely, in the stead of their present names and surnames, and also for the male descendants of the said son Charles, to take upon himself and themselves the surname of Ridgely and also to use and bear the coat of arms and armorial bearings of the family of Ridgely . . . and that the said Charles Carnan be from henceforth called by the name of Charles Ridgely.'

I am obliged for the notice of this interesting item to Mr Harry W. Newman, writing in *The Augustan*, vol x, no 7, 1967, who goes on to comment: 'Captain Charles Ridgely of Hampton died without issue and willed his estate of Hampton with its 117 slaves to Charles Ridgely Carnan, the son and heir of his sister who had married Robert Carnan, with the proviso that he assume the name of Ridgely. The estate remained in the family until a few years ago when it was purchased by a benefactress and presented to the State of Maryland. Over the portal to the great hall of Hampton is the Ridgely coat of arms, and the arms are also found on one of the mirrors as well as silver of the family.'

Here is a transaction completely in accord with English family practice over the last 200 years, the name and arms clause in a will, and the giving effect to the wishes of the deceased, only in this case not by royal sign manual in the College of Arms, but by an Act of the legislature. Even in the latter, the parallel to English custom can be matched for, as we mentioned on page 71, the name and arms of Fountaine were taken by an Act of Parliament.

It would seem, then, that a new direction has been given to American heraldry by the Maryland initiative, which carries to a logical conclusion the work of the New England Committee on Heraldry. How far it will progress cannot, of course, be predicted, but if the experiment endures it must inevitably reduce the flow of armorial petitions to heraldic offices in other countries.

The arms of the American College of Arms are: gules an American bald eagle argent arising from the ashes proper. The authorities of the college explain that 'helms or coronets are excluded from grants of arms in America to individuals. In certain cases corporate arms may contain a coronet in the arms but not in the crest. In the confirmation of existing legitimate arms in America, the helm of the arms may be retained if it was included in the original grant but a coronet of a peer is not carried on in American heraldry unless the title has been confirmed to the existing applicant with documentation by a legal heraldic authority, or by the Ministry or Department of Justice of the nation confirming the said arms.'

From the same authorities of the American College of Arms, I have learned that the college was, immediately on its foundation, registered with the trademark section of the US Patent Office, from which an international patent was received. Legislation is being pushed in the US Department of Commerce and through the US Congress to clamp down on firms which send litho reproductions of arms through the US mail. The college holds that it is fraudulent use of the mail to claim that 'we will mail you your family arms for $5.00 if you send us your name'.

Judging by the documentation required by the college in a pedigree claim for confirmation, registration and grants of arms, the standards it sets will bear comparison with anything required by authorities in the Old World, and are actually more rigorous than anything hitherto required in America. It is not surprising to learn that, by January 1969, the college had turned down over a thousand requests for recognition of either assumed arms or errors in genealogy.

The officials of the college are : Chief Herald, Gordon M. F. Stick; Herald Marshal, Donald F. Stewart; Herald Genealogist, William Henry Lloyd; and Herald Chancellor, Charles Francis Stein.

The college has recently created arms for Spiro T. Agnew, Vice-President of the USA, and who is also President of the US Senate. On June 10 1968 the college granted arms to President Lyndon B. Johnson at the White House, and subsequently presented a grant of arms to President Richard M. Nixon. This procedure is in very marked contrast to that described at the beginning of this chapter.

As an example of the work of the American College of Arms, the grant to Vice-President Agnew is here reproduced verbatim :

'To all and Singular, to whom these presents shall come, the honourable Gordon Malvern Fair Stick, Chief Herald of the American College of Arms, sends greetings : Whereas—Spiro Theodore Agnew, the Fifty-Fifth Elected Governor of the State of Maryland, being the Seventh State in the United States of America, That the said Governor, Spiro Theodore Agnew, is herewith granted his Armorial Bearings, to be borne by him and his descendants, upon Device or Badge, and used by the Memorialist, and used upon Standards or Otherwise, That the said Spiro Theodore Agnew, Fifty-Fifth Governor of Maryland, born in the City of Baltimore, the 9th day of November in the year 1918. That the said Spiro Theodore Agnew was educated in the Baltimore Public Schools, where he later was appointed as an instructor. In the year 1957, the said Spiro Theodore Agnew was appointed as a minority member to the Baltimore County Board of Appeals, and was elected as the Executive Officer of Baltimore County in 1962. That the said Spiro Theodore Agnew was elected as the Fifty-Fifth Governor of the Free State of Maryland on the 8th day of November 1966. That the said Spiro Theodore Agnew, Served as Company Commander of the 10th Armoured Division during World War II, and later saw service during the Korean Conflict. That the said Spiro Theodore Agnew did intermarry with Elinor Isabel Zudefind on the 27th day of May in the year 1942, and had issue : Pamela Lee (born the 5th of July 1945) James Rand (born the 9th of September, 1946), Susan Scott (born the 23rd of October 1947) and Elinor Kimberly (born the 9th of December 1953). That we, the Chief Herald, in the person of Gordon Malvern Fair Stick, and the Chief Herald Marshal, in the person of Donald Franklin Stewart, by virtue of the Letters Patent, and do assign unto the said Spiro Theodore Agnew, the Arms following :

'On a shield azure, four horses' heads couped argent, dexter chief, sinister chief canton, dexter canton of base, and sinister canton of base, and a cross of the same, surmounted by a cross botony gules. Crest : a hand couped and proper, holding a sceptre of office. Supporters : dexter a Greek statesman, robed proper, and sinister a Greek warrior of the same. Motto : Do all Good.

'In Witness whereof We, the said Chief Herald Marshal, have to these presents subscribed our names and affixed the seal of Our Office, this 1st day of October in the year of Our Lord and Saviour, One Thousand, Nine Hundred and Sixty Eight.'

CHAPTER 8

Continental Heraldry - I

DESPITE the vast amount of heraldry which existed on the Continent, and still exists, there is great difficuty in obtaining information on the subject, the main obstacle being that of language. In countries such as Sweden and Poland the heraldic literature remains in the original languages, and this is also the position in nearly all western European countries. Where, however, French is the language of heraldic writing, most people possess the key to understanding, and this is the case not only in France and Belgium, but also for the transactions at most international conferences. Perhaps Spanish and Italian literature is sufficiently read by English-speaking people for the heraldry of those countries to be understood, but comparatively few read the Scandinavian languages, or Polish or Dutch.

In the present and the next chapter, then, we cannot have a complete account of European heraldry though something can be said of most countries. Another factor making for ignorance of European armory is that the Continent has been subjected to so many political changes that most of the old traditional institutions have disappeared. Thus monarchy in Europe is now confined to the three Scandinavian states, to Holland and Belgium, Luxemburg, Monaco and, until recently, faraway Greece. In any event the last-named does not count heraldically, as there are no coats of arms in Greece. In the other countries mentioned, heraldry is far from moribund but it is exercised mainly in connection with arms of public bodies and not with arms grants to private individuals. Nor are such arms any longer the business of an heraldic institution, for in most Continental countries the kings of arms have departed with the kings their masters. The College of Arms in London and the Lyon Office in Edinburgh have no proper counterpart on the Continent. It is often said that the Swiss republic has state heralds, but this is quite wrong. When the throne has gone, the office of king of arms has no meaning, nor is there any official control of nobility.

Fortunately, however, there are private associations in several lands which have been formed to maintain records and to endeavour to prevent the misuse of titles and arms. A very healthy movement is that of the International Congresses of Heraldry and Genealogy which has developed since the 1939–45 war. It is performing the very useful service of bringing together from all parts of the world persons who are interested in the study of heraldry and who can thus exchange information and experience. The first of the international congresses on the two sciences of heraldry and genealogy was held in Barcelona in 1928. At this meeting an effort was made to establish a statute concerning Spanish nobility, but this object was frustrated by the advent of the Spanish Republic in 1931 and the ensuing civil war. A second congress was held at Rome and Naples in 1953 under the presidency of Baron de Giura which had lasting success. An international organisation was established, El Instituto Internacional de Genealogia y Heraldica, with its office in Madrid. Under the auspices of the Instituto a third congress took place at Madrid in 1955, at which some twenty nations were represented. The congress was supported by the Spanish government and was opened by the Minister of Justice. Following the congress, there was the opportunity to visit some of the Spanish archives in other cities. It was planned that there should be a congress every two years, but as the next centre was to be Brussels, the Belgian organisers postponed the meeting until 1958 in order that it should coincide with the Brussels International Exhibition. In all these meetings almost as much importance attaches to the social contacts and to visits to places of heraldic interest as to the reading of papers in the congress sessions. The fifth congress was held in the attractive setting of Stockholm in 1960, under the patronage of Prince Bertil of Sweden. Stockholm's immense charm, especially in the Old City, together with the opportunity of visiting other parts of Scandinavia, contributed not a little to the enjoyment of congressists from thirty countries. The sixth congress took place in 1962 in Edinburgh; the seventh in 1964 at the Hague; the eighth was in Paris in 1966, and the ninth was in Berne in 1968.

In most cases the proceedings of the congress are subsequently published and afford useful records on many subjects. It is not always possible to attend every lecture and, even if it were, language remains a serious problem. The languages of the congresses are, usually, French, German, English, Spanish and Italian. To provide interpreters for every session would be very expensive, but a method of summarisation in each of the major tongues would be welcome. The publication of papers does, however, go far to solve the problem of communication.

France

French heraldry has undergone a complete *volte face* which no lover of the noble science can contemplate without deep regret. '*Depuis le XIX*ᵉ *siècle, la France est devenue le pays où la science héraldique est la plus méconnue, aprés avoir été l'un de ceux où elle était la plus florissante.*' wrote the best writer on French heraldry, Remi Mathieu, *Le Systeme Héraldique Français,* 1946, p 256. The very language of heraldry is French and, as we have seen, a plausible case can be made out for the science of heraldry having originated in France. Yet heraldry in France is now completely unregulated, and largely because of this, is unknown to the majority of French people.

One of the main causes of this lamentable decay in heraldry

is the failure of the French heralds to make for themselves any strong position. On this subject the present Garter King of Arms has expressed a forthright opinion. After pointing out that the French heralds had no power to grant arms and had allowed many of their old functions to pass away in the sixteenth century without substituting new ones, he added : 'By 1615, their armorial competence was so slight that Louis XIII created the new office of *juge général d'armes de France* to try heraldic causes, thereby in effect robbing them of what was left. The heralds were indeed given the function of assessors in the court of the *juge d'armes* but, from jealousy or incompetence, took little part in it.' (Sir Anthony Wagner, *Heralds of England*, HMSO, 1967, p 164.)

Lest anyone should think the above opinion biased by national feeling, we may compare with it the statement of M. Mathieu : 'In England, from the start of the fifteenth century, the kings and heralds of arms were able, on their own authority, to grant certified arms peculiar to an individual on a petition made to them : the French officers of arms were always very far from having such powers and the right to grant arms was in France reserved exclusively to the sovereign, at least from the beginning of the sixteenth century.' (*op cit*, p 186.)

Consequently, when the monarchical or imperial system was finally replaced by the republican after 1870, there was no body of heralds in any way resembling the College of Arms, nor indeed had such a body existed to be abolished in the revolution of 1792. In some European countries which have become republics after having been monarchies, there has existed some kind of institution or association capable of becoming the centre for heraldic studies, and which has a position of prestige though not of authority. In France this is not so. The historical background of the present position is of great interest.

As in the rest of western Europe, arms appeared in France in the twelfth century for purposes of distinction between one armoured combatant and another. The arms of non-combatants,

ladies and ecclesiastics, came later but even so it is remarkable
how early they appear in France. Arms of ladies were rare before
the thirteenth century, but the earliest example is that of Rohaire
de Claire who died in 1156, and on whose seal appear seven
chevrons. Even if there were few other cases of feminine arms
at that date, such an example, just past the middle twelfth
century, indicated how very quickly the custom of arms-bearing
had spread to allow a non-warlike use of it to become possible so
soon after the origin of heraldry.[1] Ecclesiastical arms appear at
the earliest between 1209 and 1219, when the arms of the see
of Langres are found on coins of the bishop, Guillaume de Join-
ville. (Arms: *d'azure semé de fleurs-de-lis d'or, au sautoir de
queules brochant sur le tout.*)

Even more remarkable, and destined to have a very long
history, was the development in the use of arms outside the most
important medieval classes, the nobles and the clergy. Fairly
early in the thirteenth century appear the arms of the roturier, or
peasant class. The first instance recorded is on the seal of Guillaume de Martinvast (in the *Manche au Cherbourg*, cant.
Octeville). He used a cinquefoil. Many other instances of bourgeois bearing arms are cited by French sources in the thirteenth
century. The classes of nobles and bourgeois were not rigidly
separated one from the other. There were noblemen who were
bourgeois, but they were careful to state their condition. When
they did not do so the bourgeois may be taken to be roturiers.
Clearly, by the end of the thirteenth century, the use of arms
by persons who were not of the nobility was widespread in
France. From bourgeois of the towns to the rural class from which
came the townsmen, the use of arms spread to the simple peasants. In France, the earliest example to be found of the arms
used by a peasant is that of Jaquier le Brebiet in 1369. He had a
canting coat with three sheep held by a girl.

The arms of corporate concerns are found in the latter part

---

[1] See Note 1, Arms of Ladies, at end of chapter.

of the twelfth century, when Alphonsus II, King of Aragon, gave the town of Millau the right to bear his banner and his arms suitably differenced.

Thus, within about 150 years of the origins of heraldry, a large number of roturiers bore arms, coloured emblems of heraldic character which are not to be distinguished from those of the nobles, and which were hereditary. The possession of arms by the burghers and peasants did not make them noble, unlike conditions in England and Scotland. There, the absence of anything resembling the Continental noblesse, and the consequent existence of so many untitled aristocracy, gave arms-bearing a nobiliary status. No such thing as peasant or bourgeois arms is known in Great Britain or Ireland. The possession of arms stamps the impress of gentility on the bearer.

The view held of the widespread French use of arms in the middle ages is that arms were taken to be, like surnames, a sign used to distinguish men from each other. This was the opinion expressed by the earliest heraldic writer, Bartholus de Sassoferrato: '*Un fait est certain: dès le XIIIe siècle, des roturiers portent sur des écus les emblèmes en coleur de caractère héraldique et soumis aux règles du blazon: ces emblèmes sont hérédicaire comme ceux des nobles.*' (Mathieu, *op cit*, p 40.) Even some of the Jews, not exactly a favoured class in medieval times, bore arms.

Many writers have been found to uphold the view that arms were one of the prerogatives of the nobles. In fact, they would be more correct in saying that arms originated with the nobles but that, owing to the great utility and decorativeness of heraldic devices, their use spread among all classes of the community. Especially was this so when heraldry was used apart from warfare, as on seals. Various ordinances cited to prove that the French kings limited the use of arms to their nobles are not in any sense conclusive and amount at most to a mandate that arms should not be taken without permission of the sovereign. It appears, however, that very large numbers of people all over

France went on quite happily using arms without obtaining royal permission, a fact partly explainable by the difficulty of exercising heraldic control. One small class, however, was precluded from using arms, that of the children or descendants of condemned criminals whose armorial bearings were destroyed by the executioners. The famous Gilles de Rais, one of the companions-in-arms of Joan of Arc, who was later convicted of some appalling crimes, should by his bad conduct have rendered the use of arms by his descendants out of the question. Yet, Prégént de Coetivy, who married Marie, daughter of Gilles, bore the arms of Rais. It was open to anyone in this class, though unable to bear their paternal, forfeited arms, to petition the sovereign for a new grant.

Among the arguments advanced to prove that arms belong of right only to the nobles, has been that the use of a helmet above the shield was the prerogative of the nobility alone. Numerous examples, on the contrary, prove that in the middle ages roturiers placed a helmet above their arms, whereas very many nobles did not. The matter was, in fact, unregulated in any way, and it was only in the fifteenth century that the nobles began to display their helms in representations of their arms. The helmet appears to have been regarded not as a sign of rank but as an ornament, or fitting conclusion to the design of the shield. Anyone who has seen an illustration of arms with a crest but minus a helmet in some English heraldic drawings will be inclined to agree with the French bourgeoisie.

An edict of Charles V in 1371 is sometimes quoted as having permitted the Paris bourgeois to put helmets in their arms, but the Latin text will not bear this translation. *Usique fuerunt secundum meritum et facultates personarum loriis auratis et aliis ornamentis ad statum milicie pertinentibus nec non jure assumendi miliciam armatam, prout nobiles genere et origine regni nostri.* 'They have been wont to use according to the merit and abilities of persons the gilded reins and other ornaments pertaining to the military status, and of taking up military (or chivalric) arms as do the nobles of our kingdom.' The reference to arms here is the primary sense of the word, ie, that the Parisian burghers may, if they wish, arm themselves on horseback as do the nobles. It has nothing to do with coats of arms. In 1409, Charles VI confirmed this privilege in terms even more explicit, removing any possibility of reference to coat armour. It is correct that later, in the sixteenth century, the use of the helm began to be restricted to the nobles. The frequent reiteration of such edicts proves, of course, that the bourgeois did continue to use the helm.

It seems almost superfluous in view of the frequent use of arms by the bourgeois and the peasants to state that, in France, the majority of arms were freely chosen by their first possessors. This, too, was the position in England, despite all the artificial nonsense put forward. The arms of many great English families, such as the Percies, the Courtenays, Nevilles etc, must of necessity antedate not only the College of Arms but also the first appearance of the heralds. They were, in fact, assumed.

The marvellous feature in connection with heraldic development is the abiding nature of the rules. No one existed to issue rules, there was no central authority in Europe, yet in each country the bases of heraldry remained the same : the heraldic metals, furs and colours, the mode of adding the charges, the mode of showing the shield, helm and crest, and the distinctions of arms bearing by men and women, ecclesiastics, colleges, cities etc.

In France, as in England, many cases occurred in which a man, in consideration of being left some property, would assume the name and arms of the testator. Again as a general rule the arms of women were shown on a lozenge, without the use of helm and crest. When a woman took part in war, her arms were treated in the same way as those of a man. Thus, Charles VII on 11 June 1429 granted arms to Joan of Arc, who was allowed to have a crest and the full appurtenances of a masculine coat of arms. The time during which arms could be used so as to confer upon the bearer a right to them, was a hundred years, not unlike the sixty years grudgingly admitted sometimes in England as conferring a right to arms. It was considered that the fleurs-de-lis in the royal arms should not be used by a subject, but there were numerous exceptions, as with the Villiers family who were allowed to keep their coat with the blazon, *d'azur semè de fleurs-de-lis d'or*.

What was the position as regards the control and regulation of heraldic matters in France? No doubt the Crown in the last resort, but exercising its power largely through the ordinary institutions of the law. This is a state of affairs very different from that in England, where the law courts—as that term is generally understood—take no cognizance of coats of arms, except when the name and arms clause occurs in a will.

It must be premised that all the following details, unless otherwise stated, relate to the *ancien régime* before the French revolution.

I. First comes the jurisdiction of the common law as exercised by the tribunals of the provosts, the baillies, and the seneschals. Up to the end of the fifteenth century, heraldic cases, such as a question relating to the placing of arms on monuments in a church, could and did come before tribunals of these officials. At the turn of the century such heraldic jurisdiction as the latter possessed would appear to have passed to—

II, Parliaments, meaning the ancient courts of justice—to which were brought all types of legal problems and cases. Disputes as to arms were referred to the parliaments, and might, for instance, concern the right to bear undifferenced arms, or how to deal with the wishes of a testator (the equivalent of the English name and arms clause), or the misappropriation of arms. In some matters the cause became of a criminal nature, as when anyone had damaged the arms of another. In 1624, the Parliament of Paris ordered that an armorial banner which had been damaged in a church should be restored to its proper condition. The parliaments also heard appeals from the lower tribunals mentioned under I above.

III. There were exceptional jurisdictions: (a) the King's

Council dealt with cases in which treason was said to have occurred and when, the charge being proved, the culprit would lose the right to arms; (b) the tribunal of the Marshal and the Constable of France. Here we seem to be approximating to the English Court of Chivalry, but whereas the latter dealt with all heraldic cases, as part of the law of honour, the French court had primarily a competence for affairs of honour among gentlemen which would possibly entail armorial matters. There is one interesting parallel to the Court of Chivalry; and that is that after 1607, when the office of the Constable was suppressed, the marshals sat alone.

IV. Finally, we come to the specialised jurisdictions and that of the heralds themselves. In France as in England, and no doubt elsewhere, the heralds had a lowly origin, having been servants in the great households along with the jesters and minstrels. They were gradually differentiated from the others by their presence at tournaments and by their knowledge and skill in dealing with the arms of knights and nobles. In the course of 300 years much progress was made and in 1407 Charles VI created a College of Heralds which was installed in the chapel of St Antoine in Paris. As in other lands, there were the three classes of officers: kings of arms, heralds and pursuivants, the last-named being the young entrants to what had by then become a learned profession. In 1489, Charles VIII appointed a herald whom he named Maréchal d'Armes des Français and who had the power to draw up a list of the arms of the French nobles, and to amend anything which he found inconsistent with, or contrary to the law of arms. A step would thus appear to have been taken to give the royal heralds considerable control over the use of arms. Two deficiencies must, however, be noted. The French heralds had no right to grant arms on their own initiative. When the king granted arms on a petition, they alone had the right to draw up the arms of the petitioner, but they could not receive and act upon a petition themselves. It can easily be understood that because of this the volume of heraldic business was much smaller than in England.

The second weakness of the French heralds lay in their lack of heraldic jurisdiction. Even when the Marshal of Arms had been appointed, he did not receive jurisdictional powers. Some cases of heraldic disputes did come to the heralds, but most went before parliament, which did however use the services of the heralds as assessors or advisers. For reasons which are by no means clear, the heralds after some 200 years of progress in their profession began to decline in the sixteenth century. In 1615 the appointment of a *juge d'armes* who was not one of the heralds very greatly accelerated their decline. In 1645 Hector le Breton de la Doineterie, a king of arms, is described as one of the few official heralds who was fully capable of discharging his duties.

The appointment of a *juge général d'armes de France* in 1615 was made by Louis XIII, and the holder of the office was also appointed with the title of *conseillor du roi*. His position in many respects resembled that of the Lord Lyon, as his powers were great and included full heraldic jurisdiction. Appeal from his decision lay to the tribunal of the Marshals of France. From 1641 the office remained in the Hozier family until the Revolution, somewhat parallel to the Earl Marshalship hereditary in the family of the Duke of Norfolk. Probably due to being overlooked and by-passed by the appointment of this functionary, the heralds greatly neglected their duties and many of them did not bother to come to Paris even when summoned by officers of the crown.

The Edict of 1696

Not even the appointment of a *juge d'armes* appears to have removed all heraldic abuses. In 1696, Louis XIV made an order that certain masters should be created who would each in his own area be responsible for registering arms. Everyone who wished to bear arms had to present himself before these masters or commissioners. The tone of the edict sounded as though the Crown was determined to regulate the use of arms. The real reason was the necessity for the king to raise sufficient money to meet the heavy costs of his prolonged campaigning, and the

registration of arms was accompanied by payments of fees by the
arms bearers. Millions of livres were involved, and the financial
objective of the exercise was completely revealed in the further
edict of 1700. During the course of the registration, the office
of *juge d'armes* was suppressed but restored in 1701.

The edict of 1696 was most unpopular, understandably so
considering the way in which it was carried out. As the main
concern of the commissioners was to bring money into the royal
coffers, they not only registered the arms of those who came
forward but, as sufficient registrations were not forthcoming, it
was decided to bestow arms upon large numbers of suitable
persons. All sorts and conditions of men were thus swept into
the armorial net, the bureaus which entered the registrations
being empowered to grant arms to them. It is amusing to study
the results of their work. By the advice of the temporarily displaced *juge*, Charles D'Hozier, a sort of *en bloc* arrangement was
made of a series of heraldic charges, for use as regards office
holders. Whereas in England during the Visitations all manner
of men were trying to be armigerous gentlemen, the poor French
tried to avoid armorial honours. Nothing could save them, and
even the ecclesiastics were forced to receive coats of arms, often
of the most unsuitable kind. A curé whose name was Claude
Bonnamour was given as his charge a cupid holding in his right
hand a flaming red heart. Five canons of the Sainte Chapelle at
Dijon tried to prove that they were non-armigerous but were
forced to pay. A most unfortunate canting coat given to one
Gabriel Emfert, though of true heraldic simplicity, was sable
charged with a fiend argent, equipped with a long tail and cloven
feet. Later still came the ordinance of 1760 which was never
applied because the Parliament of Paris refused to allow it to be
carried out, on the grounds that it was contrary to the laws,
maxims and usages of the kingdom. The terms of the ordinance
were very severe; the classes of persons who were allowed arms
and who were not of the nobility were carefully defined. For the
most part these classes were those of the functionaries in various

civil or military posts. From the lists were excluded the majority of the lesser townsfolk, artisans and peasants. The rules formulated in the ordinance make it certain that it was not, like the edict of 1696, merely a fiscal measure but was designed to regulate the state of arms-bearing throughout France. It was, in short, a radical reform in the use of arms which would have removed from the many non-noble classes a use of arms which they had exercised for 500 years. This was contrary to the usages of the realm.

The Revolution

The exact and carefully set out ordinance of 1760 preceded by only thirty years the total suppression of arms in France. Under the new constitution heraldry was among the first victims, as it was considered to be one of the signs of the old feudalism. Louis XVI, by letters patent of 23 June 1790, approved or at least agreed to confirm the Assembly's decree of 19 June. By this decree, hereditary nobility was abolished for ever, and with it went the use of livery and arms. The distinction between noble and non-noble persons was completely disregarded by the members of the Assembly. Anyone who was a peasant or artisan and who bore arms had, therefore, the satisfaction of knowing that he was regarded by the Assembly as a nobleman. As the decree was so stringent, it was followed by a law of 20 April 1791 to the effect that armorial devices had to disappear throughout France within a period of two months.

These regulations were speedily put into force, especially after the abolition of the monarchy in 1792, when all outward symbols of royalty also had to go. Fortunately, the revolutionaries had the good sense not to deface works of art and so ruin them, as would have been the case if all heraldic symbols had been removed from every building or other object.

Under the brief Consulate, while Napoleon was preparing his own elevation, titles and dignities began to come back, especially after the creation of the Légion d'Honneur in 1802. In 1804, on becoming Emperor of the French, Napoleon started to bestow kingdoms and principalities on the members of his family. His outlook on life was essentially feudal. He regarded himself as a second Charlemagne, a kind of Grand Suzerain, with a regular hierarchy of sub-kings and other potentates, including the Pope, under his sway. It was natural for such a man to set up a new nobility with, of course, accompanying heraldry. The old nobility were not allowed to use their arms, unless they received, as they often did, new titles from the Emperor. Arms could not be used unless granted by the latter. Towns and other corporations were allowed to apply for arms. There was, however, a marked difference between the arms granted by Napoleon and those of the old régime. The new shields tended to be overcharged; they usually carried items designed specifically to show the office held by the bearer. Another very unpleasant feature was the liberal use of the letter 'N', or other letters in connection with escutcheons of the Napoleonic era, a usage not confined to that period but then accentuated.

The Napoleonic empire, like the Hitlerite régime, lasted a dozen years instead of the millenium expected in each case by its founder. Napoleonic heraldry went out at the Bourbon restoration, though the titles and arms of the Napoleonic creations were maintained by Louis XVIII, if he were requested to recognise them. The ancient noble titles and arms returned with the Bourbons. When the Second Republic was set up in 1852 the old titles were abolished, but nothing was said or done about the bearing of arms. Under the Second Empire of Napoleon III, return was made to the statute of 1808 which had regulated the arms bearers under Napoleon I. No legislation concerning heraldry in France has occured under the Third, Fourth or Fifth Republics.

It does not, however, follow that anyone in France can do as he likes as regards arms. Should anyone take the arms of a family to use them in commerce or as an advertisement, he may well find himself the subject of litigation. This happened to a merchant who placed on the bottles used in his business some arms which he found on the gates of a château that he had purchased. He was defeated in the courts and ordered to remove the arms from the labels. The law, therefore, recognises the theft of arms.

Arms of towns are controlled by the Ministries of the Interior and of National Education.

The best French armorial is the *Grand Armorial de France*, which mentions some 40,000 coats of arms in seven volumes, and is obtainable from La Societé du Grand Armorial de France, 179 boulevard Haussmann, Paris. There is a Société d'Héraldique et de Sigillographie, 113 rue de Courcelles, Paris 17, of which the president is M. Meurgey de Tupigny.

Belgium

Perhaps the most interesting fact about the present position of Belgian heraldry is the presence in the country of such a large number of nobles—one for every thousand of the population. From the reorganisation of the noblesse in 1815 to the present day, the Belgian nobility has numbered 1,238 families, of whom 762 were of the old régime; of this last total 359, about 45 per cent, have become extinct. At present, making allowance for the extinctions and new royal grants, there are not more than 786 noble families, of whom 404 belong to the old régime. This seems a fairly generous allowance of nobility in a country of about eight million people. The large number of nobility from older times may well be explained by the origin of the kingdom of Belgium, which was formed from the old Spanish and later Austrian Netherlands, the Catholic provinces which remained faithful to the Crown of Spain when the northern provinces revolted and formed themselves into the Dutch Republic. In addition, modern Belgium includes the ecclesiastical principality of Liège, whose allegiance was to the Holy Roman Empire. As several of the Hapsburg rulers of the Low Countries were also emperors, there would be plenty of opportunity for the creation of titles of nobility and, correspondingly, of arms. All titles had either to be granted or recognised by the sovereign following the heraldic edict of Philip II in 1595.

During the middle ages and later, the principles of cadency for all except the head of a family applied, but today, as in England, only the royal house observes the rules by the use of a label for the eldest son, the Duke of Brabant, and of a bordure for other members of the royal family. In noble families some branches bear as part of their arms the original cadency mark which their ancestor first bore. This is much the same as in England.

The coronet of noblesse does not exist in Belgian heraldry, apart from the cap of a baron and the coronet of a feudal viscount. Cadets of titled families are allowed a coronetted helmet surmounted by a crest, but not placed directly above the shield.

Apart from the nobles, there are many coats of arms in Belgium properly borne. Most of the Belgian municipalities use an armorial seal, either granted or recognised by the Crown. Many small places bear the arms of their old proprietor. The nine Belgian provinces derive their arms, except for those of Anvers and Liège, from three primitive shields, of Flanders, Brabant and Limbourg. Hainault and Namur took the lion of Flanders; Luxembourg received that of Limbourg, while the lion of Brabant is the charge in the arms of the kingdom.

The Conseil Héraldique was established by a decree of 6 February 1844 of King Leopold I of the Belgians, after a resolution in 1843 that a consultative commission should be set up for the purpose of verifying titles and examining requests for recognition of nobility. There are seven members and a registrar. The council is consulted when the Ministry of Foreign Affairs presents a report to the sovereign, or a request for recognition or confirmation of nobility or of title. It is required to agree on the noble status of anyone who requires an elevation in rank, extension of his titles to other members of his family, a change in his arms or the recognition or confirmation of letters patent which have been granted by a foreign sovereign. The Minister of Foreign

Affairs sends to the council a despatch concerning the decrees by which the sovereign grants titles of nobility, in order that the commission may submit its observations on the proposal for letters patent, arms and other details of the order. The council holds the roll of nobility and the register of letters patent, can deliver attestations of affiliation and can certify the possession and use of arms. It keeps duplicate copies of genealogies, of blazons, and of all matters produced in support of favourable decisions taken by the council. A work published in 1896 by M. M. Arerdt and De Ridder, *Législation Héraldique de la Belgique*, 1595–1895, *Jurisprudence de Conseil Héraldique*, 1844–1895, gives an account of Belgian nobiliary legislation. In Belgium, everyone has the right to choose a coat of arms but noble emblems may be used only by a person entitled to nobility. The coat of arms of another family, even though extinct, may not be adopted unless by authority.

Spain

Spanish heraldry shares with English and Scottish heraldry the common attribute of diffusion over a very large area of the world. In the New World, all countries from Mexico to Cape Horn, except for Brazil, derived their settlement from Spain; also the Philippines and Cuba. Any heraldry in this vast area had its origin in Spain. Yet this enormous development proceeds and has proceeded for a long time without any control by a central body such as the College of Arms. In fact, Spanish writers on heraldry appear to be either uninterested in the kings of arms or positively hostile to them. A well-known Spanish heraldic treatise by José Asensio y Torres (*Tratado de Héraldica y Blasón*, edition of 1929) makes no mention of the heralds, although the work is comprehensive and includes a chapter on the military orders, most of which are now obsolete.

Even more pointed than this silence is a forthright condemnation by the late Lucas de Palacio, a Mexican heraldic and archaeological writer. In one of his works, he writes of the func-

tions of the Spanish heralds, common throughout Christendom
in the middle ages, in announcing the entry of knights into the
lists, blazoning and registering their arms, and undertaking ambas-
sadorial and diplomatic duties. The king of arms who was the

Shield of the de Palacio family

chief herald presided at the chapter of the heralds, and had
jurisdiction over arms. He then adds: 'In Spain, in the course
of years, the importance of the king of arms greatly diminished.
He was converted into a technical consultor in heraldic matters.
His certifications did not have the legal force which those properly
termed official possessed. Many of the genealogical and heraldic

certifications sent out by the kings of arms to the "Indians" had gaps and serious errors. There are Spanish American families which base their superiority on certificates of the kings of arms which have no more value than the parchment so beautifully prepared, with seals of vellum or velvet and beautifully worked silver.' (*De Genealogiá y Héraldica*, 1946, p 37.) In another passage this author says: 'The certificates of the kings of arms are for most part confusing.' (He means in respect of genealogical knowledge, and then goes on to quote another source on the same subject.) 'In this respect the priest, Don Mateo Escagedo Salmòn, says in his *Solares Montaneses*, "The old kings of arms tended to the stupid flattery of those with whose drafts (of pedigree) they were charged, of those who sought from them magnificent parchments as void of documentation as they were blown up with legends, rather than to the conscientious knowledge and documentation of their work" ' (*op cit*, p 16).

It is clear that the Spanish, like the French heralds, lost their one-time importance, possibly through failure to make proper study of their science. This could well have happened to the English heralds, too, had they all been content to go along with the worst practices of Tudor times.

In Spanish heraldry, as in all other national forms of this universal science, there are many interesting variations, among them the following. The bar, or bend sinister, extending from the left top to the right base of the shield is said by Spanish writers to serve commonly to denote natural children, quite contrary to the English usage. With respect, it may be doubted whether any such usage was at all general, since the bend sinister is classed in Spanish, as in English heraldry, as an honourable ordinary.

More peculiarly Hispanic is the label, not extended right across the top of the shield, but confined within the shield. The Spanish chevron is generally prolonged to the base of the shield. The *campada* is the same as a fesse (a figure also used in Spain) but placed at the base of the shield. The grant of a bordure is described as a special concession by the King of Spain, which is quite common among families; but the bordure has not been used as a brisure, though the first Bourbon king, Philip V, used it as such when he was Duke of Anjou. In the French royal house this brisure was a mark of cadency, but the practice was not followed with rigour in Spain. Again, in Spain, the canton is used sometimes on the right, sometimes on the left of the shield, and many variations and combinations of ordinaries are employed. The chief and the pale are combined in the *jefe palo*, a T-shaped figure; sometimes this is of the same metal or colour of the field, when it is termed *jefe sosido*, and it is then well nigh indistinguishable from the rest of the shield. The *jefe cheurrón* is a combination of the chief with a chevron, the head of which is couped by the chief. The *jefe sostenido* has a third lowest part of the chief of a different colour from the rest. The *jefe surmontado*, on the contrary, has the different coloured third portion at the top of the chief. The *jefe bande* and *jefe barra* have the chief plus the bend drawn from them to right or left, as the case may be, towards the bottom of the shield. The *jefe orlado* has an inset in the chief. There are Spanish varieties of pale and bend.

Metals and colours are classed together as enamels, and there is a strict adherence to five colours, the English use of others, such as sanguine, being marked as an exception to the general rule. The furs (*forros*, or linings) are much the same as elsewhere.

There was anciently much misuse of coronets by persons who were not allowed to possess them. This misuse occasioned an edict of King Philip II in 1586, in which he declared, 'In order to remedy the great disorder and excess which has been and still is in placing crowns on the shields of arms in seals and other objects; we ordain and command that no one can or shall place coronets in the said seals or on other objects, nor on anything else where arms are used, except for dukes, marquesses and counts, of whom we hold it good that they should use coronets, provided that they are used soberly and in no other manner, and that the (other) coronets in use up to the present shall be removed and be used no more.' A fine of 10,000 maravedis was incurred by any breach of this rule. It is stated that, besides the exceptions named in the edict, there were others, such as the viscounts and barons, towns and other places which had been given the privilege by Philip's father, Charles V. Included in the exceptions were the city of Madrid, called the crowned, and also some families which had received the grant of a coronet from one of the previous Spanish kings.

Helmets followed the usual rules, gold, full-fronted and open for kings, similar but of silver for princes and sovereign dukes; silver for a marquess with closed visor. Silver was used for a count, with helmet in profile, visor closed; helmets of a viscount or baron of silver, visor closed with coronets of rank on their helmets. Helmets of hidalgos were of steel surmounted by feathers.

There is considerable use of mantles as the background of the arms, and these vary according to the rank of the bearer. That of the Constable has two right hands armed with swords issuing from a cloud against the background. Generals have crossed batons behind their shields; the major-domo of the royal household had crossed batons likewise, but of a larger and more ornate variety. The Grand Chamberlain bore a shield with crossed keys behind it, in the same way as the English Lord Great Chamberlain has the insignia of his office crossed behind his shield.

Distinction is made between holders *(tenantes)* and supporters. The former are of angels or human figures, the latter of animals. Only kings and princes may use angels, unless the privilege has been granted by the Crown. Supporters are not precisely hereditary as with arms, because they are subject to change.

Account must always be taken in Spain of the great military orders which were founded there or associated with the country. The presence of Moslems in Spain for so many centuries gave to Spanish nationalist aspirations the nature of a crusade, which ended only when the last Moorish kingdom, Granada, was taken by King Ferdinand and Queen Isabella in 1492. The Military Order of Santiago is supposed to have been founded in 848, though more probably in the eleventh or early twelfth century. The Order of Calatrava was founded in 1158 by Sancho III, King of Castile. The Order of Alcantara dates from 1176, its founder being Ferdinand II, King of Leon. The Order of Montesa was founded in 1317 by King James II of Aragon. These four great Spanish religious orders were just as much crusading orders as those of the Knights Templars, of the Holy Sepulchre, or of the Knights of St John of Jerusalem, or of Malta. In addition, Spain has many magnificent orders of chivalry which still exist, among them one of the greatest orders in the whole world, that of the Golden Fleece founded in 1429 by Philip II, 'Philip the Good', Duke of Burgundy.

Mention is also to be made of some associations which still exist in Spain—the Maestranzas, literally 'riding schools' of Seville, Granada, Ronda, Valencia and Zaragoza. These very old societies of gentlemen were instituted for the practice of equitation and, originally, as schools for the use of weapons on horseback. They were reorganised in the eighteenth century.

As regards the Spanish kings of arms, some reforms were instituted by a royal decree of 29 July 1915, of the Ministry of Grace and Justice. No institution comparable to the College of Arms existed in Spain, but under the arrangement of 1915 examinations were held to test the fitness of aspirants to the posts of kings of arms. A further decree of 13 April 1951 of the Ministry of Justice regulated the matter again. The title of King of Arms was replaced by that of Chronicler of Arms *(Cronista de Armas)*. Those who pass the examination are bound to be senior in age and graduates in law, philosophy or literature. They are appointed by a ministerial order and only those who have the official title of Chronicler of Arms, as approved by the Ministry of Justice, can supply certificates on arms or other matters mentioned. By a law of 4 May 1948, legislation anterior to 14 April 1931 (when the Republic was set up after the departure of Alfonso XIII) was re-established for the recognition, transmission and rehabilitation of noble titles; the subject comes under the control of the Ministry of Justice.

There are in Spain many publications which deal with heraldry. A vast work is the *Enciclopidia Héraldica y Genealógica Hispano-Americana* (Heraldic and Genealogical Encyclopedia: Spanish-American) by Alberto and Arturo Garcia Caraffa, of which more than fifty-five volumes have been published. According to some statements, the letter 'R' was reached only with the seventy-ninth volume. The size of this more than massive compilation may be appreciated when it is realised that it contains the arms and genealogies of a multitude of families not only in Spain but also in Latin-American colonies. This encyclopedia is found in every Spanish library of importance. In addition, the following are useful: *Armeria y Nobiliario de los Reinos Españoles* (Armory and Nobility of the Spanish Kingdoms) which is in process of being published by the International Institute. The *Diccionario Nobiliario* (Nobiliary Dictionary), by Julia Atienza, which it is understood is still in print and published by Aguilar, contains the heraldry of a large number of Spanish families.

Sources: Lucas de Palacio, *De Genealogia y heraldica*, Mexico D.F., 1946; Asensio Y Torres, *Heraldica*, Madrid, 1929.

Italy

Having been a republic since 1946, Italy takes no congnizance of heraldry or of rank, and therefore gives no protection against the misuse or appropriation of arms or titles. The Consulta Araldica, which had formerly exercised authority over the nobles and had worked on the lines of the Scottish heraldic system, was suppressed. In 1853 there had been founded the Collegio Araldico, the main object of which is to promote heraldic and genealogical researches. It is an academy of experts and publishes at regular intervals the *Libro d'Oro dell Nobiltà Italiana* or 'Golden Book of the Italian Nobility'.

The Italian nobles wished to prevent the abuses likely to arise from the unregulated conditions under the Republic. King Umberto II of Italy has never abdicated and can therefore be properly regarded as the Fountain of Honours in his realm; accordingly his decisions would be respected by all Italian nobles. The organisation now to be described was therefore set up.

(1) In each of the fourteen geographical and historic regions of the Italian peninsula, the local nobles who were officially matriculated by the royal Consulta formed an association of their own and elected a small committee of experts who were well known for their competency in heraldry as well as being persons of standing and distinguished background. The purposes of this committee are to scrutinise all requests for admission to, and to keep up to date, the regional register of the nobility.

(2) These regional committees form collectively an assembly which is the National Heraldic Council of the Italian Nobility, and this, in its turn, elects its own presidential board to rule the organisation and represent the nobility as a body. Also a Central Heraldic Commission of fourteen members is formed by delegates from each of the regional committees, and is empowered to decide upon technical problems which cannot be solved locally.

(3) King Umberto recognises the National Heraldic Council as the only legitimate body representing his nobles and, to keep permanently in touch with their organisation and to assure liaison with their offices, he has recently appointed a member of the royal household as 'the King's Secretary for Heraldic Affairs.' [Baron A. Monti della Corte, *Heraldic Authority in Modern Italy* (*The Armorial*, vol 1, no 1, Nov. 1959).]

The Collegio Araldico issues a *Rivista Araldica*. The *Libro d'Oro dell Nobilita Italiana* mentioned above was founded in 1910; it contains over 1,200 pages of details about noble Italian families and there are some full-page armorial illustrations in full colour. The arrangement of the book is similar to that of the old *Almanach de Gotha*, which is biographical rather than genealogical. Also of value for Italian heraldry is the work of Mannucci,

Nobiliario e Blasonario del Regno d'Italia, 5 vols, which was edited in 1928 by the Collegio Araldico.

The best exposition of Italian heraldry is found in what is really a short treatise by Cesare Manaresi, a member of the R. Archivio di Stato di Milano. This is the article on *Araldico* (Heraldry) in the *Enciclopedia Italiana* 1929–37, which occupies twenty-three pages, and includes some excellent illustrations. Incidentally, as this Italian encyclopedia runs to forty volumes, it is not only chauvinistic but inaccurate to contrast it with a British or American encyclopedia. Similarly, the Spanish-written *Enciclopedia Universal Ilustrada Europeo-Americana* is much larger than any similar work in the English language, and Volume 28 (1925) contains a fourteen-page article on Heraldry.

Portugal

Throughout its history Portugal has suffered through being obscured by the greater size and overall importance of its neighbour in the Iberian peninsula. So much is this the case that heraldic authorities nearly always class Spain and Portugal together to the detriment of the smaller country. This is most unfair because the patriotic spirit of Portugal has never allowed the nation to be merged with Spain. Moreover Portugal, the first to create an overseas empire, is the last to possess one, when all her younger rivals have lost theirs. In the realm of heraldry as in other spheres, Portugal has a contribution to make.

In Portugal, as elsewhere in Europe, the use of arms was entirely private and not controlled officially until the fifteenth century, when heralds were introduced by King Joao I (1385–1433). A distinction was made as regards the use of arms by non-nobles by prohibiting the use of metals in their arms, on the lines of the efforts made in France to prevent the use of crests by burghers and peasants. In Portugal, the restrictions were more successful and, in 1512, King Manoel I forbade the use of arms altogether to those who were not classed as nobles. By 1509, there was completed the record of Portuguese arms drawn up by the Portugal King of Arms and called *Livro do Armeiro Mor*.

In the national archives of Portugal are registrations of armorial bearings, and inquiries regarding certificates of arms should be made to the Director, Arquivi Nacional da Torre do Tombo, Lisbon. Unfortunately, many of the records were lost in the great Lisbon earthquake of 1755, but a full account of those which survived was published in the last century by the Viscount Sanches de Baera.

The control of arms was exercised by the heralds until 1910, when the monarchy was replaced by the republic. However, in 1945, there was set up, under the authority of the Duke of Braganza, the pretender to the throne of Portugal, the Conselho de Nobreza, (Council of Nobility), which has a commission dealing with heraldry. The address is: Praca Luis de Camoes, 46, 2, Lisbon. In addition, there is also the Instituto Portuguese de Heraldica, Largo do Carmo, Lisbon, the president of which is the Marquess of Sao Payo. The institute is a private academy, legally incorporated, and is the only body in Portugal devoted to the study of genealogy, heraldry and nobility. Inquiries of a genealogical or heraldic nature can be considered by the Institute, which also publishes a review, *Armas e Tropeos*.

Portuguese heraldry is restricted in the sense that the number of coats of arms is small, as little perhaps as a thousand, by contrast with the many thousands for England alone which are mentioned in *Burke's General Armory*. Surnames are comparatively few and, again in contrast to English practice, were not assumed by all until the sixteenth century. As there were few surnames, those of the great families were assumed by all and sundry—rather like the procedure in Wales after Henry VIII's time.

Along with the assumption of surnames went the assumption of arms. Strict rules regarding the bearing of arms, closely resembling the Scottish system of matriculation, had been promulgated by King Manoel I, but these were by no means generally observed.

One rule was that only the chief of the lineage could bear the undifferenced arms, cadets being required to difference their arms. Many cadets did not obey this rule, and a large number of persons who assumed name and arms managed to matriculate as though they were really members of the noble families whose names they had taken. Today grants of arms do not occur, at least not to individuals, though arms are devised and registered for counties or municipalities, no doubt by government departments.

Although the arrangements of Portuguese arms are in many ways different from those in England or France, there are, not unnaturally, correspondences in heraldic practice. The name and arms clause so frequent in English wills over the last 200 years is paralleled in Portugal by a rule, abolished only in 1863, under which the heir to an entailed estate was legally obliged to take the chief name and arms of the entailer. In this way a Portuguese nobleman could, by the nineteenth century, have acquired a plurality of surnames which make the British double or treble or even quadruple surnames appear simplicity itself. The abolishment of the entails must have come as a blessed relief to the unfortunate who, along with a score of Christian names, bore nine or ten surnames. Today, Portuguese practice is much the same as the Spanish, namely to use two surnames, eg, Campos y Sousa, Payo Melo e Castro, which may indicate a mother's and father's surname in that order, or at least two surnames derived from the ancestry.

In Portugal, the sensible view was taken that arms descended to all a man's descendants, not only to those in the male line. After all, a man owes his physical make-up to both sides of his family and very often males inherit characteristics from the female side. In consequence, the Portuguese armigers bore the arms of any ancestor, more or less as they wished. The rules of arms-bearing were that the chief of a family should bear the arms of that family without difference, but should he, owing to the entail system mentioned above, be head of more than one family, then the arms were to be borne combined, eg, in quarters. Cadets were allowed to bear four quarterly coats, and difference marks were laid down, eg, for bearing a paternal grandfather's coat, one small charge which could be a crescent or a fleur-de-lis.

The volume, *O Livro do Armeiro-mor*, ('The Book of Principal Arms'), is a richly illustrated codex in vellum, which King Manoel I ordered to be made for his use, and which was drawn up and illuminated by the Chief Portugal King of Arms, Jean du Cros, a Frenchman, who finished it on 9 August 1509. It was given its title because it was placed in the head armory of the kingdom. It remained in the possession of the Kings of Portugal until 5 October 1910, the beginning of the republican régime, later being placed in the Arquivo Nacional da Torre do Tombo, where it now is.

There is a modern work, *Armaria Portuguesa*, which remains incomplete owing to the death of its author, Anselmo Braamcamp Freire. It was published in 1917 and gives descriptions of the arms of Portuguese families and of foreigners who had settled in Portugal, with large references to sources. In connection with the second class, there is the astounding and true story of Duarte Brandão, a Portuguese-born Jew who, early in life, forsook Portugal and sought his fortune in England. Here he won fame and wealth by espousing the Yorkist cause; he became a brave knight and successful commander, as well as building up a good business connection and marrying an English heiress to boot. For his success in single combat against a German he was awarded by his sovereign, Edward IV, in 1475 a grant of arms: on a field azure, two dragons respectant or their necks and tails intertwined. When the Yorkist cause went down, Sir Edward Brampton, as his name had become anglicised, returned to Portugal where he died, and having long been a Christian, was buried with pious inscription in a church in Lisbon. His career would have been deemed too fantastic for fiction had it been written as a novel, but it is a true story and has been told by the distinguished historian, Professor Cecil Roth. (*Essays and Portraits in Anglo-*

Jewish History, Jewish Publication Society of America, 1962; originally published in the proceedings of La Société Guernesaise, vol XVI (ii) 1957, Brampton having been Governor of Guernsey.)

Sir Edward Brampton, or his children, intermingled his blood with that of several Portuguese families, and his descendants exist in the Portuguese aristocracy to this day.

As might be expected, the Portuguese voyages of exploration and conquests in the fifteenth and sixteenth centuries have left their mark on the country's heraldry. Between 1438 and 1637, as many as forty-four grants or augmentations of arms are quoted, a not inconsiderable proportion in view of the small number of arms given above for Portugal (Antonio Machado de Faria de Pina Cabral, *Simbolismo Heraldica dos Descobrimintos e Conquistas Portugueses. Proceedings of 3rd International Congress 1955.*) A useful guide to Portuguese heraldry is *Manual de Heráldica Portuguesa* by Armand de Mattos (1941).

NOTE 1. Arms of Ladies. Occasionally in the middle ages a lady did bear a full coat of arms with helmet and shield, usually because she engaged in the fighting. Britomart of Spenser's *Faërie Queene* was by no means merely a figure of fiction. The arms granted to Joan of Arc were: *d'azur à une épée d'argent garnie d'or soutenant une couronne royale du même et accostée de deux fleurs-de-lis d'or.*

NOTE 2. Ancestry of Napoleon. Napoleon appears to have thought little of his own ancestry. To a genealogist who wished to deduce the Napoleonic descent from a line of Gothic princes, his answer was that he dated his patent of nobility from the battle of Montenotte, his first victory. His arms, as placed over a house at Waterloo which he had occupied, show the imperial eagle surrounded by a bordure of fleurs-de-lis. Yet the Bonapartes were an armigerous family, with descent traced from the middle ages, the ancestral names being entered in the Golden Book of Treviso. Why, then, did Napoleon not use his family arms?

CHAPTER 9

Continental Heraldry - II

Poland

IT is not easy to obtain much information about Polish heraldry, quite apart from the fact that most books on the subject are in Polish. Poland is the only Slav country to come within the fold of the Latin Church, and then not before 956, the date of its conversion to Christianity. Even after this great event which, in most other countries, was signalised by the beginnings of record-keeping, very little is known about the nation's institutions. More information comes with the thirteenth and fourteenth centuries, and from the nature of Polish heraldry it is reasonable to infer some facts about Polish nobility.

Briefly, heraldry in Poland is of runic character, and from this it may be deduced that the nobles were of Viking or Scandinavian origin. 'The nobility were indeed a caste, and this made ennoblement from below difficult for some considerable time. It ensured that the plebeians were discouraged in any way from pretending to the attributes of nobility. Consequently, arms were not adopted by non-noble burgesses, whatever might from time to time have been the case in adjacent Germanic territories.' (Lt-Col R. Gayre, *The Nature of Arms*, 1961, p 90.) There is no question of roturier arms as in France.

The nobles in Poland are found in the fourteenth century as a highly organised body, holding their lands as their own property, and not as fiefs from the sovereign, which was the normal rule in Europe under the feudal system. The nobles were all equal among themselves, and one suspects that subordination to the monarchy was often hardly even nominal. All the nobility bore the same type of helmet, surmounted by the same crest of three ostrich feathers. The only coronet used corresponded to that of a marquess.

The nobles formed clans, rather on the Scottish Highland model, where all the clansmen were supposed to be related to one another. Unlike the Highlanders, the Poles all bore the same undifferenced arms, but these were quite dissimilar from those in western heraldry, though placed as insignia of the clan in the warriors' shields. Thus the Sapieha family had for its blazon an arrow-like object crossed by two straight lines on the shield. This design could not be heraldically described, but it is quite likely to be derived from the old runic symbols, the origin and meaning of which had been lost by the fourteenth century. After all, the Normans who conquered England had forgotten their Norse tongue and origin in 150 years, so that the Poles could easily have lost the knowledge of a similar ancestral background in the course of some four centuries.

The nobles had a personal military obligation and appear to have governed strongholds throughout the country as representatives of the king. In theory, the chiefs of the clans were related to the monarch, who would thus be, as in Scotland, the chief of chiefs. These military leaders had signs derived from Nordic symbols which were gradually transformed into heraldic blazons. The arrow-like sign was the emblem of the god Thor, the Norse war god, and this was combined with other runic signs. The cadet lines used a symbol with the Thor emblem as a kind of difference, which must have been a later development if, originally, they had all borne the same insignia. As so frequently happened when a people became Christians, the Church did not try to remove the pagan symbols but added to them the sign of the Cross, which was not difficult in view of the use of simple lines in the early symbols.

In time, the Polish cavaliers began to participate in the tournaments and other heraldic occasions of the west. It must have been very hard for a herald to know how to describe the arms of the Polish knights; in their own country they could easily be known

Examples of early Polish heraldic emblems

by the name given to their blazon, but this would mean nothing to the foreigner. It was therefore necesesary to find a resemblance between the ancestral emblems and some heraldic charge which might correspond to it. This was the explanation of the flèche or arrow name given to the rune of Thor as the nearest heraldic object. Other runes in which half circles appear conjoined with straight lines were made into various objects whose resemblance to the originals can still be seen, once the runic basis of Polish armory is understood. Thus the blazon of Sas is a crescent surmounted by an arrow; that of Leliwa a crescent with a six-pointed star above. These are comparatively simple illustrations, but neither they nor the more involved blazons are likely to be anything but surprising to the western student until he knows the rudimentary designs from which Polish arms have been derived.

Further changes occurred in the fifteenth and sixteenth centuries, when clan territories had ceased to correspond with clan distribution, and when families began to take surnames from their properties. Still the same arms were used, but in the passage of 200 years it could easily happen that two branches of the same family bearing the same arms but different surnames would have lost the knowledge of their common genealogy.

The exclusivity of the Polish noblesse derived from their clan origin, which was vastly different from that of their western compeers. The power of the sovereign to create noblemen was not admitted in Poland. There the nobility was a closed caste, entry into which could be made only by adoption into a clan. When the King of Poland tried to ennoble certain men for their services, the entire Polish nobility objected and even passed a law in 1572 to deprive the sovereign of the power to create nobility. There was to be no Polish Fountain of Honour; the only exception to this rule was ennoblement on the battlefield for outstanding bravery.

The ranks of the nobility were augmented to some extent when, in the fourteenth century, Poland and Lithuania were united, and the nobles of the new territories were taken into the Polish noblesse, partly by adoption. The number of blazons known at the end of the eighteenth century was only about 500. No creations are thought to have taken place since then, owing to the political history of Poland. Partitioned between three great powers—Austria, Prussia and Russia—it disappeared from the map until after the 1914–18 war.

Titles were also refused by Polish nobles, though in the 1939–45 war instances occurred in the Polish armed forces of the use of the title 'Prince'. In general, the caste attitude of the Polish nobility, joined with their later elective monarchy and the em-

M

ployment of the *liberum veto* in their Diet, contributed greatly to the ruin and dismemberment of Poland in the eighteenth century.

No special heraldic archives exist in Poland. The records of the old heraldry of the Polish kingdom were destroyed by fire in the 1939–45 war. Some information on noble families and their coats of arms can be found in voivodship archives (corresponding roughly to English counties), or in the main Historical Records Archive (Archiwum Głownym Akt Dawnych, Warsaw, ul. Długa 7).

Norway

All available publications on heraldry are kept in the library of the University of Oslo, Universitetsbiblioteket i Oslo, Drammensveien 42B, Oslo. Since 1814 there have been no titled families in Norway and since 1821 it has not been necessary for family arms to be registered or regulated in any way. Proposals in regard to official heraldry are dealt with at ministerial level, with professional assistance from the Riksarkivet, or National Archives. There are in the latter, collections of some coats of arms and there are also small collections in some local files.

Such might be an official summing up of Norwegian heraldry, and I am indebted to the work of Mr Hans A. K. T. Cappelen, for the further account which follows. He gave a paper on this subject at the IXth International Congress (see page 146) in 1968, and in March 1969 a book written by him and Director Didrik R. Heyerdahl was published under the title *Norske Slektsväpen*, ('Norwegian Family Coats of Arms'). This book has a summary in English upon which I have drawn for the following, as well as upon Mr Cappelen's paper, read at Berne. I wish to acknowledge this very valuable and courteous assistance, and more so because it has been impossible for me to avoid using the author's actual sentences or paragraphs.

Norwegian heraldic history differs from that of other European states mainly because of the country's geographical position and scattered population. There was hardly any court life in Norway before the thirteenth century, there has not been any powerful hereditary nobility since the middle ages, and the tournaments which contributed so much to the development of heraldry elsewhere were held far away and seldom visited by Norwegian knights.

Until quite recently, Norwegian authorities had paid little attention to heraldry, apart from royal arms. There has been no supervision of arms-bearing, except in a few cases of Norwegians who were granted patents of nobility. The amount of literature on heraldry is small, and is untranslated, which of course renders Mr Cappelen's work the more valuable. Published family histories contain little heraldic information.

There are few distinguishing features in modern Norwegian family heraldry, but it is marked by great simplicity in the composition of shields, so that the elaborately marshalled arms found in other lands are rare in Norway. Arms which are still used in Norway have been derived from different areas and ages. Those designed in Norway are in the minority but are the most important as they determine the concept of Norwegian heraldry throughout the 700 years of its existence.

The first known example of a coat of arms on a seal born by a non-royal person is that of the knight, Basse Guttormson, in 1286. In the fourteenth century the number of seals showing arms increased and in arms of this period there is some difference between those of the nobles and of others.

The arms of the few great nobles were often influenced by Scottish and French heraldry, with tressures flory counter flory as well as other bordures and combinations. Examples of these arms are found mostly on seals but they also occur on drinking horns, which have shields affixed or engraved upon them, and on works of enamel, textiles and in illuminations in manuscripts. Other medieval arms show the continuance of pagan influences.

The details on the arms and the accessory figures make clear that the arms did not originate in a feudal society with a well-organised knighthood. Only a few coats could have been used on a shield or helmet in actual conflict.

The number of fourteenth-century seals showing coats of arms complete with shield, helmet, crest and mantling is strictly limited. The earliest seal displaying complete arms is that of Bjorne Erlingsön, which dates from 1347.

Fathers, sons and brothers often bore different arms. In many cases the bearing is of a personal allusion, as of an office held by the armigerous man. Thus a magistrate bears the representation of the castle in Bergen, Smiths have hammer and tongs. The Christian name Hank (hawk) is represented by a hawk on a fesse; Olav is shown by an axe, thus referring to the Saint, King Olav, who was slain with an axe, the latter becoming a national symbol. The boar in the arms of the family Galtung probably refers to the Christian name Gaute, borne by some early member in the fourteenth century. The family still uses the arms, and in 1648 it received a confirmation of nobility with the name Goltung.

The Black Death in the mid-fourteenth century had serious consequences in most European countries. In Norway, it caused a decrease in the population of about one-third. The number of seals which are known in 1348 is forty, in 1349 ten, and in 1350 only three. After 1350, there are never more than thirty new seals in any year.

From this period, too, Norway came to be dominated by Denmark, with the ruling class tending to be Danish. Many seals from the fifteenth and sixteenth centuries show arms which were originally Danish and they often adhere more strictly to heraldic rules than do the Norwegian arms. As the freeholding yeomanry gradually started to use seals, and as the original nobility merged with the yeomanry, it was common for house marks, private marks, and manual signs to replace arms in the seals. The marks are formed by simple geometrical lines. Private marks are often of runic origin but they can also be unintelligible marks dating from pre-runic times. In seals, the runes are often placed beside small figures such as a cross, a heart, an axe, a bow, an arrow or a sword.

During the fifteenth to sixteenth centuries few new Norwegian arms originated. In the sixteenth to seventeenth centuries many foreigners came to Norway to settle—and gradually came to form a Norwegian upper class, which has left many heraldic records of changing styles. Most modern Norwegian arms date from the seventeenth century. Many were brought to Norway by foreigners, some have originated in Norway, and some have been taken by families of foreign extraction after settling in Norway. From the alien influx were largely recruited the civil service and the trading class. From them, the custom of bearing arms spread to other classes, artisans, sailors, and yeomen. The quality of these arms was very varied.

In the eighteenth century it became customary for most civil servants to acquire arms or allegorical symbols on their seals. In Norway, the authorities have never denied anyone the right to bear arms, and the right has been widely and freely used. The arms of maternal and female line ancestors were used if male line ancestors had not been armigerous, or if the former were socially superior.

The motives of the arms often lack originality and vary to a greater or lesser extent from generation to generation. The arms give expression to common ideals, and are thus not particularly identifying. Religious allegories, known from contemporary church decorations, appear in arms from all strata of society in the seventeenth century but are later primarily used by the clergy. The skull and crossbones were commonly used as a *momento mori*. Later, three flowers were added as symbols of eternal life. The dove with an olive branch is known from many seals (eg, Dietrichson, Krong, and Lange). *Agnus Dei*, the symbol of Christ, has been used (Faye, Omsted), and also the other symbol of Our Lord, the pelican feeding its young with its own blood.

Profane allegories are well known from contemporary art and

literature, and as a rule they are not heraldically very satisfying. Merchants and sailors often bore as their symbol the figure of the goddess of fortune, viewed as the protectress of trade and navigation. The symbol of hope is a woman with an anchor in one hand and a dove in the other, and it appears on many seals, while the staff of Aesculapius and also that of Mercury was used. Symbols denoting a profession are the compasses and triangle in the arms of Stang, whose ancestor was a builder of fortresses, and the three crossed tanner's instruments in the arms of the Berner family, they having been tanners for several generations. Army families often display as crest a mailed arm holding a sword.

Many seventeenth- and eighteenth-century arms show a deer appearing from behind a tree. This may indicate a *novus homo*, or someone who comes into the open in a particular sense. The figure of the naked savage wreathed round the middle with a leafy garland, so common in Scottish heraldry, is often used as a charge.

The union with Denmark up to 1814 led naturally to the assimilation of Norwegian to Danish heraldry. Some Swedish families also moved to Norway, eg, Arbin from Arboga. The municipal arms of Arboga show an eagle, the head of which has been adopted by Arbin, who has added another two heads with a chevron between them. Again, many families from Germany and other countries came to Norway via Sweden. Some of these altered their arms or took new ones. Many English and Scottish families settled in Norway (eg, Christie, Grieg, Collett and Wright), and these for the most part retained their arms unaltered. Belgium, Holland, France and Switzerland all contributed their quota of armigerous families to Norway.

An occurrence very similar to happenings in England was the adoption of the arms of noble families by persons having no other proof of relationship except similarity in name. This followed the publication of a book in Copenhagen, *Lexicon over Adelige Familier i Danmark Norge og Hertugdømmerne* (1782–1813), a

Seal of King of Denmark, 1500

(*Above*) Seal of Elsinore, 1610

(*left*) Seal of Odense, 1598

(*below*) Seal of Malmö, 1421

work which therefore served much the same purpose as *Burke's General Armory*. As so often happens with similar cases in England, genealogical research does not prove that identity of name necessarily denotes identity of family.

With regard to the legal protection of arms in Norway, this does not strictly extend beyond the arms of the state of Norway or other countries. The unauthorised use of these is forbidden by the Criminal Code of 22 May 1902, s.328. The Trade Mark Act, 3 March 1961, para 14, forbids the registration of trade marks if they include Norwegian or international arms, flags, seals or other badges.

The position as regards other arms, ie, of families or of individuals, is not quite clear. It would seem that the strong Left-wing bias of Norwegian politics might tend to associate heraldry with class consciousness, though arms might be considered by the Norwegian courts as being entitled to the same protection as family names. There is thought by some authorities to be an analogy with the provisions of the Personal Names Act of 29 May 1964. In Norway, the custom has long prevailed whereby the maternal arms are borne if the father's family are non-armigerous. To bear maternal arms without differencing them may probably be accepted if a person has been granted the right to assume his mother's maiden name in accordance with s.9 of the Names' Act. Except in particular circumstances, permission to assume the maternal maiden surname is a formality. Hyphenated names are not used, except where the mother's maiden name is used before the father's surname.

It is clear that, apart from special cases, family arms already in use may not be adopted—in analogy with the usage as to surnames. According, however, to para 7 of the Names' Act, the right to assume an uncommon name may be granted, provided that whose who already bear it give their consent. The use of family arms by those with the same surname could analogously be justified if all the present bearers acquiesce. Again, s.6 states that the right to assume historical, extinct or foreign names well known in Norway should not be granted, so family arms of this type should not be adopted. Arms which give the impression of being foreign, as by being elaborately marshalled, should not be assumed.

Para 7 of the Names' Act denies the right to assume an identical name, unless the applicant has some reasonable connection with it. Similar considerations should apply to the adoption of arms merely because surnames are identical.

Finally, the use of arms is not common in Norway today, apart from royal arms and those of corporate institutions. Usage is, however, perhaps more frequent now than in the last hundred years. Bookplates are less used now than in earlier times and few new ones are designed. One recent example is the bookplate of Mr Trygve Lie the former secretary-general of the United Nations. It shows a crossed club and quill pen with a standing sword superimposed, surrounded by four roses. This symbol, without the roses, in silver with a red background, can be seen on Mr Lie's shield in Fredericksborg Castle, near Copenhagen, he having been a Knight Grand Cross of the Order of the Dannebrog of Denmark.

Sweden

Sweden has an official known as the Riksheraldiker, whose task is to draw up or examine drafts of coats of arms for new towns, and also to examine coats of arms which are to be fixed on public buildings, flag standards and coins. He also makes drafts for private individuals of seals, stamps etc. In earlier times, he was required to prepare drafts of coats of arms for those who were made noblemen. The Riddarhuset (House of the Nobles) ceased to be part of the legislature when the new constitution was made in 1866. The building remains and contains a very fine collection of the arms of the old Swedish nobility. Any claim to nobility, as for the revival of a title which has been in abeyance, goes before the directorate of the House of Nobles and, if passed by this board, the arms will be set up in the Riddarhuset.

Arms of Mgr B. B. Heim,
Apostolic Delegate to Scandinavia

As an example of the modern exercise of heraldic powers in Sweden we may take the approval of the Crown of arms for the *härads*, or jurisdictional districts of the country. The following account of the matter is from the summary in English by the Chief Herald of Sweden in his pamphlet, *De Halländska Häradsvapnen.*

The coats of arms of the *härads* of Halland' (this is a province of south-western Sweden)
Since 1946 the Crown has approved coats of arms for sixty-one of the *härads* of Sweden. During the years 1958–

62, coats of arms have been approved for the eight *härads* of Halland.

Ever since its creation in 1953, the Heraldic Section of the Swedish National Archives has tried, in designing coats of arms, to respect the special character of heraldry whilst making use of modern artistic means of expression—in other words a method which gives pride of place to colour and thus results in the simplification of form and the exclusion of everything which is contrary to two dimensionality.

In Halland Faurås *härad* had a seal as early as 1484— its design is unfortunately unknown. Other *härads* began to use seals during the period 1509–84. In this connection it is interesting to note that in all cases the choice of motif was based upon folk mythology. All the designs can be traced back to the names of the *härads*.

It must be stressed that the designs of the seals are time-honoured, many having been in use for four centuries or more, and they must remain intact. The task is thus to establish the original meaning of the seal designs. Once the sphragistic design has been determined, it must be transferred to a coat of arms with its demands on colour composition and stricter stylisation. It is not, however, a matter of revising the traditional motifs in accordance with the findings of modern linguistic research.

Now within the short space of five years the coats of arms of Halland's *härads* are being published for the third time. The reason for this is the desire to present the series in colour, and at the same time to reproduce seals from the period after 1645 when Halland became a Swedish province. (It had previously belonged to Denmark, like much else in southern Sweden.)

There is a beautiful simplicity about the arms mentioned above. Thus, argent a fesse gules in the blazon of Fauräs *harad*; azure a wheat sheaf or, of Halmstads; gules a hawk or beaked and legged azure, for Höks.

Other examples of recent Swedish municipal arms are the following : the commune of Hille on the Bothnian Gulf, based on a parochial seal of the seventeenth century and devised by

Mr Hans Schlyter of Sundovall. The blazon is : argent a maiden's head and bust the hair hanging azure, about the neck a necklace or.

By royal decree of 18 December 1964 the arms of the rural commune of Ramsjö in the province of Hälsingland in Sweden were confirmed. The commune had adopted a coat of arms, having reference to the meaning of its name, derived from two words which signify an eagle and a lake : quarterly per fesse wavy, or and sable in chief two ravens respectant one wing elevated and in base two bars wavy all countercharged. The Forest Owners' Association of the province of Medelpad have an heraldic flag : argent semée of pines vert.

Heraldiska Toilaget in Malmö, Sweden, has begun the publication of *Skandinavisk Vapenrulla*, ('Scandinavian Roll of Arms') with the coats of arms of Danish, Norwegian, Swedish and Finnish families. The text is in the language of the family, the Finns using Swedish. In the third section occur the arms of Mgr Bruno Heim whose work on church heraldry has been mentioned on page 116. These rolls are excellently illustrated in colour with the written blazon and some notes on the family.

Denmark

Many heraldic memorials are to be found in Denmark but there is no official body of heralds nor any great interest in the subject. There is, however, an official, the Heraldic Counsellor of the Danish State, who is concerned mainly with the arms of municipalities. In olden times, coats of arms were granted by the kings by letters patent in which the arms were depicted. This was done when someone was ennobled, but there were grants or confirmations of arms without ennoblement. The letters patent were registered in ministries and these granted arms were never duplications, although they had no legal protection. Some arms were not granted but assumed, as in other countries. If duplication took place, the oldest owner could appeal to the king, who then decided to whom the disputed arms were to belong. Nowadays it is possible to have arms legally protected by registering them as a trade mark, eg, as for a family society in the *Official Gazette*.

A very considerable display of arms can be seen in the beautiful castle of Frederiksborg. Here is the chapel of the great Danish orders, those of the Elephant, and of Dannebrog, all of whose members must have a shield of arms for display in the chapel. Copies of the arms are in the office of the orders.

With regard to the orders of chivalry, there is not technically a grant of arms, but when a new knight is appointed the chapter of the order ask for a coat of arms to be painted on the stall plate and hung in Frederiksborg Castle. Naturally an old family coat of arms would be applicable, but where arms are not already in use the painter of the royal chapter may be asked to create a coat. Thus the arms of Sir Winston Churchill were immediately available when he was made a knight of the Order of the Elephant; on the other hand, when the same distinction was given to General Dwight D. Eisenhower, a coat of arms had to be created. (See page 132.)

Finland

There is no registration now in Finland of any coats of arms but in previous centuries, when the country possessed a House of the Nobility, the coats of arms of noblemen introduced into the House were confirmed by the Grand Duke of Finland. Thus the noble families have properly registered coats of arms. From 1157–1809, Finland belonged to Sweden but was then ceded to Russia and became a grand-dukedom, the Tzar of Russia being Grand Duke until the fall of the Russian monarchy. Finnish nobility survived throughout these centuries of Swedish and Russian control, though apart from such noble arms, no coats of arms have been officially registered. In the sixteenth and seventeenth centuries, many non-nobles used arms. Likewise, coats of arms are now used by families who in some cases with right, and in other cases without, call themselves descendants of the nobles.

A Finnish coat of arms

Some Finns have devised their own arms, as they have a perfect right to do.

Iceland

This country has very little heraldry and has never had any hereditary nobility. Several Icelanders were knighted by the Kings of Norway and Denmark in the thirteenth to the sixteenth centuries, but knowledge of their coats of arms is now very rare.

Switzerland

Despite the great riches of Swiss heraldry, there are no official or state heralds in Switzerland. The Confederation, the cantons, and most of the towns and villages have arms, or some heraldic emblems. Some of these are very simple, eg, per fesse gules and argent (Solothurn), argent a fesse azure (Zug), per bend argent and azure (Zurich); others are in the worst modern style, eg, per fesse argent and vert, in the upper part the words *Liberté et Patrie* (Vared).

If there is no Swiss College of Arms there is no lack of learned interest in the heraldic wealth of the country. There is a Swiss Heraldic Society—La Société Suisse d'Héraldique, Schweizzerische Heraldische Gesellschaft, address Zwinglistrasse 28, St Gall. The society was founded nearly eighty years ago and publishes two excellent periodicals which are not only good in themselves but which keep their readers in touch with heraldic happenings and literature in all parts of the world. These publications are : *Archivium Heraldicum*, (Editor-in-chief : Dr Olivier Clotter), 2072 Saint Blaise, Neuchatel (Suisse); and *Archives Héraldiques Suisses (Schwizer Archiv für Heraldik, Archivio Araldico Svizzero)*. Dr Clotter is the French-language editor of this latter publication; the German-language editor is E. Schneiter, Elizabethanstrasse 26, 8004 Zurich. The society collects copies of all heraldic monuments in Switzerland, as well as copies of the coats of arms of Swiss families. It owns a fine library, is always ready to supply information about Swiss heraldry, and does its best to prevent the incorrect use of arms. Members have the right to borrow books from the society's library and meet once a year in a general assembly. The IXth International Congress was held at Berne in July 1968 under the Society's auspices and was certainly one of the most successful of these gatherings.

There is a great deal of splendid heraldic glass in Switzerland and rolls of arms are also to be found from 1345. Seals, too, are numerous, the earliest communal seal dating from 1224.

Germany

No European country is richer in heraldic sources than Germany, but here again as in Poland, Sweden, etc, the problem is linguistic. There is much German heraldic writing, but as it remains untranslated into French or English it remains a closed book to many students. Moreover, as with genealogical researches

In Germany, the collection of material has been made particularly difficult by the existence for so long of so many separate states.

In Germany, seals are numerous. Rolls of arms on the English and French model are not known but their absence is adequately compensated by the existence of splendidly-painted book collections of arms in the later middle ages. Paintings of arms and carvings on tombstones are to be found in great numbers.

German heraldry has a great preference for figures in shields, eg, of armed men, which differentiate the style of this country from others. There is a great use of crests, often running to several in one family. They are used to distinguish the branches of a family rather than by the use of cadency marks or brisures. This is the more remarkable in a country so much concerned with nobiliary distinctions. One would have expected the doctrine of the *Seize Quartiers* to have brought in its train an elaborate system of differencing. Such is not the case. The use of different crests with the same shield served apparently to separate one branch from others of the same family. In Germany, too, as quartering of arms became widespread, the individual or family would use several crests in heraldic pictures, as in the case of the Prince Consort's arms (the husband of Queen Victoria).

Despite the intense pre-occupation with nobility, arms were used in Germany by merchants or bourgeois, peasants and Jews. To distinguish themselves from such persons, the nobility made the barred helmet exclusive to themselves from the middle of the sixteenth century; the use of coronets came in a century later.

Heralds had a very short existence in Germany, becoming extinct in the 1700s. Today, the main source of heraldic information is Der Herold, Verein für Heraldik, Genealogie und verwandte Wissenschaften. The head of the society is Dr Ottfried Neubecker, 62 Wiesbaden, Dieselstrasse 24. This association keeps the Deutsche Wappenrolle (German Roll of Arms). There is also a printed register of all known German arms—the Kenfenheuer.

Austria

There was never an official centre in Austria for recording armorial bearings, which seems strange for what was the centre of a great empire and an ancient monarchy. In the public records are to be found all papers about granting coats of arms, whether the grant was with or without nobility. From about 1760, it was forbidden for a family which was not noble to bear a coat of arms without a specific grant from the Emperor. Such grants were few. In 1919, when the Austrian Republic began, a law was made which forbade the use of coats of arms in any official sense. The Heraldisch-Genealogische Gesellschaft Adler (founded 1870), Vienna II, Haarhof 4 a, began in 1950 the private registration of coats of arms in the Osterreichische Wappenrolle (Austrian Roll of Arms).

The Netherlands

Although a kingdom, the Netherlands have no legislation as to armorial bearings, and anyone who wishes may have a coat of arms. There is no official registration of arms, with the exception of those granted to the nobility. In the latter connection there is the Hoge Raad van Adel (Supreme Court of Nobility) 71b Zeestraat, The Hague. It consists of a president and four members, all appointed by the Queen, and has a secretary and other staff. It advises the Queen in matters of (i) nobility, (ii) flags and coats of arms of provinces, towns and villages, (iii) emblems of units of the armed forces and, (iv) admission to the Teutonic Order and the Order of Malta. Much heraldic information is given in the publications of the Dutch genealogical societies. These are, (1) Koninklijk Nederlandsch Genootschap voor Geslacht en Wapenkunde (Royal Society for Genealogy and Heraldry), which issues a monthly periodical, *De Nederlandsche Leeuw*, from 5 Bleijenburg, The Hague; and, (2) Nederlandse Genealogische Vereniging, which publishes about every two months a periodical, *Gens Nostra*, the address being, Post-Box 976, Amsterdam.

There is also, (3) Central Bureau voor Genealogie, which possesses the heraldic collection known as Muschart, and an iconographical collection. It publishes a yearbook, *Nederlands Patriciaat*, and provides the secretariat for the *Nederlands Adelsbock* ('Year Book of the Dutch Nobility'). Address: 18 Nassaulaan, The Hague.

Luxembourg

Arms grants in Luxembourg are in the power of the Grand Duchess, but are seldom made. In such matters the sovereign acts on the advice of the Council of Ministers. The government archives contain a registry of arms and titles of nobility which give the texts of the decrees, with reproduction of the arms. This goes back to the period when the King of Holland was also sovereign of the grand duchy. For the period before Dutch rule, reference must be made to the Registry of Patents of the Provincial Council for Commissions and Declarations from 1544 to 1791. In this collection are often found concessions or grants of arms which are not preserved in Luxembourg, but which are found in Brussels in the Archives du Royaume, Départment de la Noblesse. The history of Luxembourg has been very chequered. It has been the property of Burgundy, France, Austria and Spain. At the Congress of Vienna in 1814-15 it was made a grand duchy but did not become independent until 1867. In 1890, on the death of King William III of the Netherlands without male issue, it passed to the Walramian branch of the Orange Nassau family.

As to heraldic societies, there was a Luxembourg Heraldic Society, founded in 1947, from which was afterward formed the Association of Friends of History, (Les Amis de l'Histoire, or Letzeburger Geschichtsfrienn), whose object is to propagate and popularise the study of national history in the widest sense. One of the sections of the association is Le Conseil Héraldique, which deals with matters of heraldry, sigillography and symbolism. For

N

further information, application should be made to M. Robert Matagne, membre con. Instit. Grd. Ducal sect. histor., Délégue aux Relations Exterieures du Conseil Héraldique de Luxembourg, 25 Rue Bertholet, Luxembourg.

Latvia

Once, like Estonia and Lithuania, a province of the Russian Empire, Latvia, again like the other two, became an independent republic in 1918. Its independence ended in 1940 when the three small countries once more came under Russian control. In Latvia, there was an heraldic committee under the auspices of the President, which dealt with the state and municipal coats of arms. There were indications that with time, the use, and possibly the registration, of family arms would have come. There was in olden days a Latvian nobility formed of German noble families who had settled there, and who had their family emblems. In Germany, a body exists under the title of Union of Members of the Baltic Knighthoods : Verband der Angehorigen der Baltischen Ritterschaften, c/o Munchen 13, Elisabethstrasse 5/1, Germany.

Lithuania

In the middle ages Lithuania was a grand duchy, and the use of coats of arms began in 1413. *The Lithuanian Encyclopedia* (vol VIII), indicates that the *bajorai* (nobility) were using coats of arms even before that date. The escutcheon of the Grand Duke Gediminas (1316–41)—a knight on a white horse, charging and known as Vytis—became the arms of the Lithuanian dynasty of Gediminas (1316–1572), and so of the grand duchy itself as with other royal arms (see Chapter 11). In 1796, Lithuania was taken over by Russia and most of the state records, including those dealing with heraldry and nobility, were removed to St Petersburg (Leningrad), where they became part of a general office of heraldry of the Russian Empire (see opposite, under Russia).

In 1918, the newly promulgated constitution of Lithuania

abolished privileges based on class or religion. The ancient coats of arms of various provinces and cities in Lithuania were in use and publicly recognised during the Republic's independence (1918–40). In 1928, an Association of Lithuanian Nobility was formed and registered in the state register of associations. It interested itself in matters pertaining to Lithuanian heraldry but, like all the other free associations in Lithuania, was closed by the Russian invaders.

Russia

The use of armorial bearings in Russia began with Peter the Great, who probably introduced the system as part of his policy of modernisation. Arms went with nobility and nobility was reached by tenure of office, either in military or civil posts. This conception of nobility was not anciently held in Russia. There, as in all other countries of medieval Europe, there was a noble class, members of which were called the boyars and who figure very largely in the history of the old monarchy of Russia. The Mongol savages known as the Tartars overran Russia in the thirteenth century, destroying the fine civilisation of the south. The princes of Moscow known as the grand dukes managed to remain servilely independent by adopting the role of tax collectors for the Tartars. Eventually, the Grand Duke Ivan III (1440–1505) felt strong enough to rebel, and in 1547 Ivan IV took the title of Tzar of all the Russias. By this time, officials of the court were included among the boyars, and the principle became established that those who occupied government posts should be nobles. Under the Romanovs who succeeded to the throne in 1613, the principle had become a tradition. The princes of Russia were compelled by the Tzar to come on a level with the boyars and a register of nobility (*Rodoslovnoia Knega*) was compiled. This register was copied in the reign of Ivan IV (1533–84), 'Ivan the Terrible', and copied again for the last time under Theodore III (1676–82), by which time it included all noble families accepted from the time of the previous copying. It came to be called the Velvet Book (*Barhatnaia Knega*), from its binding in red velvet.

Peter the Great (1689–1725) introduced titles, and in 1722 he decreed that all officers of the armed forces and civilian officials who had attained a certain rank should acquire hereditary nobility and the right to arms. In 1722 he established a House of Nobles under a Herald Marshal. The Velvet Book was preserved in the Heraldic Office of the Senate at St Petersburg. An official record of armorial bearings for the arms of the nobility was begun by the emperor Paul (1796–1801). Of this armorial, ten volumes were published; fourteen more were ready for printing but were never published. Many coats of arms for those who had acquired nobility by tenure of military or civil positions were established but never printed. The Russian Empire came to include many states which are now the satellites of the Soviet Union. Welcome was extended to the nobilities of those lands—Poland, Lithuania, Estonia, Latvia, Georgia, Finland and others, and the records of these nobles were carefully kept.

Czechoslovakia

Czechoslovakia lost its independence in 1621, when it became part of the Austrian Empire. Before 1621, coats of arms were registered in Prague, at the royal court. Under the empire, coats of arms for all parts of the empire were registered in Vienna up to 1918. Much information on heraldry exists in the archives of the National Museum and the state publishing house, Artia Ltd of Prague, has issued several works on the heraldry of the country.

Yugoslavia

Arms were much in use here in the middle ages, being imitated from their western neighbours. They may also have originated from ancient belief in their magical power for combating spells. Among the south Slavs, arms came into use during the twelfth and thirteenth centuries, upon the formation of South Slav states in the modern regions. The old Slav coats of arms have not been sufficiently studied. Some heraldic manuals with lists and drawings of arms exist from the sixteenth and seventeenth centuries, but these are not entirely reliable.

The state coat of arms of the Yugoslav kingdom was determined under the Vidovdan Constitution of 1921. It was composed of the coat of arms of the kingdom of Serbia, the coat of arms of Croatia, and the Illyrian-Slovenian-Celje coat of arms. The composite coat of arms had this appearance : a white eagle poised for flight on a field gules. Both heads of the white two-headed eagle were topped by the royal crown. Superimposed on the eagle's breast was an escutcheon as follows : Serbia—a white cross on red ground with one ocellus in each quarter; Croatia—a checkered shield with twenty-five alternate red and silver squares; Slovenia—three golden six-pointed stars on a blue shield. Below this was a white crescent. (This loosely worded description is from official Yugoslav sources, as is also the following account).

The Constitution of the Federal People's Republic of Yugoslavia from 31 January 1946 determined the appearance of the coat of arms as follows : 'The state coat of arms of the Federal People's Republic of Yugoslavia represents a field encircled by sheaves of wheat. At the base the sheaves are tied with a ribbon on which is inscribed the date 29–XI–1943. Between the tops of the ears is a five-pointed star. In the centre of the field five torches are laid obliquely, their several flames merging into a single flame'.

Hungary

Like Poland, Hungary saw the rise and growth of a tribal rather than a feudal nobility. A recent authority writing on Hungarian arms states that it is to the fourteenth century that we must look for the general adoption of arms in Hungary. 'The Hungarian nobles who accompanied Sigismund of Luxembourg, King of Hungary and Holy Roman Emperor, to the Council of Constance (1414–18) saw the arms of foreign nobles displayed above their dwellings in Constance, and they thereupon asked

Sigismund for permission to assume similar *tesserae nobilitatis*. At first, the greater nobles adopted prescriptively their own arms, but after 1400, especially those close to the Court, asked for letters patent'. (Lt-Col R. Gayre of Gayre and Nigg—*The Nature of Arms*, 1961, p 88.) In these circumstances, with so late a development of heraldry, it is not surprising that organisations to register arms did not exist.

The superior authority of the nobility was the Minister of the Interior and it was he who authenticated coats of arms on the basis of data kept in the National Archives. Letters patent given under the great seals were promulgated at the general assembly of the county in which the grantee lived. After 1526 these grants were, with changing regularity, matriculated in the so-called *Libri Regii*. A sort of central register was kept separately for Hungary and for Transylvania—before 1867 in Vienna and after that date in the International Archives in Budapest. Hungarian nationals, wishing to bear arms legally or use their titles of nobility (including territorial designations) in the kingdom of Hungary, were obliged to matriculate in the public register of arms and titles, which was kept and conducted by the Ministry of the Interior in Budapest. The National Archives acted in these cases as experts for the Ministry. The *Libri Regii* and this register have been published.

Law IV of 1947 abolished all noble and aristocratic ranks and prohibited the use of titles of nobility, coats of arms and similar devices.

CHAPTER 10

Oriental Heraldry

Japan

WHILE many instances of the use of symbolism are known in Asiatic nations, only in Japan can a properly heraldic system be found. This is the system of the *mon*, a Japanese term which has been rendered by various words in different European languages but which is most accurately translated in English as 'badge'. In certain circumstances a mon may be described as a crest, but a coat of arms it most certainly is not.

The mon system originated in Japan in the twelfth century, as did heraldry in Europe. It was used in connection with armour but not, as in the west, for the purposes of identification. Anyone who has seen suits of Japanese armour in museums and art galleries and noted the minute size of the mon on the helmet, or other armour, will appreciate that it would not serve for identification except at very close quarters. Japanese armour was made of metal or leather, and looks like wickerwork; the helmets were of metal. The armour was used until a quite late period in warfare, and, right up to the end of the nineteenth century for ceremonial purposes.[1]

In warfare, in order to distinguish one body of men from others, banners were used on which the mon was prominently

[1] See Note 1, Japanese Armour, at end of chapter.

199

displayed. In addition to its warlike employment, the mon also came to be used in a large number of ways in peacetime.

It is considered by those who have studied Japanese heraldry that the mon had a twofold origin, on the clothes of the great nobles and, simultaneously, on the banners and accoutrements of the warriors. Later, the mon came to be used on castles and houses and, in common with European heraldic practice, successive owners of a great building would place their arms on or within it. In this way, as in England and France, the history of the ownership of a castle can be traced. In later periods of Japanese history, from the seventeenth century onwards, the mon was used to mark and adorn all manner of domestic belongings, and this practice subsequently spread to the lower classes, from farmers and merchants to actors and other entertainers. When actors used a mon, it was not restricted to that of their own family; many designs of others could and would be employed.

The two centuries from the seventeenth to the nineteenth were in Japan an age of seclusion, a period when the country was sealed off by its rulers from any intercourse with the rest of the world. This was the feudal age when the daimios, or great lords, and their followers the samurai, really ruled the country. Yet these haughty feudal knights, with whom the system of the mon had originated, apparently did not object to the use of similar devices by their social inferiors.

Japanese heraldry developed without any assistance from any heraldic college. That it evolved as it has done, without very much misappropriation or ugliness, is a tribute to the good sense and artistic feeling of the Japanese. This is the more impressive because the Japanese sovereigns for the greater part of their history have never exercised much authority. Honoured more in theory than in practice, the emperors have been completely overshadowed by their powerful nobles. Sometimes emperors have retired, some have even known great poverty. When the country was finally reopened to Europeans in the mid-nineteenth century, the western negotiators thought that the Shogun was the titular as well as the real ruler of Japan. It was a surprise to discover that behind the Shogunate was the imperial throne.

Without royal control or a college of arms, Japanese heraldry developed without fuss or bother. The earliest use of the mon by the knights was in 1156, when two powerful but warring clans, the Minamoto and the Taira, required means of identification on their banners. By the next century the use of the mon had become general among the warrior class. One of the most interesting designs, from a western point of view, was that of the Lord of Oka, who bore what may be described as a cross potent within a ring, having a ring around the centre of the cross. Another mon of this nobleman was that of oak leaves.

By the sixteenth century the position of the mon on the clothing had become fixed and settled. On the ceremonial dress of the warriors the mon was worn in five places, on the breasts, sleeves and back. Later, they were used in three places, as Fox-Davies has stated : 'A Japanese of the upper classes always has his mon in three places upon his kimono, usually at the back just below the collar and on either sleeve.' (*A Complete Guide to Heraldry*, 1961, p 12.) In some Japanese writings of the period a great warrior would be described by the name of his mon, rather than by his clan or family surname. Here, too, is a resemblance to some poetic western usages, with the ramping lion mentioned as denoting Scotland, or the three lions for England.

As in Europe, there was bound to have been confusion in the use of the same mon by unrelated families, and no doubt there were specialists in such matters, even though no official class of heralds existed. At length, in 1642, the Shogun Iyemitsu, who held that post from 1632–51, decreed that all the knightly families were to register their mon. This decree also required at least two mon to be registered and stipulated that, thereafter, no deviation from their use would be allowed. We do not know what happened when a Japanese equivalent of *Scrope v Grosvenor* or *Carminow v Scrope* occurred, although it is certain that a considerable amount of duplication did exist in the badges of the great families. By this time, too, the mon had been in use for about a century by priests, scholars and substantial townsmen outside the warrior class. Yet another parallel with the European use of badges was that more than one mon might be owned by the same family or by the same person, just as many historical English families are known to have used more than one badge. The Nevilles, for instance, used a bull, a double staple, in one branch, and a rose and a portcullis in another as their badges. So with the leading Japanese families. They had a fixed mon or *jomon* for the most important functions; and a *kayemon* or lesser device for general use. The retainers of a lord wore his *jomon* on their clothing, and this badge was also used on his great standard.

From the early eighteenth century there was considerable employment of the mon purely as an ornament without any reference to heraldic or clannish significance. In a nation as artistically sensitive as the Japanese this development was inevitable.

The use of the mon received an extra fillip in the era known as the Meiji Era ('Enlightened Government') which began in 1868. All Japanese were then required to take surnames—just as earlier in the same century, all Danes had had to adopt surnames, previously the prerogative of the nobles. When the Japanese acquired surnames, they usually adopted a mon as well, and most of them have such designs today. As mentioned earlier, the crest was sometimes the equivalent of the mon and took the form of a device which could be attached to the socket on the front of some Japanese helmets. When used in this way it was often a variant of the mon; eg, the Havabusa clan used a single wild goose as crest but bore three geese as the mon. As to the design of the mon, the best description of it is in the words of Dr Carroll Parish :

'Each mon is founded upon a single definite motive or charge, as a western herald would say, or a combination of two motives. The main motive may be depicted singly or repeated one or more times in definite order. It may stand free or be enclosed in a circle, square or other regular form. At first, mon were realistic and, therefore, irregular in form. Later, they became stylized and symmetrical.' (*The Augustan*, vol XI, no 1, 1968.) Dr Parish mentions that in a publication of 1880 there were over 3,000 mon listed as belonging to some 500 prominent Japanese families. From early times the mon had been hereditary in families. In *The Japan Gazette—The Peerage of Japan*, published in 1912, each article on a noble family is headed by the mon in use in that house. Robert Standish's well-known novel, *The Three Bamboos*, derived its title from the emblem adopted by the Fureno family, the name which he gave to his distinguished Japanese house. From the seventeenth century, a directory of the mon of the great families has been kept.

The subject matter of the mon is very different from European heraldic styles. The figures are mainly of vegetables, flowers or inanimate objects, rarely of animals. This is probably due to the influence over many centuries of Buddhism, the only great religion to give kindly consideration to animals. Doves occur in the mon of a Taira clan member, owing, so legend asserts, to an event which occurred—the flight of doves from a tree. Readers can easily remember many such stories, some of them true, of the origin of charges in a coat of arms in England.

The conferring of a mon by a great lord upon a lesser person was very frequent in Japan, as there was no central control of devices. Mon were taken and discarded easily—that is before the decree of 1642—and very likely with equal facility soon after and to the present time. Frequently the subject of a mon was chosen with reference to the name of the bearer, thus resembling the punning arms in western heraldry.

As far back as the reign of the Emperor Gotoba, the chrysanthemum had been adopted as the imperial device; also the paulownie, the tree in which the fabulous phoenix sat. There are many designs of the chrysanthemum, each varying according to the number of petals in the symbol. For the emperor is reserved the sixteen-petal chrysanthemum, while the imperial sons and brothers bear the flower with fourteen petals.

Many of the mon are derived from religious symbols, and others come from Chinese or Japanese written characters. A very interesting parallel occurs between the Scottish rule of inheritance of the whole arms by the chief alone and the Japanese principle of primogeniture. Only the eldest son could inherit both the family estate and the headship of the clan, with everything which went with it, including the mon. It was necessary for the younger sons to strike out on their own and, because of this, variations of the family mon were created to be symbols of the clan branches. When anyone was adopted into a family he would often take the mon of that family. It is considered bad form and a breach of etiquette for a non-royal person to use the chrysanthemum and, as with some royal unions in the west, new designs of the mon are made when a member of the Japanese royal family marries.

The great reverence for the royal symbols was shown in the last century when, in imitation of the western practice, the emperor instituted orders of chivalry. The most important is the Order of the Chrysanthemum, 1876, which is usually given only to royalty, either members of the Japanese house or sovereigns or heads of state. Next to this comes the Order of the Paulownia Sun (1888), again a distinction of very high degree.

Passing from the Japanese system which is universally agreed to be heraldic, the question arises as to how far the worldwide use of symbolism can be equated with heraldry. It has already been stated that only in western Europe and in Japan can a genuine heraldic system be found, originating in both cases in the twelfth century. Can any other region claim an incipient heraldry, as in the case of the devices used by the twelve tribes of Israel, symbols which did not develop into an heraldic system? If the heraldry in Europe did really derive from participation in the Crusades then some credit for the employment of a few heraldic charges can be given to the Moslem races with whom the Crusaders came into contact. On this subject the words of A. C. Fox-Davies are worth quoting: 'The Saracens and Moors, to whom we owe the origin of so many of our recognised heraldic charges and the derivation of some of our terms (eg, 'gules' from the Persian *gul* and 'azure' from the Persian *lazurd*), had evidently on their part something more than the rudiments of armoury.' (*A Complete Guide to Heraldry*, 1961, p 13.) He then gives some illustrations which certainly contain heraldic features. The device of the Emir Arkatây shows what looks like a fesse and one of the Kings of Granada, Abu Abdullah, Mohammed Ibu Naer (1231–1272) had a shield with a typical heraldic band across it from the dexter to the sinister. Enthusiasts have built from this small foundation a Saracenic heraldry, even deriving our term 'ungulated' from a non-Latin source (its real origin is Latin *unguis*, a nail). Even the origin of 'gules' from Persian is challenged by an alternative derivation from Latin *gula*, throat.

India

Were there rudiments of armoury anywhere else in Asia? Lt-Col James Tod, the historian of Rajast'han, had no doubts at all as to the answer. 'The martial Rajpoots are not strangers to armorial bearings, now so indiscriminately used in Europe. The great banner of Mewar exhibits a golden sun on a crimson field: those of the chiefs bear a dagger. Amber displays the panchranga or five-coloured flag. The lion rampant on an argent field is extinct with the state of Chanderi. In Europe, these customs were not introduced till the period of the Crusades, and were copied from the Saracens; while the use of them amongst the Rajpoot tribes can be traced to a period anterior to the war of Troy. In the Mahabharat, or great war, twelve hundred years before Christ, we find the hero Bheesama exulting over his trophy, the banner of Arjoova, its field adorned with the figure of the Indian Hanuman (ie, the monkey god). These emblems had a religious reference amongst the Hindus, and were taken from their mythology, the origin of all devices.' (J. Tod, *Annals and Antiquities of Rajast'han or the Central and Western Rajpoot state of*

India, originally published 1829, new edition 1950, two volumes in one, vol 1, pp 113–4.)

In fact the Rajputs, like all other races, had symbols which were capable of being developed into heraldic devices when the Rajputs came into contact with the western heraldic system. Allowance must be made in Tod's book for the enthusiasm of the explorer. The first European, in 1807, to traverse the wild country of Chanderi, he opened the archives of Rajast'han, and, like Warren Hastings when translating from oriental tongues, became so enamoured of his discoveries that he compares Indian with European achievement to the disadvantage of the latter.

The attribution of heraldry to the ancient races of India is to be taken, along with the ascription of many thousands of years' history to the peninsula, *cum grano salis.* Granted that the history of India is imperfectly known, it is unlikely that the present estimate of the country's antiquity will ever be extended beyond four to four and a half thousand years. The discovery of sites at Mohenjo-Daro in Sind, and at Halappa in the Punjab, reveal a civilisation dated approximately 2500 BC, which was destroyed by invaders. The ancestors of the Hindus are known as the Indo-Aryans and invaded India about 1500 BC, gradually mixing with the inhabitants whom they termed Dasas, or slaves. The two vast epics of India, the Ramayana and the Mahabharata, were written about 300–400 BC, and give an account, necessarily overlaid with myths and legends, of the great war referred to by Tod.

There is no room for heraldic devices going back five thousand years—the history of India as now known does not warrant the idea. In the nineteenth century, especially after the Indian Mutiny in 1857, most of the Indian princes had come under British protection. In increasing measure they became British-educated and adopted many western customs. In 1877 to mark a great imperial occasion, a member of the Bengal civil service, Robert Taylor, designed coats of arms for the princes, and some writers have complained that he did not seem aware of the heraldic background of the princes. It was not that, like Col Tod, he regarded the ancient Indian symbols as heraldic, but that he translated them into western heraldic styles with many charges which were usually allusive to some fact, legend or myth in a particular prince's genealogy. The reigning houses of Mewar had the sun as their emblem, as mentioned by Tod. This was adapted by Taylor in the form of the sun in splendour, ie, with a human face, as in western heraldry. The sun in splendour also appeared in some of the Mewar shields as the main charge, as in the arms of Idar. For Barwani, the sun charge was on a canton, the blazon of the arms devised by Taylor being: vairy three barrulets gules, a chief wavy argent on a canton of the second, a sun in splendour. There is a crest and there are supporters. The motto has been translated as 'Lord of the road, pass and mart'. The charges of the coat of arms of this state of Barwani have been explained as denoting, in the three barrulets, the road, pass and mart in the state as its chief sources of revenue, while the vairy field signifies the jungle of the country and the wavy chief, the river Nerbudda. This explanation shows a coat very much in accord with the principles on which many English coats of arms have been prepared, eg, the representation of the Thames in the arms of the Westminster Bank, and the six fountains denoting springs in the shield of Lord Stourton.

Robert Taylor's designs were emblazoned on banners which were presented by the Viceroy to ruling chiefs entitled to a salute at the Delhi Durbar in 1877. In 1902, a complete set of Taylor's designs, together with his notes, were obtained by the Indian government and reproduced in a volume entitled, *The Princely Armory*.[1] It is stated that Taylor obtained information from local political agents about the ruling families and based his designs on these details.

By the time of the Delhi Durbar in 1911 for King George V, most of the Indian princes were using arms. A book was compiled, it is understood, which showed the arms of the princes as in 1911, but subsequently they were 'regularised' by registration in the

[1] See Note 2, Arms of the Indian Princes, at end of chapter.

College of Arms. At the Durbar of 1911, the foundations of New Delhi were laid, and in the Chamber of Princes the arms of the various princes were placed in alphabetical order on metal plaques.

To a British viewer, these coats often appear overloaded, and of course they contain many features unknown or unfamiliar to us. Here is the description of the arms of the ruler of Sandur, a small state to the north of Mysore : bhagwa (salmon pink or medium shade of rose doré) on a fesse argent, a ghorpad (ie, a monitor lizard) proper; in chief a pindi (a turreted erection) vert, entwined by a five-headed cobra with hoods expanded above and tail suspended all proper between two towers or, in base a field gun or. Crest : an open chattra (ie, umbrella) bhagwa or, issuing from the helmet or, displaying mantling sable and argent. Supporters : dexter and sinister an elephant with trunk erect proper.

The arms of the Maharaja of Travancore, a state on the south coast of India, show a design far removed from the European style, because no shield is given and the centre of the arms is simply the conch, the symbol of Travancore, surrounded by a wreath of greyish foliage. On either side is an elephant with trunk raised above the wreath; each elephant faces the conch. The whole stands on a version of the Victorian gas-bracket already mentioned in connection with the degenerate heraldry of Britain in the last century. The description supplied from the government of Travancore is : 'The coat of arms of the Travancore State is represented by a conch, supported by two elephants, one on either side thereof, together with a motto in Sanskrit, "Dharmosmatkuladaivatam", which means "Dharma is our household divinity". The conch and the elephants are emblazoned in white on a red background. The conch is one of the prominent weapons of Sri Padmanabha (an aspect of Mahavishnu, the sustaining and protecting god of the Hindu Trinity), the family deity of the Maharajas of Travancore. It is believed to be an emblem of purity, auspiciousness, victory and prosperity. The conch is a product of the sea, and Travancore, which has the longest seaboard among

Arms of Travancore state

o

the Indian states, is aptly symbolised by it. The elephants form a distinguishing feature of Travancore, being very common in its forests. They, too, are emblematic of auspiciousness and victory. The motto signifies that righteousness is the watchword of the Rulers of Travancore.'

In the arms of Cooch Behar, the ground of the shield is purple

Arms of Maharaja of Cooch Behar

with a balance and a ring in gold, plus a gold-hilted sword and what appears to be a green sheaf saltirewise. The supporters are : dexter a rampant lion, sinister an elephant. The crest is a globe of the world, seated thereon a representation of Hanuman.

Tagore has a standard and a badge. The latter is a rose between two sprigs of leaves rising from an eastern antique crown. The standard has next to the staff the arms of Tagore, azure a sun in splendour or, within a bordure or, eight roses gules. The badge is shown on the standard three times against a background of or and azure.

The coat of arms of the Maharaja of Jaipur is one of the most elaborate. It is quarterly : 1, a bullock argent on a green field; 2, a chariot with four horses and two occupants (the horses argent, the human figures or), on a green field; 3, vert, an elephant sable; 4, vert, a castle on a hill argent. The supporters are : dexter a rampant lion proper, sinister a horse argent on its hind legs, saddled and bridled or having a saddle gules. The crest shows the lotus on top of the helmet and thereon a male and female figure. There is a pavilion behind the achievement decorated with six flags at the top and two cannons below.

The principle that the English College of Arms should deal with applications for arms from anyone in the British Empire explains the grant of arms to some Indian knights and baronets, and the only Indian peer, Lord Sinha. The position of the princes was very different. They were sovereign princes who had come voluntarily under the protection of the British government. The Emperor of India was their suzerain; it would perhaps not be improper for an Indian prince to petition his emperor, through the latter's Earl Marshal, for a grant of arms. On the other hand, as sovereign rulers themselves, with lineages going back many hundreds of years, the princes would quite naturally assume their own coats of arms, especially after acquaintance with the arms of the Governor-Generals. Mr Robert Taylor's enterprise in devising arms for the various Indian rulers must have proceeded quite independently of the College of Arms. The so-called regularising of arms for the princes, which was mentioned to me in 1939 by an officer of the College of Arms, meant in all probability the usual differencing procedure employed when the College confirms a coat of arms.

NOTE 1 : Japanese Armour. Japanese armour deserves more detailed mention. The description—wickerwork—is not entirely adequate. In its earliest form Japanese armour was, it seems, of leather with plates of metal; there was also a cuirass of metal rivetted and laced. The former type has some resemblance to the European chain-mail armour of the eleventh century. Probably any form of metal armour must have a leather foundation. During the eighth to the twelfth centuries, the influence from the Asian mainland began to be felt, but as with most foreign importations, the Japanese adapted the new styles to suit themselves. Naturally, the armour of the great men was more elaborate than that of the common soldiers. The Japanese did not use a shield as they needed both hands for their weapons. At first, up to the twelfth century, they fought on horseback, wielding both the bow and arrow or a long, heavy sword. At this time armour was fairly weighty and the more important warriors had helmets and arm and shoulder protectors, the latter taking the place of shields. The common soldiers did not have helmets or shoulder pieces and their armour was much lighter and less protective. From the thirteenth century, the gap between these two types of equipment lessened: 'greaves, first introduced about the eleventh century and a sort of armoured apron under the tassets to give additional protection to the thighs, were generally adopted and the face and neck were covered with an iron mask, often of ferocious aspect, and a laced gorget. Some form of horns and forecrest on the helmet became almost universal, and the bearskin boots of the earlier mounted warriors gave place to more practical sandals. Mail was used to protect the forearms'. (*Arms and Armour of Old Japan*, HMSO, 1951, p 11.)

Armour was last worn in battle in the time of the changeover from the Shogunate in the nineteenth century, when suits mostly made of cowhide proved quite practical. In the work quoted above there are some excellent photographs of Japanese armour. The helmets are very unlike those of Europe, though in the sixteenth century they began to have a brim, probably due to imitation of Spanish models. Three small prints show the putting-on of armour. There are two complete suits, one from the Kamakura (medieval) period, the other of Doi armour. These are excellent examples which serve to show the wicker-work appearance of so much Japanese armour. The extreme sharpness of the Japanese swords would serve to demonstrate that only strong armour would keep out a good stroke. Yet the Japanese, like the rest of the oriental nations, managed to fight many fiercely contested engagements without wearing armour which was complete and enveloping from head to toe. No example brings this out so well as the figure of Honda Tadakatsu (1548–1610) which, like the rest of the illustrations mentioned, is on view at the Victoria and Albert Museum in London. This figure shows the mounted warrior, and inevitably one is led to compare and contrast him with the knight in the famous illustration of the Luttrell Psalter. Whereas the western knight has heraldic devices on shield, surcoat, lance, and horse trappings, the Japanese bears the mon only on the small flag which he carries, though it was probably on his helmet and other armour. He is incomparably the lighter figure. One wonders why European knights did not adapt themselves to eastern warfare by wearing lighter armour. After all, they must have been badly handicapped when fighting in the sandy wastes of Syria and Palestine against the much more mobile Saracens.

NOTE 2: Arms of the Indian Princes. *The Princely Armory* has for subtitle: 'Being a display of the arms of the ruling chiefs of India prepared for the Imperial Assembly held at Delhi on the 1st day of January, 1877.' The book was devised by Robert Taylor, MA, Cantab., Bengal Civil Service. Printed for the Government of India at the Government Central Printing Office, 8 Hastings Street, Calcutta, 1902.' Only twenty-five copies were printed.

The preface to this work is quite explicit in stating that Taylor made up the arms. Ninety coats of arms are illustrated and eleven more are mentioned but without a picture. The only colour used is a very pale red (perhaps identical with the *bhagwa* mentioned on p 253). Taylor explains in the introduction that he was asked by his civil service chief in 1869 to prepare banners for knights of the Order of the Star of India, and again in 1875 for the forthcoming visit to India of the Prince of Wales. 'For the older families at all events I thought that there would be no difficulty in making characteristic bearings such in fact as we might suppose would have grown into use if western heraldry had been introduced into India before the Mohammedan invasion.' (p 3.) Again (p 133), Taylor in his notes about the arms of the Thakur of Bhownugur writes that 'for him, Mr Macnaghten (of the Rajkumar College) had devised a shield'; but Taylor rejected the crowns in this design and also substituted sanguine for gules. 'The Thakur objected to any change unless it left as handsome a coat as the old one'. It is thus abundantly clear that Taylor composed the arms of the ninety banners bestowed in 1877. He asked the political agents in the princely states for information as to symbols used, in order that he might at least have something to go on in preparing his designs. From the agents he received very little and when he did, as in the case of Bhownugur above, the resultant arms were a device based upon a device drawn up in Bhownugur by a European, and based in its turn on—what? Something in the form of a symbol, no doubt, but of so impermanent a nature that the ruler himself did not object to its disappearance, provided that the ensuing arms were attractive.

It is clear from Taylor's account that he had a good knowledge of heraldry, but that he undertook the task of devising these arms very unwillingly, as can be understood in view of the extra amount of work involved. He acted mainly out of regard for his chief, who was ill and heavily overworked.

Taylor's achievement started the development of Indian heraldry. Ninety coats of arms to be worked out in approximately eighteen months was a burdensome task, but as there were over 500 Indian princes recognised by the British government it could not be supposed that the remaining majority of princes would be willing to acquiesce in armorial oblivion, nor did they. In fact, in 1868, before Taylor's work had begun, the Maharajah of Burdwan had applied to the College of Arms for armorial bearings and had been granted them with supporters. The College of Arms did not in this case discriminate between one Indian prince and another. Burdwan was a great noble but not a territorial ruler in the sense that Hyderabad or Jaipur or Travancore could be classed. The Indian government exercised the most scrupulous care in its treatment of the princes, who had come into treaty relations with the British somewhat on the lines of the medieval princes in Europe who remained independent inside their own lands but acknowledged a suzerain. The Indian princes were not British subjects. Consequently, when the College of Arms came to be concerned with Indian princely coats, it met with a most determined opposition from the Indian government. Briefly, the College heard of the grants of arms—for that is what they were—made by the Viceroy through the medium of Robert Taylor, and the kings of arms strove to have them regularised. A correspondence ensued between the Garter King of Arms and the Secretary of State for India, the former taking his stand on the virtually worldwide jurisdiction of the College. The opinion of the law officers of the Crown was taken (13 August 1913, and on another occasion) on this subject and confirmed the view of the College. 'The proposition (with which we agree) that the Earl Marshal has also an Imperial Jurisdiction in respect of persons not domiciled in the United Kingdom etc.' At another time the word 'colonial' was used as the adjective instead of 'imperial'. One of the signatories of the law officers' opinion was Rufus Isaacs, later to be Viceroy of India, by which time his views may have undergone some change. Following upon the claim of jurisdiction over British subjects outside the United Kingdom, the Garter King of Arms in 1916 stated to the Secretary of State for India that he considered the arms assigned in 1877 to be heraldically inadequate in many respects and that they should certainly be revised. A memorandum was prepared setting out the proposed revision and how it was to be achieved, but the Indian government declined to accede to these proposals. In 1904, the Maharajah of Tagore (see p 210) had applied to the College for a grant of arms with supporters, on the lines of the Burdwan grant. At the request of the Indian government, the College did not grant supporters to Tagore, though it granted arms. The government's objection to supporters was based on considerations of its own carefully worked-out tables of protocol among the princes.

In 1919 the College under a new Garter King of Arms, Sir Henry Farnham Burke (son of Sir Bernard Burke and grandson of the founder of the Burke publications, John Burke), returned to the assault. Burke told the Secretary of State for India that banners with armorial devices had been presented to certain Indian princes on the occasion of the Delhi Durbar in 1877, but that they were not passed through the College or recorded there. The matter was thoroughly investigated by the Indian government, who set forth certain principles. As the Indian princes were not British subjects, this effectively disposed of the plea that they came under the imperial or colonial jurisdiction of the College. Instead of being subjects of the Crown, they were regarded by the Indian government as being in subordinate alliance with the British government. Their position armorially was, therefore, quite different from that of a native of British India, who was created a baronet or knight, or who petitioned the Crown via the College for arms. In addition, very serious considerations of etiquette and policy were involved. In 1877, the heraldic banners were presented to the princes by the Viceroy, the representative of the Queen Empress, and those princes to whom they were awarded could reasonably conclude that they had received them from their suzerain. How, then, after half a century, could approach be made to them to state that the banners were wrong and that the princely recipients should now petition the Earl Marshal for a revised grant?

Such considerations involving high policy were irrefutable and Sir Henry Burke was informed in 1922 by the Secretary of State that the latter did not consider it desirable to take action in the manner suggested by Sir

Henry's predecessor as Garter, Sir A. Scott Gatty. There, presumably, the matter rested, though the statement that the princes had mostly regularised their position as to arms implies that many of the rulers did, in fact, petition the College. Whether these were identical with the ninety of 1877, or were from the lesser princes, cannot be decided.

In the course of the seven years of argument between the College and the government, some unflattering views of the former were expressed by servants of the latter, all of whom were Englishmen or Britons, and not Indians. On one occasion a senior civil servant, with understandable if somewhat inaccurate exasperation, described the 'College of Heralds as a bugbear' from which India had the good fortune to be free. Another went even further, 'this appears to me to be the greatest nonsense and I dislike the whole business. What has the College of Arms here or Garter got to do with India and why have they (or he) been allowed to interfere? Is it anything more than an attempt by the College to exploit a new and promising field of fees? The less any Indian (or for the matter of that, anyone else) has to do with the College, the better for him.'

CHAPTER 11

Royal Arms and Arms of Dominion

Sweden

AFTER the separation of Norway and Sweden in 1905, an Act was passed in Sweden on 15 May 1908 concerning the two coats of arms of that kingdom, the Great and the Small Coat of Arms. The Small Coat of Arms is azure three crowns or. As with other countries, including England, the arms of a dynasty became those of the country, for when Albrecht of Mecklenburg made himself King of Sweden in 1364 he adopted the design of the three crowns instead of his family device of a crowned bull's head. From a seal of 1376 it can be seen that King Albrecht used a coat of arms with one crown on occasions. It may have been that the idea of a crown came to him from its use on his paternal coat.

This coat with the three crowns became the Small Coat of Arms in Sweden. The Great Coat of Arms is quarterly with an escutcheon bearing the arms of the reigning dynasty. The 1st and 4th quarters show the three crowns, while the 2nd and 3rd quarters are azure three bends argent sinister wavy over all a crowned lion rampant or (the arms of the Folkungs). The quarters are divided by a filet cross formy or, in order to separate two fields of the same tincture. This arrangement of the Great

Royal Arms of Sweden

Coat dates from 1448, when King Karl VIII Knutson used it. Since the accession of Bernadotte, one of Napoleon's marshals, to the Swedish throne as King Karl XIV Johan (1818–44), the arms of the Bernadotte family have been shown on the escutcheon of the Great Coat of Arms. These arms are of an impaled coat, the dexter being the arms of Vasa, on the sinister, Bernadotte. The Vasas reigned from 1523–1654 but King Karl XIII, who adopted Bernadotte, was proud of his descent from the Vasas. Therefore Karl XIV used the Vasa arms in the dexter half of his shield. They are tierced bendwise azure, argent and gules, overall a vase or. This charge dates from the middle ages and has been represented under several different figures. The Bernadotte arms are : azure in base a bridge emerging from waters argent, in chief an eagle under the constellation of Charles's Wain or. The bridge represents the principality of Ponte Corvo in South Italy, which was given to Bernadotte by Napoleon. The eagle symbol was awarded by Napoleon to persons of princely rank. The stars were added when Bernadotte became heir to the Swedish crown. The royal arms have a closed crown, two crowned lions as supporters and the insignia of the great Order of the Seraphim are hung round the shield. The supporting lions have forked tails. There is a crowned mantle which envelopes the Great Coat of Arms.

Norway

Here, too, the arms of the Sverre dynasty, which show gules a lion rampant crowned or holding in the paws an axe, became the coat of arms of Norway, which remained unaltered by any subsequent dynasty. It appears to have been after 1280 that King Eric Magnusson of Norway put the axe into the royal arms.

Iceland

Had been independent until 1262–64, when the country submitted to the Norwegian king. The arms commonly given as the old arms of Iceland are : gules a stock or codfish argent crowned or, but this blazon does not appear before the sixteenth century. Mr Paul Warming, Heraldic Counsellor of the Danish State, has shown from an examination of the *Armorial Wijnbergen* that Iceland in the thirteenth century, at the time of the union with Norway, bore arms thus : barruly of twelve argent and azure a chief or, over all a lion rampant gules holding an axe azure on the chief and or on the barruly. When Norway was united with Denmark in the fourteenth century, Iceland also was associated with these two countries. In 1815, Norway was separated from Denmark but Iceland remained Danish. The Icelandic arms with the stockfish charge were replaced in 1903 by others : azure a falcon argent. In 1919 yet another blazon appeared : azure a cross argent charged with a cross gules, supported by four legendary figures from the Norse sagas and surmounted by the royal Icelandic crown. This blazon disappeared after the proclamation of the Republic of Iceland in 1944. There is still an Order of the Icelandic Falcon which is bestowed by the Republic. (*Les Armes de l'Islande et du Danemark dans l'Armorial Wijnbergen*, by Paul Warming.)

Denmark

The arms of Denmark : or semée of hearts gules three lions passant azure, are those of the Valdemar family which reigned in Denmark from 1157. They form the small Danish Coat of Arms and are an important part of the Great Coat. The crest with these arms was formed by two oxhorns. The Great Coat of Arms is arranged as an impalement. In the dexter half, the upper part of the shield shows the original Valdemar arms, the lower half being different. In the sinister half, the Valdemar arms are used but having in base a gold dragon in a field gules. The supporters are two Hercules armed with clubs, there is a royal crown surmounting the whole with the usual mantle, and the shield is surrounded by the insignia of Denmark's principal order, that of the Elephant.

Finland

Was originally a Swedish province and the Folkung arms were used there until, in 1569, the device of a lion was adopted.

In 1397 the Nordic Union of Kalmar brought together Norway, Denmark and Sweden. Eric, Duke of Pomerania, became King of Denmark in 1398 and his shield of arms included : 1st quarter, Denmark (the three lions); 2, the Kalmar Union, ie, the three crowns as in the Small Coat of Sweden; 3, the arms of the Folkungs mentioned above; 4, the griffin of Pomerania, King Eric's family arms. There was an inescutcheon, bearing the arms of Norway, the lion of Norway, these being the Danish royal family arms from the time of King Olav, the son of Haakon VI by Queen Margaret.

Spain

The story of Spain being that of the gradual coalescence of a number of small states—Leon, Castile, Navarre and Aragon—it was natural that the royal arms of Spain should have illustrated this heraldically. Eventually, these kingdoms were united by the marriage of Isabella of Castile and Ferdinand of Aragon. In 1479, Ferdinand succeeded to the Aragonese throne and Isabella was recognised as Queen of Castile. The last Moorish kingdom was conquered in 1492. Up to that time the arms were those of the four kingdoms mentioned above. The kings of Asturias-Leon used only the Cross of Victory, known as the Cross of Covadonga and so named to commemorate the victory gained there by Pelayo in 718, the traditional date given by Spaniards for the start of the re-conquest of their country from the Moors who had invaded it in 711. It was not until the time of Alfonso VII, who reigned 1126–57 over Leon and Castile, that the traditional lion of Leon appeared on the seals and coins of the kingdom, without, however, displacing the Cross from the arms. At first, the lion was passant, but by the reign of Fernando II (1157–88) the first rampant lions were being used in the shield of Leon, sometimes in purple, at other times without any colour, sometimes on a gold, at others on a silver field.

Alfonso VIII of Castile (1158–1214) adopted the familiar castle for the arms of his country. Ferdinand III, who finally united the kingdoms of Leon and Castile in 1230, signified this union by quartering the shield between the arms of the two countries, showing the castles and the lions, both of these being canting or punning arms derived from the name of the kingdom.

The shield was thus one of sovereignty or dominion, ie, national. Personal badges were used by some of the Spanish kings, as they were in England (see pp 80–2, The Queen's Beasts), but these were not permanent additions to the shield.

Aragon was formed of the original small northern kingdom plus the countship of Barcelona and the lordship of Montpellier, to which was added Valencia and Mallorca by conquest, each territory being denoted in the shield by bars. Later, the arms of Sicily were added to the shields, and Juan II (1406–54) used six bars. These arms were symbolical of the various constituents of the kingdom, as was the case with the fourth Spanish kingdom, that of Navarre. Considerable variety existed in the charges until the thirteenth century. Rays were used to denote power, with a carbuncle at centre; later, the rays were interpreted as chains and this symbolism was related to the great victory gained over the Muslims in 1212 at the battle of Las Navas de Tolosa. A Spanish herald thus describes the fortunes of the arms of Navarre, 'The chains disappeared from the shield of Spain, without any reason to justify it, in the time of the Austrian dynasty (ie, the house of Hapsburg), the Bourbons did not replace them, they were re-introduced by Joseph Bonaparte, forgotten by Ferdinand VII and Isabella II, appeared fleetingly on the seals of Carlos Maria Isidro and were definitely restored by the revolution of 1868 to the national arms.'

When Castile and Aragon were united, the national shield (Castile and Leon) was organised with that of Aragon and Sicily. Under the Hapsburgs the shield became dynastic, showing the marriage alliance of the Spanish heiress Juana (Joan) the Mad with her German husband, Philip the Fair. The child of this marriage was the Holy Roman emperor, Charles V, who was Charles I of Spain. A vastly complicated coat of arms showing the devices of the house of Austria, of Burgundy, Brabant etc, along with those of old Spain, was then in use, to which Charles I added Jerusalem, Naples etc. Under his son, Philip II (whose first wife was Mary I of England), an escutcheon was added for the conquest of Portugal but dropped by succeeding monarchs when Portugal valiantly refused to become Spanish. In 1700 Philip V, a Bourbon and grandson of Louis XIV, succeeded to the Spanish throne. He used the arms, charging them with an inescutcheon within a bordure gules containing the three fleurs-de-lis. Charles III totally altered the arms, making a quartered shield of Castile and Leon, in point Granada, and around, in a form of rays, the quarters of Aragon, Sicily, Austria, Artois, Tuscany, Parma etc (over some of which he did not reign) and ignored completely the colonial dominions. Strange to relate, it was the most outrageous of usurpers of the Spanish throne, Joseph Bonaparte, who gave to the arms of Spain their ancient national character—Castile, Leon, Aragon, Navarre and Granada—plus Ultramar, to signify the vast overseas Spanish dominions—the last being represented by the two columns of Hercules—the whole being charged with an inescutcheon of the Napoleonic eagle. Perhaps it is not so strange that King Joseph should have reverted to this simpler coat for he had, of course, no Bourbon or Hapsburg connection and was compelled to represent himself as a quasi Spanish nationalist.

The brief republic of 1868 followed much the same lines as Joseph's construction of the national shield. Today, the position is as follows: quarterly 1 and 4, Castile and Leon, 2 and 3, Aragon and Navarre; in base Granada. The crown of the Catholic kings forms the helmet, and overall an eagle; accompanied by the two pillars of Hercules, and below the shield the yoke and the arrows used as badges by the Catholic kings and now employed as a symbol of national unity. The national arms of the several Spanish kingdoms, later unified, have thus once again become the symbols of the country.

The Netherlands

Have the same arms for the State as for the royal house and they are of very ancient origin. In their present form they date from a royal decree of 24 August 1815 made by William I. At that time the United Netherlands included Belgium and Luxembourg as well as Holland. The arms as laid down in 1815 were modified in 1907 and were settled by a statute passed in 1954, when the Netherlands were united with Surinam and the Antilles. The arms of the Netherlands are : azure a lion rampant or, semée of billets bearing a crown heraldic with two jewels or, holding in the dexter paw a drawn sword and in the sinister a bundle of arrows, pointed or, their points upward, and the arrows bound by a band or. The supporters are two lions. The crest is a lion sejant or between two trunks azure semée of billets or, rising out of a crown or.

These arms are described in the decree as the sovereign's hereditary arms of Nassau. As far back as 1198, on a seal of Count Waleran of Laurenbourg, ancestor of the Counts of Nassau, is found a lion in a double bordure componée. From 1221 the lion was billetty. In the *Armorial of Wijnbergen* in the thirteenth century, published in the *Archives Héraldiques Suisse* (1951–54), the Count of Nassau in 1288 bears azure a lion billety or. The States General of the Netherlands (1581–1795) used these arms, the lion being crowned and equipped with the sword and the bundle of arrows. Of the seventeen provinces of the Netherlands, at least twelve bore the lion in their arms, possibly from connection with the Counts of Nassau. The crown on the lion is more strange because the titular sovereign of the Netherlands was Philip II of Spain, against whom the Netherlands were in revolt. The sword was the symbol of defence. The bundle of arrows signified unity, but this symbol can be traced to the badges of the Spanish kings and is now one of the emblems of national unity in Spain. In 1522 the Emperor Charles V, in addressing the States General, exhorted them to keep to unity in accordance with the old story of the dying man who demonstrated to his sons that unity made for strength through the familiar medium of a bundle of sticks. This unity the Netherlands were to obtain only as a result of their successful struggle against Charles's son, Philip II. As we see in the account of the Spanish arms mentioned earlier, the bundle of arrows is one of the national symbols of modern Spain, as well as having been the badge of some of her ancient kings.

Italy

The royal house of the Italian kings, that of Savoy, is traced to one Humbert of the White Castles, or White Hands, who was Count of Savoy and Seigneur of Chablais and of Valais between 1024 and 1048. His successors used an eagle as their device, which was also used in the arms of Savoy in the seventeenth and eighteenth centuries. The famous White Cross of Savoy was used in 1258 by Amadeus V the Great. The winged lion also became the crest of the family. The lions as supporters of the arms appeared at the beginning of the eighteenth century.

Canada

The arms of the Dominion of Canada and the Canadian provinces are of great interest because Canada saw the first official heraldic development outside Great Britain. Conquered from the French in 1759, Canada remained in the British Empire despite every effort by the Americans to capture it. On the passing of the British North American Act of 1867, Canada became a self-governing state under the British Crown and the prototype of the Dominions. From 1868 there existed, under a royal warrant of 26 May of that year, a Great Seal for Canada which showed in quarterly form the arms of Ontario, Quebec, New Brunswick and Nova Scotia. This was used as though it represented the arms of the Sovereign of Canada and, unofficially, the arms of the various newly-created provinces were sometimes added to reproductions of the seal. On 21 November 1921, the royal arms of the Sovereign of Canada were authorised by George V as follows : tierced in fesse the first and second divisions quarterly gules, three lions passant guardant in pale or (for England); 2, Scotland; 3, Ireland (these, of course, as in the British royal arms); 4, azure three fleurs-de-lis or (in allusion to the French settlers), and the third division argent, three maple leaves conjoined on one stem proper (the heraldic representation of Canada's emblem). Crest : on a royal helmet a lion guardant or imperially crowned proper holding in the dexter paw a maple leaf gules. Supporters : dexter a lion rampant or holding a lance argent point or, flying therefrom to the dexter the Union flag; sinister a unicorn argent armed crined unguled or, gorged with a coronet composed of crosses patée and fleurs-de-lis a chain affixed thereto reflexed of the last, and holding a like lance flying therefrom to the sinister a like banner azure charged with three fleurs-de-lis or. The whole is ensigned with the Imperial Crown proper, and below the shield upon a compartment strewn with roses, thistles, shamrocks and lilies, a scroll azure inscribed with the motto : *A mari usque ad mare* 'From sea to sea', this being a quotation from Psalm 72, v 8. 'He shall have dominion also from sea to sea; and from the river unto the ends of the earth.' The title of 'Dominion' was taken from this passage after various alternatives such as Kingdom of Canada (rejected as offensive to the USA) had been considered. The presence of the fleurs-de-lis in shield, supporters and compartment refers, of course, to the French settlement of Canada. For 460 years the English kings had used the fleurs-de-lis of France in their arms, and had borne the vain title of Kings of France. In 1801, George III dropped both arms and title; yet within three generations his descendants were to be able with complete propriety to place the fleurs-de-lis in the arms of their sovereignty over Canada.

With regard to the Canadian provinces, their arms are given below in the order in which they were granted.

Nova Scotia

Granted by Charles I when this country was colonised, and the oldest escutcheon of a British territory outside the British Isles. The arms are : argent a cross of St Andrew azure charged with an escutcheon of the royal arms of Scotland. Crest : a branch of laurel and a thistle issuing from two hands

P

conjoined, the one being armed and the other naked all proper. Supporters : dexter a unicorn argent armed, crined and unguled or, and crowned with the Imperial crown proper, and gorged with a coronet composed of crosses pattée and fleurs-de-lis, a chain affixed thereto passing through the forelegs and reflexed over the back, gold; on the sinister, a savage holding in the exterior hand an arrow. Motto (over the crest, as usual with Scottish arms): *Munit haec et altera vincit.* 'One defends, the other conquers'— in allusion to the two hands in the crest, the one to exercise the royal power of defence of the subjects, the other to indicate the latter's success in colonising the wild land of Nova Scotia.

This coat of arms is essentially Scottish and, in granting it, Charles I was evidently acting in his capacity as King of Scots, the time being nearly a century before the union of Scotland and England. (An entry of the arms is in the Lyon Register for 1805– 10, the entry for 1625 having been lost.) When the design for the Great Seal was made in 1868, this grant of 1625 was overlooked or forgotten and a new coat granted for Nova Scotia, but in 1929 George V restored the former armorial bearings granted by Charles I. The savage shown as the sinister supporter is a very familiar figure in Scots armory, but in the representation of the Nova Scotia coat he has been given a trans-Atlantic touch by being represented as a Red Indian.

Newfoundland

Was until 1949 a separate British dominion, possessing as part of its territory a strip of the Labrador coast of Canada. It is now a province of Canada and bears these arms, granted in 1638 : gules a cross argent between in 1st and 4th quarters a lion passant guardant crowned or, and in 2nd and 3rd quarters a unicorn passant of the second armed crined and unguled gold gorged with a coronet a chain affixed thereto passing between its forelegs and reflexed over the back of the last. Crest : an elk passant proper. Supporters : on each side a savage of the area armed and clothed as for war. Motto : *Quaerite prime regnum Dei.* 'Seek ye first the kingdom of God.' The savages being described 'as of the area' are clearly meant to be Red Indian and would be the first representation in English heraldry of colonial devices. It is possible however that the Nova Scotian savage was meant to be an Indian from the first, which would make this the first colonial device used in heraldry in Great Britain.

Ontario

Arms were granted in 1868, as were those of New Brunswick and Quebec. Formerly known as Upper Canada, Ontario was formed by those persons who refused to live under the government of the United States after it parted from Great Britain. For this reason, the local authorities asked for the cross of St George to be shown in their arms and, after the customary argumentation from the College of Arms, their request was granted. The arms are : vert a sprig of three leaves of maple slipped or, on a chief argent the cross of St George. Crest : a bear passant sable. Supporters : dexter a moose, sinister a Canadian deer, both proper. Motto : *Ut incepit fidelis sic permanet.* 'Begun in loyalty, may it so remain.'

It may be noted that, as with the elk in the crest of Newfoundland, the fauna of Canada have provided for the supporters animals new to heraldry, and which have become the forerunners of many others.

New Brunswick

Arms are : or on waves a lymphad with oars in action proper on a chief gules a lion passant guardant or. This province was founded by United Empire Loyalists, as those British citizens were called who left the USA for British territory. The lymphad, or ship, is a reference to the ship-building industry which in former times was a feature of the province; the lion is a British emblem appropriate to the loyal settlers. These arms were granted in 1868.

Quebec

Had no coat of arms when under French rule, but armorial
bearings were granted in 1868 and the blazon was redesigned
in 1939 to read: per fesse azure and or, on a fesse gules a lion
passant reguardant of the second, between in chief three fleurs-
de-lis of the same, and in base a sugar maple sprig with three
leaves vert, veined also gold. Motto: *Je me souviens*. The original
blazon was: or on a fess gules between two fleurs-de-lis in chief
azure, and a sprig of three leaves of maple slipped, vert in base,
a lion passant guardant gold. The 1939 version has not received
royal sanction but it is the form of arms now in use. The change
was made by a provincial Order in Council, and the provincial
flag of Quebec was produced in 1948 from the same source.

Manitoba

Was formed out of part of the vast area of central Canada
which had been administered by the Hudson Bay Company. In
the arms of the company the chief charge was the red cross of
St George, and when the province was granted arms in 1905 they
contained this charge. The arms are: vert on a rock a buffalo
statant proper on a chief argent the cross of St George gules.
Green is clearly appropriate for a prairie province of which the
buffalo was formerly the principal animal, roaming in vast herds
across the area.

Prince Edward Island

Did not join Canada until 1873, nor obtain arms until 1905.
They are: argent on an island vert to the sinister an oak tree
fructed to the dexter three oak saplings sprouting all proper, on
a chief gules a lion passant guardant or. Motto: *Parva sub
ingenti*, 'Small things under huge', which is thought to be an
allusion, like that of the oak saplings and the full-grown tree, to
the fact that the island was the scene of the conferences which
led to the formation of the Dominion of Canada. Thus, in a way,

Prince Edward Island is the parent of the whole vast country. The representation of an island in the arms is, of course, one of the instances of the ancient canting principle in heraldry.

British Columbia

Bears arms, granted in 1906, which are a beautiful representation in heraldry of features in the country's situation. They are : argent three bars wavy azure issuant from the base a demi sun in splendour proper, on a chief the Union device charged in the centre with an antique crown or. Motto : *Splendor sine occasu,* 'Splendour without setting or end'. The sun setting in splendour in the waves is an allusion to the furthest west position of the province. The use of the Union Jack serves to recall that only the patriotism and loyalty of the British settlers saved this territory from being lost to the British Empire and to Canada. At first, Spain from the south and Russia from Alaska seemed likely to divide the Pacific coast between them. Then, when Spain renounced her rights in 1819, a far more formidable power appeared. It seemed that America from the south would join her territory to the Russian border, but the firmness of British settlers ensured that Columbia remained British and she joined the Dominion of Canada in 1871.

Saskatchewan

Has had arms since 1906. They are : vert three garbs in fesse or, on a chief of the last a lion passant guardant gules. The reference is to the main industry of the province, agriculture.

Alberta

Has arms which bear witness to its physical features and main occupations : azure in front of a range of snow-topped mountains proper a range of hills vert, in base a wheat field surmounted by a prairie both also proper, on a chief argent a St George's Cross gules. The last, as in Manitoba's blazon, is an allusion to the fact that the province was formerly part of the Hudson Bay territory.

The arms were granted in 1907. In addition to the provinces listed above, Canada has two territories which were formed from the Hudson Bay area.

The Yukon Territory

Has arms which were granted in 1956 : azure on a pallet wavy argent a like pallet of the field issuant from base two piles reversed gules edged also argent each charged with two bezants in pale, on a chief argent a cross gules surmounted of a roundel vair. Crest : a husky dog standing on a mount of snow proper. The allusions here to the territory and its development are more recondite for the layman, but the heraldic student will find little difficulty in identifying the pallet wavy with the Yukon river, while the two piles reversed indicate the mountains, the gold discs reminding us that it was to the discovery of gold that the Yukon owed its development. Mostly this was done by Englishmen, hence the St George's Cross. The roundel vair alludes to the fur trade, and the husky as a crest is an armorial tribute to a brave and useful animal.

The Northwest Territories

Have arms which were granted in 1956. These are : per bend wavy gules and vert billety or in sinister chief the mask of an arctic fox argent, on a chief indented also argent a barrulet wavy azure. Crest : a compass rose proper between two narwhals hauriant and addorsed or. Dr Swan, to whose study I am indebted for the blazons given above, thus explains this somewhat involved coat : 'The green and red of the field separated by a wavy line represent the Mackenzie Valley and the tundra, respectively, divided by the tree line. The gold billets and the mask of a white fox refer to the important mineral and fur resources of the territory. The constant attempts in marine history to discover the Northwest Passage to China and the Orient are alluded to in the chief by a wavy blue line passing through an icefield. The gold narwhals of the crest protect a compass rose, symbolic of the north magnetic pole which is situated in the North-West Territories.' (*The Canadian Arms of Dominion and Sovereignty,* Conrad M. J. F. Swan, in *Recueil V Congres Internationale des Sciences Genealogique et Heraldique a Stockholm,* 1960.)

Commonwealth Symbols

Information about the state symbols of some of the numerous states formerly in the British Empire which are now sovereign and independent may also be of interest. These symbols, though not heraldic in origin, are described by the governments which possess them in heraldic terms. The most interesting is the symbol of India, the emblem which replaced the crown on government buildings and suchlike in 1950. This symbol shows the profile of the Lion Capitol at Sarnath as it is now. The crest consists of the three lions on an abacus which has in bas relief a wheel in the centre, with a bull on the right and a horse on the left. On the extreme right and left of the abacus there appear outlines of the other wheels. The Wheel of the Law is the Dharma Chakra and is the symbol of a great ideal, the law which all must obey. It also appears on the Indian national flag. The Sarnath Lion pillar, which dates from the first century BC, was erected to mark the spot where Gautama, the Buddha or founder of Buddhism, proclaimed his teaching. It is associated with the great Indian monarch, Asoka, who reigned from 264 to 227 BC over a very large part of modern India. The most easily accessible account of Asoka for English readers is in H. G. Wells' *Outline of History* (1951 edition, p 402), in which there is the following glowing tribute to the Indian monarch who endeavoured to put his Buddhist faith into practice. 'For eight and twenty years Asoka worked sanely for the real needs of men. Amidst the tens of thousands of names of monarchs that crowd the columns of history, their majesties and graciousnesses and serenities and royal highnesses and the like, the name of Asoka shines, and shines almost alone, a star. From the Volga to Japan his name is still honoured. China, Tibet and even India, though it has left his

doctrine, preserve the tradition of his greatness. More living men
cherish his memory today than have ever heard the names of
Constantine and Charlemagne.'

However much Wellsian exaggeration is here, there is no doubt
that, in choosing as crest the lions of Asoka, India has honoured
a very great man.

In India's fellow republic, Pakistan, the national flag is green
(with white next to the pole), while on the green background is
a crescent, the familiar Islamic symbol, representing progress, and
a five-pointed star representing light and knowledge. In one picture of the arms of Pakistan the crescent and star are shown
above the quarterly shield, which is surrounded on three sides
by a spray of flowers. The quarterly shield shows in each quarter
vegetables or crops, as one would expect in an Islamic country
where religious prohibitions forbid depictment of human forms,
or even animals.

This rule, however, is not always respected, and the arms of
Iraq show supporters of a lion (dexter) and a horse (sinister). The
Iraqui shield has been well described as 'more picturesque than
heraldic . . . a sketch of the country intersected by the rivers
Euphrates and Tigris. An outstanding group of date palms,
corresponding with some wheat and cotton beneath the shield,
indicates the main growths. Pen and sword are signs of culture
and war'. (Heraldica, *The Symbols of Islam,* Martin Ellehange,
No 2, 1958).

In conclusion, one may note the flamboyant symbols which
marked the Messianic or almost deified state of Kwame Nkrumah
during his period as President of Ghana. A souvenir brochure of
the state regalia of Ghana was issued, 'together with a recent
portrait of President Nkrumah' for Republic Day, 1 July 1960.
This showed, in colour, the flag of Ghana, its coat of arms,
the sword of state, the President's portrait, his personal standard
pole, the Ghana mace, and—perhaps most important—the
President's personal standard. The only interest now of this
last is in the heraldic terms used in describing it : 'This stan-

dard consists of the Ghana presidential coat of arms on a blue background. The coat of arms is made up of the black star and the flying eagles of Ghana, with the following two traditional symbols: 1, the three concentric circles "Adinkerahene" symbol of sovereignty; 2, the cross "Kerapa", otherwise known as "Musuyide", symbol of good luck and sanctity.'

Glossary

(Of terms used in the text, but not explained there.)

Accostée: Placed side by side.
Addorsed: Placed back to back.
Affrontée: Full faced.
Annulet: Ring.
Argent: Silver.
Armigerous: Arms bearing.
Azure: Blue.

Bar: Diminutive of the fesse, and taking up one-fifth of the shield.
Barbed: Term used to describe the natural colouring of the five leaves which appear on the outside of a full-blown rose.
Barrulet: Diminutive of the bar.
Barruly: Covered with ten or more barrulets.
Barry: When the field or charge is divided by horizontal lines.
Bend: Two lines drawn diagonally from dexter chief to sinister base.
Bend sinister: When the bend is drawn from the sinister chief.
Bezant: Ancient gold coin of the Byzantine Empire, a round, flat gold piece.
Bezantée: Semée or strewn of bezants.
Billets: Oblong square.
Billetty: Semée of billets.
Bordure: Border on the inside of a shield and occupying one-fifth of the shield.

Botonny: Applied to a cross whose arms resemble a trefoil.
Brisure: Mark of cadency.

Cadency: Marks or arrangements on a shield to denote junior
   lines or members of a family.
Cadet: Younger son or junior member of a family.
Canting: Punning.
Canton: Division of one-third of the chief in the right-hand
   corner.
Chapeau: Cap of maintenance, ie, headgear of crimson velvet
   turned up with ermine, used originally by barons in Parlia-
   ment.
Charge: Any figure borne on the field.
Chevron: Division occupying one-third or one-fifth of the shield,
   like an inverted stripe in a sergeant's badge of rank.
Chevronel: Diminutive of the chevron.
Chief: Upper part of a shield.
Compartment: Base on which the shield rests, particularly when
   the shield has supporters.
Counter changed: Where a field is divided per bend etc, and the
   charges in each section are of the tincture of the field in the
   other section.
Couped: Cut off by a straight line, applied to the head or limbs
   of an animal.
Crined: When the beard or hair of an object differs in tincture
   from the body.
Cross potent: When each arm ends in a two-lined bar.
Cubit arm: The hand and arm cut off at the elbow.

Dancetty: When lines of which the teeth, or indents, are larger
   or wider than those of the line indented.
Dexter: Right.
Differenced: Implies marks of cadency.
Dimidiation: Division into two equal parts.

Enfiled: When a charge is pieced by the blade of a sword or other weapon.

Engrailed: Partition line scalloped.

Eponym: One who gives his name to something, especially to a people or place.

Erased: In contrast to couped, means forcibly torn off the body, leaving the severed part jagged.

Ermine: White fur with black spots.

Ermines: Black fur with white spots.

Escutcheon: Shield.

Escutcheon of Pretence: Small shield placed in the middle of a man's shield and bearing upon it the arms of his wife, when the latter is an heraldic heiress.

Fesse: Formed by two horizontal lines across the shield taking up one-third of the area.

Field: Surface of the shield on which charges may be borne.

Filet: A diminutive.

Formée: Pattée.

Fructed: Fruited, bearing fruit.

Fusil: Narrow lozenge.

Gamb: The whole foreleg of a beast, as apart from a paw, which is shown as couped or erased from the middle joint.

Garb: Wheatsheaf.

Garnée: Garnished, ie, ornamented.

Gorged: Wearing a collar.

Griffin: Mythical animal, the upper half an eagle, the lower a lion. The male version has no wings.

Guardant: Full-faced.

Gules: Red.

Hauriant: When a fish is shown in the perpendicular position, as if sucking in air.

Ilk: Term used when name of family and of an estate are the same, in Scotland, eg, Swinton of Swinton=Swinton of that ilk.

Impaling: Putting two coats in the same shield in pale.

Leaved: With the leaves of a different colour.

Lozenge: Shaped like a diamond and four-sided.

Lymphad: Galley.

Marshalling: Arranging two or more coats of arms in same shield.

Martlet: Bird without feet.

Matriculation: Registration of arms in Lyon Register.

Mon : Japanese term most easily and correctly rendered as badge or crest.

Mullet: Star of five points.

Ocellus: Little eye, an eye spot.

Or: Gold.

Ordinary: Some heraldic charges very frequently used.

Orle: Inner border, which does not touch extremities of the shield.

Pale: Band placed vertically in the centre of a shield.

Palets (pallets): Diminutive of the pale.

Paly: Divided into perpendicular divisions like pales with alternate tinctures and the number of such divisions must be given as paly of six etc.

Pantheons: Mythical creatures like the wyvern and griffin.

Passant: Said of an animal walking and looking straight before it.

Pattée: Cross with each arm expanding from the centre and ending in a straight line.

Patonce: Floriated form of the cross.

Petrasancta system: One in which the colours of a coat of arms are indicated by use of lines and dots.

Pile: Like an inverted pyramid.

Poppinjay: Parrot.
Proper: Borne in its natural colour.

Quarterly: When the shield is divided into four equal sections by lines.
Queue: Tail.

Rampant: When an animal is shown standing erect on its hind legs.
Reguardant: Looking backward.
Respectant: When animals are shown face to face.
Roundels: Round figures of metal, flat—they change their names according to their tinctures.

Sable: Black.
Saltire: The ordinary formed like an 'X' or St Andrew's Cross.
Sanguine: Blood colour (also called murrey).
Seeded: When flowers are of a different tincture.
Segreant: Said of a griffin rampant, wings addorsed.
Semée: Strewed or powdered, with small charges.
Sinister: Left.
Slipped: Said of leaves and flowers when a slip or stalk is torn from the stem.
Splendour: Said of the sun shown with a human face and irradiated.
Statant: Standing.
Supporters: Figures placed on either side of a shield.

Tanist (tanistair): Person nominated by chief of a clan as his successor.
Tierced: Said of the field when it is divided into three equal areas of different colours.
Tincture: The metals (or and argent), colours, and furs (eg, ermine) used in heraldry.

Tressure: Diminutive of the orle.

Tressure flory counter flory: Royal tressure in arms of Scotland.

Unguled: When the hooves of an animal are of a different tincture from the rest of the body.

Vaire: One of the heraldic furs.

Vert: Green.

Voided: The interior of the charge is removed so as to leave the field visible.

Wattled: Term applied to the gills of a cock, etc, when the colour has to be mentioned.

Yale: Mythical creature coloured argent with spots in gold. It is maned, tufted, hoofed, horned and tusked or.

Index